THE SOUTHWEST AIRLINES WAY

Using the Power of Relationships to Achieve High Performance

JODY HOFFER GITTELL

McGraw-Hill
New York   Chicago   San Francisco
Lisbon   London   Madrid   Mexico City
Milan   New Delhi   San Juan   Seoul
Singapore   Sydney   Toronto

The McGraw·Hill Companies

First McGraw-Hill paperback edition published 2005.

6 7 8 9 0   DOC/DOC   0 9 8 7 6 5 4 (HC)
1 2 3 4 5 6 7 8 9 0   DOC/DOC   0 9 8 7 6 5 (PBK)

ISBN 0-07-139683-7 (HC)
ISBN 0-07-145827-1 (PBK)

Library of Congress Cataloging-in-Publication Data

Gittell, Jody Hoffer.
    The Southwest Airlines way : using the power of relationships
    to achieve high performance / Jody Hoffer Gittell.
        p. cm.
    Includes index.
    ISBN 0-07-139683-7 (Hardcover : alk. paper)
    ISBN 0-07-145827-1 (Paperback)
    1. Southwest Airlines Co.—Management   2. Airlines—United
    States—Management   I. Title.
    HE9803.S68 G588 2002
    387.7'42'068—dc21   2002013969

Contents

PART 1

High Performance Relationships— The Key to Southwest's Success 1

PART 3

Building High Performance Relationships—And Keeping Them   195

Preface to the Paperback Edition

The two years since this book was written have been a dynamic time for Southwest Airlines and the rest of the airline industry. Southwest Airlines has passed a tipping point. It is no longer flying "under the radar" to infiltrate existing markets and to grow new markets. Southwest is now the largest carrier of passengers in the largest market in the world—the domestic United States. It has sufficient market power to set low fares that the rest of the industry must match. Other airlines that are modeled after Southwest—like JetBlue Airways in the United States, WestJet in Canada, EasyJet in Europe, and JetStar in Australia—are growing quickly. Together they are accelerating the transformation of the industry that Southwest has begun.

The established airlines continue to innovate and respond, and their responses are wide-ranging. At times, the response is cost cutting that is almost purely focused on reducing the wages and benefits of workers, consistent with the strategies of mainstream Corporate America. At other times, we see more creative efforts to increase aircraft and employee productivity, thus enabling lower fares with less of a toll on employee standard of living. This second approach offers a mutual gains solution, but it requires full cooperation and partnership with frontline employees.

This second approach is fundamentally the Southwest Airlines Way—to focus on employees not primarily as a source of cost but rather as a valuable source of knowledge for reducing costs and for delivering high-quality, reliable service. Even more important, the Southwest Airlines Way is to see employees as individually valuable, but as much *more* valuable when they work closely together to accomplish a common goal. It is through high performance relationships of shared goals, shared knowledge, and mutual respect, at all levels of the organization and across all employee groups, that Southwest has achieved low costs, high quality, and sustained profitability.

This book describes how Southwest does it, through careful comparisons with several key competitors in the industry—American, Continental, and United Airlines. In good times and bad, Southwest invests in a set of organizational practices that support high performance relationships, such as cross-functional conflict resolution, cross-functional performance measures, and cross-functional boundary spanners. These practices are designed to ensure that pilots, flight attendants, customer service agents, ramp agents, and mechanics act with regard to the overall work process and with respect for their colleagues in every function. The Southwest Airlines Way is not rocket science, but it requires sustained attention to working relationships at every level of the organization.

One thing that has become even more evident since this book was first written is the importance of financial reserves for supporting high performance relationships through good times and bad. The book discusses financial reserves in Chap. 17 almost as an afterthought, as having been essential for Southwest to bounce back quickly after the crisis of September 11 without any layoffs, despite the disproportionate impact on its market niche—short haul travel. We now see the additional example of JetBlue Airways, which was started up with the same philosophy of high levels of financial reserves and low levels of debt. In turbulent environments, financial reserves are critical for enabling managers to preserve relationships and avoid layoffs through the ups and downs. These relationships serve as a key source of resilience during a crisis, enabling organizations like Southwest to adjust and adapt in the midst of a severe downturn and to bounce back with energy and strength when the next opportunity arises.

Speaking of opportunities, this paperback edition of *The Southwest Airlines Way* gives me an opportunity to acknowledge several people who were overlooked in the hardcover edition. First, Maurice Segall, who served on my Ph.D. dissertation committee at the Massachusetts Institute of Technology and provided a knowledgeable sounding board whenever I returned from the field full of observations and ideas. Second, Ralph Craviso, now vice president of workforce effectiveness at Lucent Technologies, who shared his insights into airline industrial relations at an early stage of the project. And third, Richard Snowden, a human resource and strategy consultant, who gave critical input into the initial draft of the book in his role as neighbor and friend. Finally, I wish to acknowledge once again the hundreds of frontline employees from Southwest, American, Continental, and United Airlines who spent time telling me how their organizations work. They helped make this book unusual among management books by giving us the perspective of the people who do the work.

Many of those acknowledged previously continue to be great sources of collegiality as I venture to understand the role of high performance relationships in the global airline industry, and in hospitals and long-term care. The greatest inspiration of all still comes from my extended family, and especially from my husband Ross and our daughters Rose and Grace.

Jody Hoffer Gittell
April 2005

Preface

Southwest Airlines is a remarkable company with a consistent record of profitability and performance in a turbulent industry. However, most popular accounts of Southwest's success have focused on the charismatic leadership style of founder, former CEO, and current chairman Herb Kelleher. Now that Kelleher has stepped down from his day-to-day leadership role, it is time to explore other underlying factors that have been critical to Southwest's success. In this book I argue that Southwest's most powerful organizational competency—the "secret ingredient" that makes it so distinctive—is its ability to build and sustain high performance relationships among managers, employees, unions, and suppliers. These relationships are characterized by shared goals, shared knowledge, and mutual respect. Although these relationships appear simple, appearances are deceptive. Over time, Southwest Airlines has carefully developed a set of organizational practices that build and sustain strong relationships among those who are critical to the organization's success.

Southwest's competitors have not found these relationships easy to achieve, as I learned while conducting field research on the airline industry, over a period of eight years, at Southwest, American, Continental, United, and other airlines. One significant obstacle has been a tradition of deep divisions among the functions that are involved in air travel: pilots, flight attendants, gate agents, ticketing agents, ramp agents, baggage transfer agents, cabin cleaners, caterers, fuelers, freight agents, operations agents, and mechanics. Much like relationships between physicians and nurses, or between design engineers, production managers, and sales reps, their relationships typically lack shared goals, shared knowledge, or respect for the roles played by the others. As a ramp agent at American Airlines explained to me:

There are employees here who think they're better than other employees. Gate and ticket agents think they're better than the ramp. The ramp think they're better than the cabin cleaners—think it's a sissy, woman's job. Then the cabin cleaners look down on the building cleaners. The mechanics think the ramp agents are a bunch of luggage handlers.

Lynn Heitman, the station manager for this particular station, had come from a prominent position at American's headquarters and had quickly observed these obstacles. She concluded that there was tremendous potential to improve station performance if cross-functional teamwork could be strengthened at the point of service delivery. Over several years of painful effort, however, she learned that there was little to no support at American Airlines for her efforts at that time. The company as a whole was not adept at building strong relationships and did not see their importance. The top management team itself was functionally divided, each member overseeing its own functional silo and protecting its own functional turf. In addition, there had been years of adversarial labor relations at American under the leadership of Robert Crandall, a former CEO who sought confrontation and fostered distrust.

As I observed Heitman's experience at American Airlines in the early 1990s, I began to hear reports of a remarkable airline with a reputation for providing reliable service, making money consistently, and giving credit for these outcomes to its frontline employees. The U.S. Department of Transportation had just put out a report documenting this airline's impact on the competitive landscape of the airline industry. The company was Southwest Airlines. Through a series of conversations, I made contact with Colleen Barrett, who at the time was executive vice president of customers and now is president and chief operating officer. Colleen was quite open to my coming and studying their operations.

My first interview at Southwest Airlines was with Rollie Lyson, the station manager for Phoenix. "I want to meet with people in each department," I said. "That should be easy enough," he replied. He described the departmental structure. "That sounds very similar to the way departments are organized at other airlines," I said, surprised. "Oh, it's identical," he said. "I'd like to see how you coordinate the flight departure process," I said. "What do you mean?" Lyson asked. "Well, do you have cross-functional teams?" I asked. "Well, it depends what you mean. We don't have meetings on a regular basis. Everybody talks to each other and they know what to do. We have a fact-finding meeting if something can't be worked out directly." I left this conversation more curious than ever about what Southwest did to achieve its remarkable performance. As I had done at American Airlines, I began to watch Southwest employees at work. I asked them what they were doing and why.

The contrasts were dramatic. The same functions existed at Southwest—pilots, flight attendants, gate agents, ticketing agents, ramp agents, baggage transfer agents, cabin cleaners, caterers, fuelers, freight agents, operations agents, and mechanics—each of which was critical for servicing aircraft, passengers, baggage, and freight in a consistent and reliable way under high-pressure conditions. But unlike what I had observed in my visits to American Airlines, relationships among these frontline employee groups were characterized by high levels of shared goals, shared knowledge, and mutual respect. A Southwest Airlines' gate agent described the importance of each function at Southwest:

> No one takes the job of another person for granted. The skycap is just as critical as the pilot. You can always count on the next guy standing there. No one department is any more important than another.

I found that relationships of shared goals, shared knowledge, and mutual respect helped to support frequent, timely, problem-solving dialogue among employees, allowing Southwest to provide high-quality service to its passengers with a highly efficient use of resources. With further visits around the Southwest system, I learned that this phenomenon had not been achieved fully in every station, but that it was widespread. Visits to Continental Airlines and United Airlines revealed some success in achieving Southwest-like relationships, but only in isolated pockets. The remainder of my research was dedicated to understanding the performance effects of strong relationships among frontline employees—and then to figuring out how Southwest has been able to excel at building these relationships, while so many of its competitors continued to struggle. This book describes what I found, and the powerful lessons I believe managers can learn from Southwest.

Jody Hoffer Gittell

Acknowledgments

For making this book possible, I thank first of all the remarkable leaders and frontline employees of Southwest Airlines. President and Chief Operating Officer Colleen Barrett and Executive Vice President of Operations Jim Wimberly have made possible my multiple research visits over the past eight years, and have responded generously to innumerable requests for data and interviews. I also thank others in the airline industry, particularly managers and employees from American, Continental, and United Airlines, who provided me with the learning laboratory without which this book could not have been written. Many impressive and dedicated people work every day in this industry under difficult conditions, and the inability of their organizations thus far to succeed on the scale of Southwest Airlines is not due to a lack of good-faith effort on their part. Though it is written for the average manager in any industry, my hope is that this book will serve as a valuable source of learning for managers in the airline industry in particular.

This book was written with the support of the Massachusetts Institute of Technology's Global Airline Industry Program and the Alfred P. Sloan Foundation. It is one of a series of industry-based research projects funded by the Sloan Foundation in industries ranging from automobiles and apparel to semiconductors and steel. For their insights into labor relations and the competitive dynamics of the airline industry, I gratefully acknowledge colleagues at MIT, particularly Thomas Kochan, Robert McKersie, Peter Belobaba, R. John Hansman, Andrew von Nordenflycht, and Victor Rivas. For their research on Southwest Airlines, I thank my former colleagues at the Harvard Business School, James Heskett, Earl Sasser, Len Schlesinger, Roger Hallowell, and Rogelio Oliva. For helping me to develop the concept of relational coordination, I thank Teresa Amabile (Harvard), Deborah Ancona

(MIT), Deborah Dougherty (Rutgers), and Jane Dutton (University of Michigan). For encouraging me to extend my findings beyond the airline industry, I thank my colleagues at Brandeis University's Heller School for Social Policy and Management. Last but not least, I thank my editor Richard Narramore for his insight in conceiving this book and his colleagues at McGraw-Hill for embracing the concept.

I dedicate this book with love to my parents John and Shirley Hoffer, my parents-in-law Marilyn and Irwin Gittell, my sisters, brothers, cousins, nieces, nephews, aunts, uncles, and my friends and neighbors. Most of all, I dedicate this book to my husband Ross Gittell and our daughters Rose and Grace, who give us never-a-dull-moment.

High Performance Relationships

The Key to Southwest's Success

From Love Field to the World's Most Successful Airline

SOUTHWEST AIRLINES HAS been profitable every year for 31 years—an unsurpassed record in the highly turbulent, frequently unprofitable, airline industry. During the same period, most of its competitors have struggled to achieve even three or four years of consecutive profitability. This record has not gone unnoticed by investors. For most of 2002 the total market value of Southwest—about $9 billion—was larger than that of all other major U.S. airlines combined. See Exhibit 1–1. The business press has celebrated Southwest, and *Fortune* magazine has called it "the most successful airline in history."[1] Southwest has also achieved high levels of employee satisfaction. It has been included in *Fortune* magazine's list of the "100 Best Companies to Work for in America" three years in a row, and has consistently enjoyed lower turnover rates than other U.S. airlines.[2]

Because of its remarkable success and the innovative ways that its success has been achieved, Southwest Airlines has the potential to transform the airline industry in the same way that Toyota transformed the auto industry in the 1980s, when its "lean" manufacturing practices swept through the industry.[3] Southwest's business model, like that of Toyota, is to provide a low-cost product by utilizing its resources effi-

Exhibit 1–1 Market Capitalization of Southwest Relative to Airline Industry*

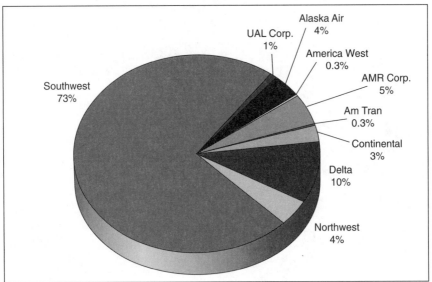

*Market capitalization (value of a total outstanding stock) at closing on Sept. 23, 2002.
Source: New York Stock Exchange

ciently, while providing record levels of reliable service. Southwest's marketplace success has been sufficiently dramatic and visible to inspire attempts by other airlines to adopt the Southwest model. Some efforts have occurred within the traditional hub-and-spoke model. Other efforts have taken the form of an "airline within an airline"—United Shuttle, Continental Lite, US Airways' MetroJet, and Delta Express. Still others have taken the form of start-ups—Morris Air, Reno, Midway, ValuJet, and most recently, JetBlue Airways. Southwest's influence has also been felt beyond the United States, with start-ups such as West-Jet in Canada, Ryanair in Ireland, Easy Jet in England, and Debonair in Belgium.[4] All of these airlines have borrowed elements of the Southwest model in hopes of achieving similar success. Just as managers around the world have learned about lean production and the Toyota Production System through accounts of the auto industry's transformation, managers are eager to better understand the principles that underlie the remarkable success of Southwest Airlines.

However, the Southwest model is still not well understood. Misconceptions are prevalent. Most people assume that Southwest Airlines has no unions, or very few unionized employees relative to the rest of the industry. A top airline industry analyst recently told a group of students at the Massachusetts Institute of Technology that "Southwest is not shackled by traditional unions." In fact, Southwest is one of the most highly unionized airlines in the U.S. airline industry, with employees who are represented by some of the most traditional unions in the United States. Similarly, people ascribe Southwest's success to its use of a single aircraft type and to its point-to-point route network, disregarding the numerous competitors—including Continental Lite, US Airways' MetroJet, and the United Shuttle—that have not succeeded despite adopting these elements.

Managers will not learn from Southwest's success until they have learned what the Southwest way actually is and how to adapt it to their companies and competitive settings. Like Toyota in the 1980s, Southwest has demonstrated its ability to outperform the rest of the industry and can no longer be ignored. If the essence of the Southwest model were well understood, others could learn from it, adapt these lessons to their situations, and transform their companies. One of the purposes of this book is to illuminate for managers what it takes to imitate Southwest's success.

For the first two decades of its existence, Southwest was considered an idiosyncratic regional airline, based out of Love Field, Texas. It was known for its flight attendants in hot pants and its wacky "LUV" culture. It was popular among price-conscious travelers in the southwestern region of the United States, but it appeared not to be very relevant for the rest of the country, much less the world. By 2002, however, Southwest was the fourth largest airline in the United States in terms of domestic passenger miles flown, serving 59 airports in 30 states. In terms of passengers flown per day, Southwest was the third largest airline in the United States, and the largest in terms of the number of flights per day.[5]

In the wake of the September 11, 2001, terrorist attacks, Southwest maintained a steady presence, refusing to lay off employees while other carriers shed both employees and unprofitable routes. Backed up by a strong cash position and the lowest debt/equity ratio in the industry, Southwest instead used these difficult times to increase its presence and expand the availability of its low-cost model to the flying public.[6] While other airlines laid off tens of thousands of employees, long-time Southwest employees saw the airline's no-layoff response as unremarkable and entirely consistent with Southwest tradition. According to one old-timer:

> That's part of our culture. We've always said we'll do whatever we can to take care of our people. So that's what we've tried to do.

How did this remarkable transformation occur? How did Southwest grow from an idiosyncratic Texas airline to an organization that managers all over the world are seeking to emulate?

Efficiency

Southwest grew by offering low fares that were designed to compete with the automobile and bus, rather than with other airlines. For managers the interesting question is how Southwest achieves the low costs that make its low fares so profitable. Southwest's low costs are not based on low wages—more of its employees are unionized than at any other major U.S. airline and they are paid around the industry average. Rather, Southwest is able to offer lower prices due in large part to the highly productive use of its major assets—its aircraft and its people.

Southwest is known for quick turnarounds of its aircraft at the gate to minimize the time its aircraft spend on the ground—non-revenue-producing time for an airline's most costly asset. When a plane spends less time on the ground, it is able to earn more revenue per day. Given the high value of aircraft, the gains from reducing turnaround times by just 5 minutes per departure are substantial. As Southwest employees are quick to point out to each other, to customers, and to visitors, "our planes don't make any money sitting on the ground—we have to get them back into the air." Southwest also benefits from record levels of employee productivity. Adjusting for its unique product mix focused on short-haul flights (more on this in Chap. 2), Southwest has by far the most productive aircraft and employees of any major U.S. airline.

Quality

When Southwest hit the industry radar screen in the early 1990s, the company became known not only for its efficiency but also for its record levels of reliability. Southwest is the only airline to have won the airline industry's "Triple Crown"—the fewest delays, the fewest complaints, and the fewest mishandled bags—not only for individual months but for entire years, from 1992 through 1996. No other airline has won the Triple Crown for more than one month at a time. Southwest is also known for its record levels of safety. Unlike any other major U.S. airline, Southwest has never suffered a fatality and was consistently found by the Federal Aviation Administration to have the fewest pilot deviations per flight departure of all the major U.S. airlines.

Controlled Growth

Although Southwest's growth seems rapid and sudden, in fact the company has grown at a nearly constant annual rate of 10 to 15 percent over the 32 years of its existence as part of a very deliberate philosophy of controlled growth. Southwest first hit the national radar screen during the 1990–1994 downturn in the industry in the wake of the Gulf War.[7] While other airlines were pulling back and reducing their presence in many markets, Southwest continued its growth and made its first move beyond the southwest region of the United States. Southwest had already begun flying into California in the early 1980s, but in 1991 it began to offer flights in the intrastate California market. Southwest dramatically caught the attention of the aviation industry when it took over the San Jose/Los Angeles market in 1991 just as American Airlines was pulling out of its unprofitable San Jose hub.

In 1993, the U.S. Department of Transportation labeled Southwest the dominant airline in the United States because of the effect it was beginning to have on the rest of the industry.[8] They coined a new term—the "Southwest effect"—the change in fares and passenger volumes that is observed when Southwest enters a market. According to the report, when Southwest announces service on a new route, other airlines serving that route almost immediately reduce their fares, and sometimes increase their frequencies as well. As a result, they reported, the net effect of Southwest's entrance into a new market had been to reduce fares by an average of 65 percent, and to increase passenger traffic at least 30 percent in every new market it entered, with a 500 percent increase in one market.

The same Department of Transportation report noted Southwest's dominance in the 100 largest U.S. city-pair markets, leading many to conclude that the Southwest point-to-point route structure was only relevant to high-density markets. Low-density markets would still require the traditional hub-and-spoke system, in which passengers traveling from small markets could be consolidated together in hubs to create the economies of scale needed for efficient service. However, what these analysts failed to recognize was that Southwest's dominance in the 100 largest city-pair markets was due in most cases to the fact that Southwest's low fares had created those high-density markets, rather than that they were high density to begin with. As Southwest's Chairman Herb Kelleher explained to an industry analyst in 1995:

> When the Transportation Department issues a report discussing Southwest's dominance in the top 100 U.S. markets, most people conclude that we only go into markets that are very dense. What people don't realize is that Southwest Airlines made those markets dense with low fares and high-frequency service; they weren't that way when we went into them. . . . After we established our Oakland-Burbank route, it soared to the 25th largest passenger market from the 179th in less than a year. Another example is our Chicago–Louisville route. Thirty days after we opened it, the market tripled in size.[9]

Theoretically, Kelleher concluded, there are no markets where the Southwest formula cannot be applied successfully.

After expanding beyond Texas and into Arizona and California, Southwest began to achieve a national network by the end of 1994, with a solid presence in the Midwest (Chicago and Cleveland) and its first presence on the East Coast (Baltimore). At the same time, Southwest began to integrate the operations of Morris Air, a Southwest look-alike acquired in 1993 for its complementary route structure in the northwestern United States, and for the expected ease of its integration into Southwest given the careful attention by its founders, June and Mitch Morris, to imitating Southwest practices. Integrating Morris Air's routes, aircraft, and employees temporarily sent Southwest above its target growth rate, but resulted in a network with a strong presence in the northwest.

Demand for Reliable Low-Fare Travel

Southwest's growth was driven by growing demand for the product that Southwest delivered so well: reliable low-cost travel. Consumer behavior shifted in the early 1990s toward greater price sensitivity, motivated by a downturn in the business cycle and made possible by increasing corporate control over business travel. The shift appeared to affect business travelers as well as leisure travelers, partly through corporate directives to cut down on travel costs. For example, the president of the West Coast division of Circuit City said:

> My directive to all my people is to fly Southwest whenever possible. We don't need the frills—just good service, a good fare, and to be there on time.[10]

Passenger willingness to pay rebounded after 1994, reflected in revenues that reached a peak of 13.5 cents per passenger mile in 2000. But from 2000 to 2001, revenue per passenger mile dropped by more than 10 percent. See Exhibit 1–2. According to United Airlines' chief financial officer, "None of us has ever seen this kind of collapse in business travel."[11] Although the decline was precipitated by the faltering economy, industry observers feared that the change in demand was more than cyclical this time. "Anybody who has a modicum of Internet capability and wants to take what is now a modest amount of time can very rapidly find out and comparison shop," said Leo Mullin, CEO of Delta Airlines. "There is almost perfect information out there." An airline analyst surmised that, based on the low cost of information, "business travelers may be in the process of retraining themselves as to what they are willing to pay for business travel tickets."[12]

After the terrorist attacks of September 2001, the decline in passenger willingness to pay for air travel declined even further. From 2000 to 2002, the average cost of a 1000-mile coach fare fell 14.7 percent.[13] "I believe what we're up against in the airline industry is much more than a cyclical problem," said Donald Carty, CEO of American Airlines. "We need to take a long hard look at literally everything we do . . . to see if they still make sense in the new reality."[14] While other airlines were wondering what to do, Southwest Airlines was well positioned to benefit from the increasingly price-savvy customer that it had helped to create.

Competitive Threats

Spurred by this change in air travel demand, airlines have woken up to Southwest's steady growth and unusually successful business model. As the

Exhibit 1-2 Revenue per Mile Earned by Major U.S. Airlines*

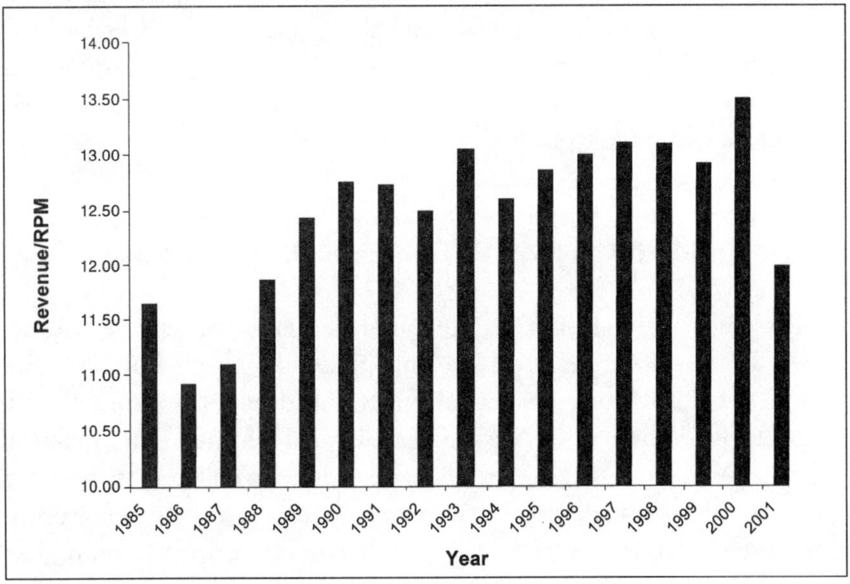

*Revenue per revenue passenger mile (cents).
Source: Air Transport Association of America

industry came out of its previous downturn in 1994, other airlines for the first time saw a real, viable threat that they could no longer ignore, and they responded by trying to imitate Southwest. Continental responded to the Southwest threat with Continental Lite, United responded with the United Shuttle, and US Airways responded with Project High Ground (the predecessor to MetroJet).

Before it became clear that these early Southwest imitators would not succeed on a large scale, fare competition from them immediately began to take a toll on Southwest's profitability, which dropped 48 percent in the fourth quarter of 1994. The United Shuttle forced fare wars in several of Southwest's West Coast markets, while Continental Lite and US Airways forced fare wars on the East Coast, particularly on Baltimore, Cleveland, and Chicago routes. In the meantime, the costs associated with the 1994 integration of Morris Air into Southwest's employment and route system were large, taking a toll on Southwest's profitability. Lower profits and the fear that other airlines would successfully imitate Southwest's business model fueled a 54 percent decline in Southwest's stock price from February to December of 1994.

These new forces generated considerable anguish throughout South-west. "There is really so much competition out there that people are really pulling together," said a customer service supervisor in Chicago. "The Shuttle is all that's on our minds right now," said the Los Angeles station manager. "We just watched a feature on television about us and the Shut-tle. They say the United system is far too rigid to provide good customer service. But our stock started at 30 this year and now it's down to 17."

In his 1995 "Message to the Field," Herb Kelleher addressed the threat posed by competitors such as Continental Lite and the United Shuttle. Continental had just given up the Lite concept, recognizing defeat. Still, Herb told employees, all airlines were now competing on costs in response to the challenge posed by Southwest. Southwest had shown a lot of discipline with its costs, even during good times, he emphasized. This was what enabled Southwest to continue making money during the 1990–1994 downturn in the industry. In fact, he pointed out, Southwest had reduced its costs even further between the fourth quarter of 1993 and 1994, from 7.11 to 6.94 cents per average seat mile. Given the billions of seat miles flown by Southwest, this cost dif-ference added up to millions of dollars in profits, he said. Without this improvement in costs, Southwest profits in the fourth quarter of 1994 would have fallen 84 percent rather than 48 percent. As Kelleher ex-plained to Southwest employees:

> We want to reduce all of our costs, except our wages and benefits and our profit sharing. This is Southwest's way of competing, unlike others who lower their wages and benefits.

The fear, in particular, was that a hub-and-spoke carrier like United would achieve lower fares on short-haul flights by successfully imitating the Southwest strategy, then have the additional advantage of a second hub-and-spoke product with longer-haul flights and a more extensive route network. Southwest was excluded from two major computerized reservations systems in 1994—Continental's System One and United's APOLLO—further fueling Southwest's fears that its competitors were trying to put it out of business.

Ultimately, Southwest held its own in California against competitive threats from United's Shuttle. Southwest turned its attention to increas-ing its presence in the Midwest and on the East Coast, where US Airways' MetroJet and Delta Express were posing similar competitive threats. Though Southwest considered these threats to be substantial, it ultimately outlasted both competitors. However, the competition is expected to intensify rather than subside, as others seek to learn from Southwest's success. Southwest currently faces a competitive threat from JetBlue Airways, the best-funded start-up in U.S. aviation history, which was founded in early 1999 by former Southwest Airlines' executives with an initial capitalization of $130 million. JetBlue's early operational success was similar to that of Southwest's, and less than three years after its founding, its market capitalization exceeded that of American Airlines (more on this in Chap. 16).

Success Factors—Leadership, Culture, Strategy, and Coordination

What are the forces underlying Southwest's remarkable performance and its self-transformation from an idiosyncratic regional carrier to a dominant national force? More important, what are the strategies and practices that managers in any industry can take away from Southwest to improve the performance of their own organizations? This book argues that Southwest's most distinctive organizational competency is its ability to build and sustain relationships characterized by shared goals, shared knowledge, and mutual respect. Although Southwest's relational competence seems simple and self-evident, this book shows that building it required a set of organizational practices that are neither simple nor self-evident. Though distinctive in many ways, Southwest is most distinctive in its intense focus on the quality of its relationships, and in its willingness to forego quick solutions to invest long-term in the maintenance of relationships among managers, employees, and business partners.

This book is not the first attempt to offer an analysis of Southwest's unusual performance. Several explanations have already been given for Southwest's success: (1) its status as a largely nonunion carrier in a highly unionized industry, (2) the extraordinary leadership of Herb Kelleher, (3) the unique culture of Southwest, (4) its quick-turnaround-at-the-gate strategy, and (5) high levels of coordination. The first explanation is surprisingly common but it is simply based on error. In fact, as noted earlier, Southwest has the highest percentage of unionized employees of any airline in the United States, and it prides itself on outstanding relationships with its unions, including traditional unions such as the International

Brotherhood of Teamsters, the International Association of Machinists, and the Transport Workers Union (more on this in Chap. 13). The other four factors—leadership, culture, strategy, and coordination—offer important insights into Southwest's success, but each one is powered by Southwest's distinctive relationship-building ability.

Leadership

Many believe that Southwest has succeeded because of the remarkable leadership of Herb Kelleher. The press has extolled the quirky qualities of Herb, and there is no point in underestimating the importance that this man has played in the success of Southwest Airlines. Perhaps most remarkable of all, Herb has remained in a leadership role at Southwest Airlines from the time of its founding until the present. As Executive Vice President Jim Wimberly noted in 2000, a year before Kelleher handed over the CEO and president positions to colleagues Jim Parker and Colleen Barrett, "There is no other air carrier that has had the same continuity of leadership as Southwest. It has shaped this culture, and we are blessed with it."[15]

Herb's leadership has been critical at Southwest, most popular accounts agree, because he has helped to shape a truly unique culture for this organization, unlike that of any other major U.S. airline. In particular, Herb has created a focus on relationships—relationships based on shared goals, shared knowledge, and mutual respect. Not only has he helped to develop the organizational practices that strengthen relationships, his personal actions have also exemplified to employees the importance of relationships. As one pilot explained:

> I can call Herb today. You don't just call and say there's a problem. He'll say, "think about it and tell me the solution that you think will work." He has an open door policy. I can call him almost 24 hours a day. If it's an emergency, he will call back in 15 minutes. He is one of the inspirations for this company. He's the guiding light. He listens to everybody. He's unbelievable when it comes to personal etiquette. If you've got a problem, he cares.

However, leadership is not confined to the CEO. Leadership is better understood as a process that can take place at any level of an organization.[16] Indeed, leadership is needed in today's organizations to motivate, support, and enable employees to work together in support of a set of shared goals. This book will describe the leadership style at Southwest—both as carried out at the top by Herb Kelleher, his top management team, and his successors (Chap. 5) and as it is exercised at the level of frontline supervisors (Chap. 6).

Culture

Another common explanation given for Southwest's success is its unique culture. Indeed, Southwest has a very different culture from that of other major U.S. airlines, as we know from the popular reports and as other management theorists have shown.[17] What is so unique about Southwest's culture? Southwest's culture has evolved over time from a culture that was idiosyncratic to a particular time and place (hot pants and LUV in the southwestern region of the United States in the 1970s, with "Come to Jesus" meetings) to a culture that is highly inclusive and diverse. However, what has remained constant over time and what lies at the root of Southwest's culture is the focus on relationships. This book goes beyond the observation that culture is important to identify what is so powerful about Southwest's particular culture.

A related question is how that culture is built and sustained, after the initial spontaneous culture of a small company is no longer sufficient. As Colleen Barrett pointed out, "We had a company culture here before I knew what it meant. The main goal is to maintain it. But it's difficult. . . . Senior officers don't even touch the workforce." In this book we will take a hard look at the role of relationships in Southwest's culture, and at the organizational practices that Southwest has developed to build and sustain those relationships.

Strategy

Alternatively, perhaps Southwest has succeeded because its quick turnaround strategy is fundamentally different from that of other major U.S. airlines. Having a point-to-point network, rather than a hub-and-spoke network, quick turnarounds are arguably more relevant to Southwest than to its competitors. Other airlines have hubs that give them pricing power. According to American Airline's senior vice president of planning, a hub generates up to 20 percent more revenue per plane than a comparable point-to-point flight.[18] Southwest, on the other hand, as a point-to-point carrier, has neither hubs nor pricing power. Southwest has instead used a quick-turnaround strategy, and the high aircraft utilization inherent in this strategy, to offer low-cost air travel to consumers. The quick-turnaround strategy requires a simple product and a configuration of assets—aircraft, routes, and maintenance facilities—that is very different from that of a hub-and-spoke operation.

This argument contains some important insights. As we will see in Chap. 2, Southwest's focus on short-haul routes has made quick turnarounds even more critical for its operational success, given the inherent productivity disadvantages of short-haul flying. However, this story about strategy, like those about leadership and culture, is made possible by Southwest's strong relationships. Relationships among frontline employee work groups are critical for coordinating the flight departure process for any airline, but especially for one that has at the centerpiece of its strategy the goal of turning the planes in record times, while doing it safely and accurately. Other airlines have tried Southwest's quick-turnaround strategy—the United Shuttle, Continental Lite, Delta Express, and US Airways' MetroJet—with nowhere near the same success. To implement this kind of strategy—a strategy based on leanness, speed, and reliability—requires highly effective working relationships among all parties involved. It is not just a matter of having a single aircraft type or a point-to-point route structure, as we will see from the detailed case studies presented in Chap. 16.

Any organization that wants to compete on the basis of leanness, speed, and reliability can benefit from Southwest's relationship focus. As we learned from Toyota in the transformation of automobile manufacturing, the principles of lean manufacturing require an intense focus on teamwork among functions that traditionally have not spoken to one another.[19] As we learned from Wal-Mart in the transformation of retailing, integrating the supply chain from customer through manufacturer requires relationships among parties all along this chain, many of whom traditionally have had few shared goals and little shared knowledge.[20] Similarly, we will see evidence in Chap. 4 of the same phenomenon in health care. As hospitals and other health-care provider organizations have responded to the need for reduced costs and shorter patient stays, strong working relationships have been critical for implementing new strategies.

Coordination

Finally, perhaps Southwest's outstanding performance has been achieved through high levels of coordination among its frontline employee groups.[21] Well-coordinated organizations have a competitive advantage through their ability to achieve higher quality at lower cost by achieving faster cycle times and by providing a more coherent interface to customers. Such organizations can change the nature of competition in an industry by pushing out the efficiency/quality frontier, rather than simply making efficiency/quality trade-offs along an existing boundary.[22] In the U.S. auto industry, major gains have already been achieved from improved coordination of the production process,[23] with additional gains being achieved through the integration of production and design. These changes have been motivated in large part by product market competition from early Japanese innovators such as Toyota.[24] Scholars have found evidence that coordination also contributes substantially to performance in the telecommunications,[25] mainframe computer,[26] and apparel[27] industries.

Coordination plays an important role in the airline industry because one of the core processes in the provision of air travel, the flight departure process, requires a high degree of coordination under time constraints for its successful completion. However, there is a tradition in the airline industry of strong functional boundaries and status differences across employee groups involved in the departure process, making coordination difficult to achieve. Coordination appears to be a source of competitive advantage for Southwest Airlines—helping it to deliver inexpensive on-time service with a speedy turnaround that lowers costs. However, coordination in its traditional sense does not fully capture what has made Southwest so successful. Instead, the coordination observed at Southwest is powered by relationships among employees—relationships of shared goals, shared knowledge, and mutual respect—described in Chap. 3 as "relational coordination." We will see in Chap. 3 that relational coordination goes beyond the more familiar concept of teamwork. Relational coordination describes not only how people act, but also how they see themselves in relationship to one another.

Behind These Success Factors—High Performance Relationships

Although leadership, culture, strategy, and coordination are critical success factors, they are only part of the story. Southwest's relationship focus, its commitment and passion for shared goals, shared knowledge, and mutual respect, joins with frequent, timely, problem-solving communication to form a powerful force called relational coordination. Part 1 of this book documents how relational coordination can drive high performance in two very different settings—flight departures and patient care.

How does Southwest craft the process that results in shared goals, shared knowledge, and mutual respect among frontline employees, managers, and external partners? Part 2 describes the specific organizational practices that turn good intentions into results. These 10 practices are neither simple nor self-evident. They require substantial investment and organizational commitment. Part 2 shows how these practices live and breathe at Southwest and how they can drive results for any organization that is willing to invest in its relationships.

The best practices and lessons learned at Southwest are transferable not only to the airline industry but to any industry. Part 3 uncovers the challenges of implementing these 10 practices in your organization. Like notes in a symphony, these practices must synchronize and harmonize with each other. Surprisingly, if only one of these practices is out of tune, it can seriously undermine your organization's investment in the others. Part 3 chronicles American, Continental, United, and JetBlue's attempts to learn and duplicate elements of the Southwest high performance model.

Relationship focus as a way of doing business not only can drive growth and profitability, it can sustain them through crises and through ups and downs in the business cycle. Part 3 will arm you with guidelines to build and sustain the relationships that can help your organization adapt successfully to the turbulence of today's challenging business world.

CHAPTER

How Southwest Uses High Performance Relationships to Overcome Strategic Challenges

S OUTHWEST AIRLINES WAS founded to serve a unique market within the airline industry. Herb Kelleher and Rollin King, Southwest's founders, wanted to provide frequent, low-cost service in busy markets of less than 500 miles. They considered the automobile and bus service their major competition. Southwest's flights were typically nonstop from originating airport to destination, although connections were available for customers who wanted them.

The Productivity Disadvantages of Short-Haul Flying

Because Southwest Airlines is well known for focusing on short-haul flights and is now the leading low-cost airline in the United States, the general public tends to think that short-haul flights are cheaper to operate than longer routes. However, the opposite is true. Short-haul flights are inherently costlier than long-haul flights, per mile flown—making Southwest's tremendous profitability record even more impressive. Short-haul flying is more expensive because planes spend more time on the ground relative to time spent in the air, reducing aircraft productivity. Also, time spent on the ground is inherently more labor-intensive than time spent in the air, reducing labor productivity. On the ground, a wide array of ground-based crews is involved in servicing the aircraft and processing the passengers. For those readers familiar with manufacturing, the reasoning is similar to the logic of "setup costs." Small batches are inherently costlier than large batches on a per-unit basis, because the setup costs for a small batch are equal to the setup costs for a large batch, but for a small batch those setup costs are spread over a smaller number of units. Similarly, short-haul flights are costlier than long-haul flights on a per-mile basis, because many of the setup costs (loading passengers, bags, and cargo, fueling, maintenance, cleaning) are incurred whether the flight is short or long, but for a short-haul flight those setup costs are spread over a smaller number of miles flown.[1]

To illustrate, Exhibit 2–1 shows the effect of flight length on costs and productivity. Considering all of the major U.S. airlines except Southwest, flight length is negatively related to costs per seat mile—the shorter the flight, the higher the costs. Similarly, flight length is positively related to aircraft and labor productivity—the shorter the flight, the lower the productivity.

Exhibit 2–1 Impact of Flight Length on Costs and Productivity*

	Flight Length[†]	
	Without Southwest	**With Southwest**
Costs per seat mile[‡]	−.18	.13
Aircraft productivity[§]	.22	−.13
Labor productivity[¶]	.14	−.24

* Correlation coefficients are shown in the table. All results are significant at the 99.99 percent confidence level, and are based on quarterly data from 1987 through 2000, for all major U.S. airlines. Data are available through the U.S. Department of Transportation, Form 41.

[†] Flight length = revenue aircraft miles per flight departure.

[‡] Costs per seat mile = total operating costs per available seat mile.

[§] Aircraft productivity = block hours per aircraft day.

[¶] Labor productivity = index of flight miles per pilot, revenue passenger miles per flight attendant, flight departures per mechanic and dispatcher, and passengers enplaned per ramp and customer service agent.

However, just by including Southwest in the equation, the results change direction. Because of Southwest's innovative attempts to reduce the costs of short-haul flying, flight length is now positively related to costs per seat mile—the shorter the flight, the lower the costs. Likewise, flight length is now negatively related to aircraft and labor productivity— the shorter the flight, the higher the productivity. Southwest's innovations have changed the underlying logic of production in the airline industry.

In short, many of Southwest's innovations were motivated by the ambitious, counterintuitive strategy of offering short-haul service at low cost. To offset the productivity disadvantages inherent in short-haul flying, Southwest focused first and foremost on achieving quick "turnarounds." Quick turnarounds mean turning aircraft around as fast as possible at the gate to minimize the time that aircraft spend on the ground, because ground time is non-revenue-producing time for an airline's most costly asset. In interviews conducted for this book, Southwest's frontline employees demonstrated that they are acutely aware that "our planes don't make any money sitting on the ground—we have to get them back into the air."

The quick turnaround is akin to reducing setup costs. If Southwest were going to offer short-haul flights economically, without relying on low wages or propeller aircraft as many of the regional airlines do, they would have to reduce setup costs. A major element of setup costs is simply the time required—in automobile production for example, Toyota moved the industry toward smaller batches to reduce expensive inventory and respond more quickly to changes in customer demand. To succeed at its strategy of providing high-quality, low-cost automobiles, however, Toyota had to figure out how to reduce setup costs, and in particular, how to increase the speed of changeovers from one batch to the next. Toyota spawned many innovations in the production process in the effort to meet the challenge of producing smaller batches economically—and speedy equipment changeovers were critical to the overall process. Southwest's quick turnarounds were the airline industry parallel to Toyota's speedy equipment changeovers. Both innovations made smaller-scale production runs more economically feasible than they had ever been before. Unless creative measures were taken to counteract the disadvantage, the short-haul strategy chosen by Southwest Airlines would have resulted in lower aircraft and labor productivity, and higher costs per seat mile flown.

In addition, Southwest lacks the hub-and-spoke system that has long been considered the most profitable way to run an airline. When airlines were suddenly exposed to new competitive pressures after deregulation, they built hub-and-spoke systems to better compete. The competitive advantage of hubs derives from economies of scale. According to experts from the MIT International Center for Air Transportation:

> The simplest manifestation of these economies of scale appear in areas such as maintenance, where staff and inventory costs can be reduced by having one central maintenance facility. A subtler and more important reason for hub-and-spoke arrangements, however, has to do with economies of scale applied to frequency and passenger preferences. . . . Market share in the airline industry is largely a function of flight frequency. A hub-and-spoke network topology has a consolidating effect that makes it possible to justify more flights to each city.[2]

Market share in turn allows greater pricing power, as we know from basic economics principles. To illustrate this pricing power, a hub generates up to 20 percent more revenue per plane for American than a comparable point-to-point flight, according to American's senior vice president of planning.[3] However, there are also disadvantages of hub-and-spoke systems: "The advantage of hub-and-spoke networks is that they concentrate traffic. The disadvantage of hub-and-spoke networks is that they concentrate traffic."[4] When airports begin to run out of capacity, as is occurring in the U.S. airline industry today, the disadvantages of consolidating flights in a hub begin to outweigh the advantages.

The temptation under the current conditions is to advocate point-to-point networks as a solution for the woes of the airline industry.[5] But point-to-point networks have disadvantages as well. Maintenance and other resources are more widely distributed, creating greater coordination challenges. Perhaps most important, point-to-point networks do not generate the same pricing power as hubs. To make up for this lack of pricing power, airlines that depend largely on point-to-point route networks have to be extremely cost-effective. There are many ways to be cost-effective, including cheap labor and cheap equipment. But Southwest chose to meet these strategic challenges through quick turnarounds of its aircraft at the gate.

Achieving Quick Turnarounds

Southwest discovered multiple ways to speed the turnaround of its aircraft at the gate. First, Southwest used only one aircraft type—the Boeing 737. Although there were differences between the early 737 Series 200 and the later Series 700, Southwest standardized cockpit configurations as much as possible to minimize extra training requirements for its pilots. Thus, crews, furnishings, and spare parts were interchangeable and maintenance was more uniform.

Second, where available, Southwest used less congested airports to avoid disrupting flight operations and to maximize aircraft time in the air (as opposed to time spent taxiing or being held at the gate due to air traffic control issues). In large cities Southwest often used older facilities, such as Dallas's Love Field or Chicago's Midway Airport, that had been abandoned when new, larger airports were constructed. Southwest often offered service to smaller airports with easy access to large metropolitan areas (e.g., New York City through Long Island Islip airport).

Third, to speed turnarounds Southwest offered limited services, specifically no in-flight meals—only beverages and snacks—and did not transfer baggage to other airlines. These practices reduced costs and turnaround time. Finally, Southwest offered open seating. This practice helped create efficiencies in several ways. First, there was no need for software to sort and hold seating assignments, nor the time and expense of printing boarding passes and then verifying them as passengers boarded the aircraft. Perhaps more important, the open seating system rewarded passengers for showing up early to the gate: the early passengers had their choice of the best seats.

Coordination through High Performance Relationships

These strategies for simplifying Southwest's "product" were important but not sufficient for achieving its goal of quick turnarounds. Quick turnarounds at the gate were impossible without a high level of coordination among 12 distinct functions: pilots, flight attendants, gate agents, ticketing agents, operations agents, ramp agents, baggage transfer agents, cargo agents, mechanics, fuelers, aircraft cleaners, and caterers. In the airline industry, these functions are divided by differences in expertise, status, and even the distinct locations in which they work—

pilots spend their time in the cockpit; flight attendants in the cabin; baggage handlers, caterers, fuelers, and mechanics on the ramp; and gate and ticket agents in the gate and ticketing areas. They do not have a history of warm cooperation in the industry as a whole.

Over time, Southwest Airlines has developed 10 organizational practices to facilitate coordination among these diverse functions, by building relationships of shared goals, shared knowledge, and mutual respect. The rest of this book explains these 10 practices and how managers in any setting can implement them to improve their business performance.

Each of these practices is designed to build relationships of shared goals, shared knowledge, and mutual respect, within Southwest and with its external partners. The practices together have produced high levels of relational coordination, enabling Southwest to turn planes quickly, achieving industry-leading levels of aircraft and employee productivity.

Other Possible Responses to the Same Challenges

Of course, a different organization facing the same strategic challenges faced by Southwest might have responded to those challenges in an entirely different way. Like Southwest, US Airways does primarily short-haul flying. Rather than looking for ways to speed gate turnarounds, US Airways has relied on pricing power at its hubs to command high fares to cover the high costs of short-haul flying. However, with the incursion of Southwest into its East Coast markets, this pricing power has been challenged, leading US Airways to look for other solutions. Regional airlines also do primarily short-haul flying, but there are three interesting differences between their approach and that of Southwest. First, they strive to reduce the inherent productivity disadvantage of short-haul flying by paying employees below the industry standard. Second, they tend to use propeller aircraft rather than jets for the same reason. And third, they act as feeders to the long-haul routes of other airlines, rather than developing their own point-to-point route structures.[6] Southwest could have overcome the productivity disadvantages of short-haul flying in these other ways, without having to rely so heavily on cross-functional coordination of the flight departure process, and the relationships that make it possible.

Why did Southwest choose to focus on relationships to solve the strategic challenge of offering low-cost short-haul flights? The explanation seems to lie in the values and backgrounds of Southwest's founders.

Herb Kelleher and Colleen Barrett, who has recently risen to the position of president and chief operating officer, both played a critical role in the founding of Southwest, and in the development of its organizational practices. Both share the values of egalitarianism and caring. Likewise, they have had the advantage in some respects of coming from outside the airline industry. The disadvantage was their need to learn from scratch what other airline executives took for granted. The advantage, however, was the same—the need to learn from scratch, for themselves, what other airline executives took for granted. One thing they absolutely did not take for granted, given their values, were the status distinctions that are so pervasive in the airline industry and throughout the world of work.

Summing Up

This chapter explains what motivated Southwest to develop the 10 principles of relationship-based performance. The primary motivation was the need to overcome the inherent productivity disadvantages of short-haul flying in order to compete in a cost-effective way with the car and the bus. However, this does not mean that the principles of relationship-based performance are relevant only for airlines with this particular strategy. Even though the principles of relationship-based performance were critical for Southwest's success, those principles are also relevant for airlines with different strategies and for organizations in different industries. The key point, as the next two chapters will show, is that strong working relationships allow organizations to achieve reliable performance in a highly efficient way. Organizations with strong relationships can move beyond traditional trade-offs between efficiency and quality, shifting out the efficiency/quality frontier to achieve higher levels of both. Relationships are not just "nice to have" but rather—if invested in consistently over the long term—can be powerful drivers of organizational performance.

Southwest versus American Airlines

The Power of Relational Coordination

There's a code, a way you respond to every individual who works for Southwest. It promotes good working relationships.

—Ramp Manager, Southwest Airlines

SOUTHWEST HAS THE fastest gate turnarounds in the airline industry, to minimize the time its aircraft spend on the ground. When a plane spends less time on the ground, it is able to earn more revenue per day. Given the value of aircraft, the gains from reducing gate times by just 5 minutes per departure are substantial. This chapter defines relational coordination and shows that relational coordination accounts for much of Southwest's industry-leading turnaround times. The sections immediately following are based on observations and interviews conducted at Southwest and American Airlines and reveal startling contrasts between the two airlines.[1] Later in the chapter, we see how relational coordination resulted in fewer delays, fewer lost bags, faster turnarounds, and higher employee productivity in a study comparing operations at Southwest, United, Continental, and American. Although relationships are relatively "soft" organizational factors and therefore tempting to neglect under challenging conditions, relationships of shared goals, shared knowledge, and mutual respect contribute *substantially* to effective coordination and therefore to quality and efficiency performance.

Communication

The flight departure process is one of the core processes of an airline's operations. Repeated hundreds of times daily in dozens of locations, the success or failure of this process can make or break an airline's reputation for reliability. In the flight departure process, representatives of 12 distinct functions, who often do not communicate well with each other, perform a complex set of tasks between the arrival of the plane and its next departure. The flight departure process is further complicated by rapid changes in weather, connections, and gate availability, such that information is often inaccurate, unavailable, or obsolete. Robert Baker, executive vice president of operations for American Airlines, called the flight departure process one of the least predictable work processes that an airline performs on a repeated basis.

In the flight departure process, coordination occurs largely through communication among pilots, flight attendants, mechanics, gate agents, ticketing agents, ramp agents, baggage transfer agents, aircraft cleaners, caterers, fuelers, freight agents, and operations agents. However, the communication observed among these functions at Southwest and American Airlines was very different.

Frequency and Timeliness of Communication

American employees interviewed for this book expressed frustration with both the absence and lateness of the communication they needed from their colleagues to make decisions and carry out their tasks. Reports of inadequate communication were common. According to a customer service supervisor at American:

> Here you don't communicate. And sometimes you end up not knowing things. . . . Everyone says we need effective communication. But it's a low priority in action. On the gates I can't tell you the number of times you get the wrong information from ops. They tend to be optimistic. We call it the

creeping delay. The hardest thing at the gates with off-schedule operations is to get information. They are leery to say the magnitude of the problem.

Similarly, an American gate agent reported:

> We have to rely on the maintenance group. If there's a delay, a problem with the operation, we have to be in touch with them. Through operations usually, but sometimes directly. It doesn't go especially well. Unfortunately those departments that don't deal directly with the public don't feel that sense of urgency. We get the brunt of it when other departments fail to load a bag, clean the cabin, tell us when there's going to be a mechanical delay. . . . Timely communication is very, very important.

While employees at American complained about the failure of their counterparts in other functions to communicate with sufficient frequency and timeliness, Southwest employees expressed pride in the frequency and timeliness of their communication. A customer service supervisor reported:

> When there are irregular operations, bags have to be moved. There is constant communication between customer service and the ramp. Customer service will advise the ramp directly or through operations.

A Southwest station manager described the normal pattern of communication regarding mechanical difficulties:

> The pilot [reports a maintenance issue] when he calls in range to operations. The mechanic is usually here to meet the plane. If something is seriously wrong, we move to an off-terminal location and cancel the flight. If it's just two hours, we do an aircraft swap. Ops keeps everyone informed. . . . It happens smoothly.

A Southwest gate agent praised the quality of communication:

> The ops agent is responsible for every bit of information going into the computer. We can tell the customer everything they need to know, because it's right there. Communication is ultimately the key.

Communication is one of the primary ways that people coordinate their work with others in a wide variety of settings.[2] Organizational experts have long recognized the power of frequent communication for coordinating work processes, and have now begun to focus on the critical importance of timely communication.[3] With frequent, timely communication, Southwest employees could respond quickly to changing circumstances in a coordinated fashion.[4] Without it, American employees could not.

Problem Solving versus Blaming

The communication observed at these two airlines also differed in the degree to which it focused on problem solving rather than blaming. At American Airlines, employees involved in the flight departure process displayed a great deal of blaming and blame avoidance toward each other for late departures and other negative outcomes. There was a tendency to hide information to avoid blame for a delay, thus detracting from the information sharing that was central to coordination. An American gate agent explained this tendency:

> Unfortunately, in this company when something goes wrong, they need to be able to pin it on someone. You should hear them fight over whose department gets charged for the delay.

A ramp supervisor at American concurred:

> If you ask anyone here, what's the last thing you think of when there's a problem? I bet your bottom dollar it's the customer. And these are guys who bust their butts every day. But they're thinking, how do I keep my ass out of the sling.

By contrast, Southwest employees communicate about the problem itself, rather than assigning blame when difficulties occur. When something goes wrong, according to a Southwest pilot:

> We figure out the cause of the delay. We do not necessarily chastise, though sometimes that comes into play. It is a matter of working together. No finger pointing, especially here, and I'm sure that's the case elsewhere at Southwest.

A Southwest station manager explained his philosophy:

> If there's a delay, we find out why it happened. . . . Say there was a 10-minute delay because freight was excessive. If I'm screaming, I won't know why it was late. [The freight handlers] will think, "He's an idiot, if only he knew." Then they'll start leaving stuff behind or they'll just shove it in and I won't know. If we ask, "Hey, what happened?" then the next day the problem is taken care of. . . . You have to be in that mode every day. There's no one person who can do it. We all succeed together—and all fail together. You have to truly live it. I think we do here.

Problem-solving communication in turn enables employees to adapt quickly and work together when things go wrong. It is a critical ingredient in coordinating flight departures. As we saw, however, when something went wrong at American, the primary focus of communication was blaming and the avoidance of blame—in contrast, when something went wrong at Southwest, the primary focus of communication was problem solving.

Other work settings also require problem-solving communication. Saul Rubinstein found that problem-solving communication among workers at the Saturn auto plant was a key aspect of coordinating work and achieving quality outcomes.[5] However, it is not easy to achieve. W. Edwards Deming, the father of Total Quality Management (TQM), argued that the resort to fault finding rather than problem solving is a common flaw in organizations, and one that undermines both performance *and* the potential to improve performance over time.[6]

Relationships

Behind these differences in communication, there seemed to be a deeper phenomenon at work. In particular, relationships of shared goals, shared knowledge, and mutual respect observed among Southwest employees were much stronger than those observed among American employees.

Shared Goals

At American, shared goals appeared to be weak. According to a customer service agent, "If I sit back here for two hours [in the break room] I feel like nobody cares." On the ramp, similar complaints were heard. According to a ramp manager, "Ninety percent of the ramp employees don't care what happens, even if the walls fall down, as long as they get their check."

As just noted, American employees did care a lot about one thing in particular, and that was avoiding blame for failing to accomplish their tasks. A pilot pointed out that American gate agents "were scared to death to take a delay." However, this fear generated a sense of competing goals rather than shared goals. Once another party was tagged as responsible for having caused a problem, others were effectively off the hook. Shared goals for performance appeared to be weak to nonexistent at American.

By contrast, shared goals at Southwest appeared to be strong. According to a Southwest customer service supervisor:

> The main thing is that everybody cares. We work in so many different areas but it doesn't matter. It's true from the top to the last one hired. . . . Sometimes my friends ask me, why do you like to work at Southwest? I feel like a dork, but it's because everybody cares.

At Southwest, managers, supervisors, and frontline employees in each functional area said that their primary goals were safety, on-time performance, and satisfying the customer. These goals seemed to be shared, in the sense that employees from each functional area referred to the same goals and could explain why they were important. When discussing the need for on-time performance, nearly everybody explained that "our aircraft are valuable and they don't earn any money sitting on the ground." A Southwest ramp supervisor explained to me:

> If we can't keep you, the customer, coming back, we are not going to stay in business.

A Southwest flight attendant supervisor explained:

> Here it's one goal—one hundred percent customer service. Whatever it takes. You can see it just walking through the terminal. Rampers will even help board a flight. There's a desire to be part of the team.

According to a Southwest pilot:

From someone who drives the bus, as it were, if you don't mind my language, people work their asses off. I've never seen so many people work so hard to do one thing. You see people checking their watches to get the on-time departure. People work real hard. Then it's over, and you're back on time.

Even outsiders recognize the shared goals of Southwest's employees. A contract fueler for Southwest explained:

This airline is very different. . . . Here, if there's something to do, people want to do it right away. At US Airways, it was "we still have 15 minutes."

From a Southwest pilot's perspective:

When you come in [to the gate] and see everybody there ready to go to work, it makes you feel great.

In their classic book on organizations, James March and Herbert Simon[7] describe the potentially disintegrative effects when employees in an organization pursue their own functional goals without reference to the over-arching goals of the larger work process. Shared goals play an especially important role when different functions are involved in delivering the same service.[8] The comparison between Southwest and American shows that when employees have the same goals regardless of their functional identity, they can respond in a coordinated way as new information becomes available.

Shared Knowledge

There were also notable differences between American and Southwest in the degree of shared knowledge observed among employees. Interviews with frontline employees at American revealed that they had little awareness of the overall work process, and instead had a tendency to understand their own piece of the process to the exclusion of the rest. When asked what they were doing and why, American employees typically explained their own tasks without reference to the overall process of flight departures. For example, ramp agents explained to me that when the bell rings, it is time to go out to meet the plane.

By contrast, interviews with Southwest frontline employees revealed that they understood the overall work process—and the links between their own jobs and the jobs performed by their counterparts in other functions. When asked to explain what they were doing and why, the answers were typically couched in reference to the overall process. These descriptions by Southwest employees typically took the form, "The pilot has to do A, B, and C before he can take off, so I need to get this to him right away." Rather than just knowing what to do, Southwest employees knew why, based on shared knowledge of how the overall process worked. One pilot explained Southwest's strength with regard to shared knowledge:

> Everyone knows exactly what to do. . . . Each part has a great relationship with the rest. . . . There are no great secrets. Every part is just as important as the rest. The lavs included. Everyone knows what everyone else is doing.

Other work settings also benefit from shared knowledge, and suffer when it is absent. Deborah Dougherty found that members of product development teams representing different functional areas often inhabit different "thought worlds" due to differences in their training, socialization, and expertise.[9] These thought worlds get in the way of effective communication and slow down the product development process. Shared knowledge of the work process by those who are participants in it can link these different thought worlds and therefore enhance coordination.

Mutual Respect

Finally, interviews revealed dramatic differences in the degree of respect shown by employees toward their colleagues in other functional areas. Status boundaries between employees in different functions pose a significant obstacle to coordination in the airline industry. Among station employees there is a tradition of name calling, such as "agent trash" and "ramp rats." As one gate agent explained, "They call them ramp rats for a reason—they're pigs." There is a hierarchy on the ramp that starts with the highly paid mechanics and ends with cabin cleaners. Some of these barriers are due to the very different work performed by each function, and to the geographic distance between these functions, even though their work is highly interdependent. The pilots are at the top of the status hierarchy. As one pilot explained:

Pilots are great at being self-righteous. It's something about the job. The major airlines treat you well. People do what you say. It brings out a certain decisiveness that becomes arrogance.

At American, status boundaries clearly pose an obstacle to coordination. The relationships between the pilots and other functions are particularly problematic. According to a station manager, ramp workers "have a tremendous inferiority complex. They think everyone is looking down on them. The pilots don't respect them." This status barrier between the two functions has clear consequences for delays, according to an American station manager:

> We had a problem . . . with parking airplanes when they arrived. Captains would have to wait for the crews to come out and direct them in. The crews wouldn't necessarily be in any hurry to get out there.

Ramp workers also perceive a lack of respect from flight attendants, and in response tend to put them down. A cabin cleaner at American explained:

> It all comes down to respect. . . . The flight attendants think they're better than [us] when they're sleeping five to an apartment and they're just waitresses in the sky.

Tensions exist among ground employees at American as well. According to a ramp supervisor at American:

> There are employees working here who think they're better than other employees. Gate and ticket agents think they're better than the ramp. The ramp think they're better than cabin services, think it's a sissy, woman's job. Then the cabin cleaners look down on the building cleaners. The mechanics think the ramp are a bunch of luggage handlers.

An American ramp crew chief confirmed these status divisions:

> Cabin cleaning is like a stepchild. All of us have that attitude. "Get out of here and do your job." It's a macho thing—we call them pillow fluffers.

A customer service supervisor at American reported the apparent lack of respect she and her colleagues received from maintenance:

> Maintenance, they are highly specialized and won't talk. They don't have a sense of urgency. You ask them what's wrong with the plane and they look at you like you're female and wouldn't understand if they told you.

She reported that maintenance communicates with the ops center and the pilots, "but they just don't seem to take seriously the 'little girl' at the gate."

Status consciousness permeates the industry and therefore also has the potential to undermine working relationships at Southwest. At Southwest, however, employees tend to treat each other with a great deal of respect. A Southwest manager of ramp and operations explained:

> There's a code, a way you respond to every individual who works for Southwest. The easiest way to get in trouble here is to offend another employee. We need people to respond favorably. It promotes good working relationships.

Southwest employees were observed to speak respectfully of their colleagues in other functions and to interact comfortably with them, whether that person's job is to empty the toilets or fly the plane. According to a Southwest customer service agent:

> No one takes the job of another person for granted. The skycap is just as critical as the pilot. You can always count on the next guy standing there. No one department is any more important than another.

An operations agent compared Southwest to other airlines:

> I would never go work at American Airlines. The animosity there is tremendous. Here it's so cool. Whether you have a college degree or a GED it doesn't matter. There's no status here, just a good work ethic.

Another Southwest operations agent had a similar comment when asked about the relationship between operations and ramp agents:

> Some of us have degrees and some of us don't. But it doesn't matter. We need all of these positions.

A Southwest pilot explained:

> We're predisposed to liking each other—I like the flight attendants and even
> that guy [an operations agent] over there and I don't even know him. I guess
> it's mutual respect.

John Van Maanen and Steve Barley's[10] work suggests that members of
distinct occupational communities are often divided by differences in status
and that these communities may bolster their own status by actively culti-
vating disrespect for the work performed by others. When members of
these distinct occupational communities are engaged in a common work
process, the potential for these divisive relationships to undermine coordination is apparent. Respect for the competence of other employees is fundamental to the coordination of work processes, whether the work involves
flight departures, research and development, or jazz improvisation.[11]

Exhibit 3–1 summarizes the dimensions of communication and relationships that are integral to effective coordination.

Coordinating through Relationships

All of the above evidence suggests that effective coordination requires
frequent, timely, problem-solving communication carried out through
relationships of shared goals, shared knowledge, and mutual respect.
This is precisely what relational coordination means. In environments
where relational coordination is weak, performance is also weak, as data
in the next section will show. With strong relationships, employees
embrace rather than reject their connections with one another, enabling
them to coordinate more effectively with each other. Shared goals motivate employees to move beyond what is best for their own narrow area
of responsibility and act with regard for the overall work process.
Shared knowledge among employees regarding how their tasks are
related to other tasks enables them to act with regard for the overall
work process. Respect for the work of others encourages employees to
value the contributions of others and to consider the impact of their
actions on others, further reinforcing the inclination to act with regard
for the overall work process.

Employees who feel disrespected by members of another function
avoid communication (and even eye contact) with members of that function. Without relationships of shared knowledge, employees are less able
to engage in timely communication when circumstances change sud-

Exhibit 3–1 Dimensions of Relational Coordination

	American	Southwest
Relationships		
Shared goals	"Ninety percent of the ramp employees don't care what happens, even if the walls fall down, as long as they get their check."	"I've never seen so many people work so hard to do one thing. You see people checking their watches to get the on-time departure. . . . Then it's over and you're back on time."
Shared knowledge	Participants revealed little awareness of the overall process. They typically explained their own set of tasks without reference to the overall process of flight departures.	Participants exhibited relatively clear mental models of the overall process— an understanding of the links between their own jobs and the jobs of other functions. Rather than just knowing what to do, they knew why, based on shared knowledge of how the overall process worked.
Mutual respect	"There are employees working here who think they're better than other employees. Gate and ticket agents think they're better than the ramp. The ramp think they're better than cabin cleaners—think it's a sissy, woman's job. Then the cabin cleaners look down on the building cleaners. The mechanics think the ramp are a bunch of luggage handlers."	"No one takes the job of another person for granted. The skycap is just as critical as the pilot. You can always count on the next guy standing there. No one department is any more important than another."

table continues

Exhibit 3–1 Dimensions of Relational Coordination (continued)

	American	Southwest
Communication		
Frequent and timely communication	"Here you don't communicate. And sometimes you end up not knowing things. . . . Everyone says we need effective communication. But it's a low priority in action. . . . The hardest thing at the gates when flights are delayed is to get information."	"There is constant communication between customer service and the ramp. When planes have to be switched and bags must be moved, customer service will advise the ramp directly or through operations." If there's an aircraft swap "operations keeps everyone informed. . . . It happens smoothly."
Problem-solving communication	"If you ask anyone here, what's the last thing you think of when there's a problem, I bet your bottom dollar it's the customer. And these are guys who work hard every day. But they're thinking, how do I keep my ass out of the sling?"	"We figure out the cause of the delay. We do not necessarily chastise, though sometimes that comes into play. It is a matter of working together. Figuring out what we can learn. Not finger pointing."

denly, not knowing with sufficient precision who needs to know what and with what urgency. Without shared goals, the easiest response to problems is to blame others for having caused the problem rather than to engage in problem solving with them.

Does relational coordination really make a difference for performance, and if so, how can managers make it happen in their own organizations? The performance question is answered in the next section, and again in the following chapter. The implementation question is answered in detail throughout Part 2 of this book.

Southwest versus Continental, American, and United: Relational Coordination Pays Off

Relational coordination isn't just a morale-boosting nicety for employees. It accounts for dramatic differences in flight departure performance between Southwest and other airlines. Relational coordination allows Southwest employees to respond rapidly to new information, resulting in fewer customer complaints, flight delays, and lost bags. Relational coordination also results in better utilization of staff and gate time because less time is wasted waiting to hear from others, conducting redundant communication, looking for missing information, etc., with the result that flight departures can be staffed more leanly and scheduled with shorter turnaround times.

These observations were confirmed with data from a study involving two Southwest sites, two Continental sites, two American sites, and three United sites. Sites included some that were considered to be high performers, as well as some that were considered to be troubled—particularly the second Southwest site, located in Los Angeles and suffering greatly at the time from rapid rates of growth, high employee turnover, and managerial inexperience. A third site of United that was considered to be very promising was then included—the launch site for the United Shuttle, designed to fight back against Southwest's incursions into the California market.

Measuring Relational Coordination and Performance

At each of these nine sites, employees were surveyed from five core functions—ticketing agents, gate agents, baggage transfer agents, ramp agents, and operations agents—about their communication and relationships with each other and with pilots, flight attendants, mechanics, caterers, cabin cleaners, fuelers, and cargo agents.[12] See Exhibit 3–2 for the survey questions used to measure relational coordination.

Quality performance was measured in three ways—customer complaints, mishandled bags, and late arrivals—the same measures that are tracked on a monthly basis by the U.S. Department of Transportation. In addition, efficiency performance was measured in two ways—turnaround time per departure and staff time per passenger.[13] Of course, other factors besides coordination affect quality and efficiency performance. Some were described in Chap. 2, where the particular challenges

Exhibit 3–2 Relational Coordination Survey Items*

Relationships	
Shared goals	Do people in these groups have the same work goals as you?
Shared knowledge	How much do people in each of these groups know about your job?
Mutual respect	How much respect do you get from the people in each of these groups?

Communication	
Frequent communication	How often do you communicate with each of these groups?
Timely communication	Do the people in these groups communicate with you in a timely way?
Problem-solving communication	When there is a problem, do the people in these groups try to solve the problem, or try to determine whose fault it was?

* Respondents were asked to answer each question with respect to each of the 12 functions involved in flight departures. Answers were in the form of a 5-point Likert scale.

of Southwest's short-haul strategy and the cost savings made possible by its simpler product were explained. To capture these product characteristics, average length of flight, number of passengers per flight, tons of cargo per flight, and percentage of passengers connecting were measured.[14] Number of flights per day at a given site was also included to capture the potential effects of operational scale. Performance and product variables are shown in Exhibit 3–3.

Findings

As expected, communication and relationships were highly correlated—employees who engaged in frequent, timely, problem-solving communication with other functions also had relationships based on shared goals, shared knowledge, and mutual respect.[15] Strong relationships fostered high-quality communication, while high-quality communication helped employees build strong relationships with each other.

In addition, there were substantial differences in overall levels of relational coordination from one site to another, even within the same airline.

Exhibit 3-3 Performance and Product Measures

Efficiency Performance	
Turnaround time	Minutes of scheduled time at the gate, per departure, equal to the average difference between scheduled arrival time for each aircraft and its scheduled departure time, excluding flights with overnight stay
Staff time	Airport employees per 1000 daily passengers, including full-time-equivalent airport personnel in the ticket, gate, operations, ramp, and cabin cleaning functions
Quality Performance	
Customer complaints	Number of airport-related customer complaints per 100,000 passengers
Lost baggage	Number of bags mishandled per 1000 passengers
Late arrivals	Percentage of flights arriving at their down-line destination more than 15 minutes late
Product Measures	
Flights per day	Number of flights departing per day
Average flight length	Average length of flights
Passengers per flight	Average number of passengers per flight
Cargo per flight	Average tons of cargo carried per flight
Passenger connections	Percentage of passengers who are making connections

Of the nine sites in this study, Southwest's Chicago site had by far the highest overall levels of relational coordination. However, the next highest level of relational coordination was found at the United Shuttle's Los Angeles site. Southwest's Los Angeles site ranked third. Because Southwest's Los Angeles site was deliberately chosen as one that was struggling with growth issues at the time, this was not surprising. Continental, United, and American Airlines each had one site with moderately high levels of relational coordination—and each also had one site with relatively low levels of relational coordination.[16] In addition to significant differences in relational coordination across these nine sites, there were also significant differences in product characteristics and performance.[17]

Using statistical techniques to account for the effects of product characteristics,[18] relational coordination was found to affect significantly the performance of the flight departure process. Relational coordination enables shorter turnaround times, greater employee productivity, fewer customer complaints, fewer lost bags, and fewer flight delays. A doubling of relational coordination among frontline employees enables a 21 percent reduction in turnaround time and a 42 percent increase in employee productivity. That same increase in relational coordination contributes to a 64 percent decrease in customer complaints, a 31 percent decrease in lost baggage, and a 50 percent decrease in flight delays.[19]

The performance effects of relational coordination are large and statistically significant. This means that you can be confident of achieving improved performance results if you can achieve an increase in relational coordination.[20] There is a simpler, more graphic way to observe the overall performance effects of relational coordination. After efficiency and quality measures were adjusted for product differences, they were combined into a single measure of performance. Overall performance for each of the nine sites was then plotted against relational coordination. Exhibit 3–4 shows a clear positive impact of relational coordination on performance.

Improving Both Quality and Efficiency

We have seen that relational coordination does not just improve the quality or the efficiency of service delivery in this setting—it improves both simultaneously. This is impressive. Many organizational practices that improve efficiency do so at the cost of reduced quality. Likewise, many organizational practices that improve quality do so at the cost of reduced efficiency. It is very unusual, and powerful, when an organizational practice leads to both increased quality and increased efficiency. The findings reported here show that relational coordination has significant positive effects on both quality and efficiency. Efficiency/quality trade-offs are the rule in most business operations, but improvements in relational coordination, like other fundamental process improvements, allow an organization to *shift* the efficiency/quality curve outward to a more favorable position.[21]

Exhibit 3–4 Impact of Relational Coordination on Flight Departure
Performance*

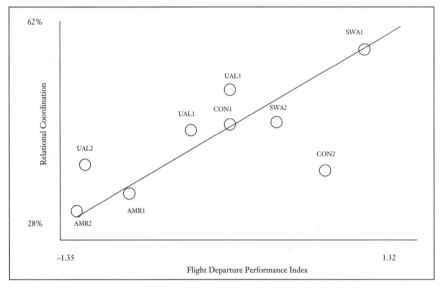

* Each circle denotes one of the nine sites included in the study. Relational coordination,
coordination carried out through relationships of shared goals, shared knowledge, and
mutual respect, is measured as the percent of cross-functional ties that are strong or very
strong, based on an employee survey. Flight departure performance is an index of quality—
customer complaints, mishandled bags, and late arrivals—as well as efficiency—turnaround
time per departure and staff time per passenger. Each performance measure was adjusted
for differences in product characteristics and combined into a single performance index.

Why Relational Coordination Works: The Power of Collective Identity

We have seen that there are three important elements of working relationships for achieving effective coordination: shared goals, shared
knowledge, and mutual respect. These relationships have powerful
effects because they shape our personal identities. Through relationships, other people influence the development of our identities, just as
we influence the development of theirs. Relationships of shared goals,
shared knowledge, and mutual respect help us to form a collective identity with others, enabling us to engage more easily in coordinated collective action. In contrast, organizations that lack shared goals, shared
knowledge, and mutual respect tend to have weak collective identities.
Individual workers do not identify with the organization strongly, and

tend not to consider what is best for the organization. Instead they focus on what is best for accomplishing their own narrow task.

Postmodernists[22] and feminist philosophers[23] have argued that the relational basis of human identity has been overlooked in our individualistic society, and that in fact our identities are "socially constructed." Indeed, as Joyce Fletcher has argued, the way people work together cannot be fully understood without this relational perspective.[24] Organizational social capital, embedded in interpersonal relationships, is therefore likely to be critical for organizational performance.[25] However, the division of labor poses a tremendous challenge. The division of labor is a powerful source of efficiency and productivity, as Adam Smith showed over 200 years ago,[26] but it results in alienation and fragmentation of human identity.[27] Strong working relationships can serve to overcome the alienation created by the division of labor by creating more holistic, social identities in place of the more partial and fragmented identities that lead people to reject their connections with others.

In sum, relationships shape our own personal identities: they define who we are. It is no wonder, then, that relationships among people who work together—particularly their shared goals, shared knowledge, and respect for one another, or lack thereof—are such powerful drivers of organizational performance.

This chapter has one critical implication for managers. Although relationships are relatively "soft" organizational factors and therefore tempting to neglect under challenging conditions, relationships of shared goals, shared knowledge, and mutual respect contribute *substantially* to effective coordination and to the quality and efficiency of organizational performance. In Part 2 of this book, we will learn how Southwest Airlines creates these high levels of relational coordination through 10 distinctive organizational practices, and how these practices can be implemented in any organization. First, however, the next chapter demonstrates that the performance effects of relational coordination are not unique to the airline industry.

How Relational Coordination Works in Other Industries

The Case of Health Care

It's not just individual brilliance that matters anymore. It's a coordinated effort.
—Chief Social Worker, Beth Israel Deaconess Medical Center

WE LEARNED IN Chap. 3 that coordination does not occur in a relational vacuum. Relational coordination is coordination carried out through relationships of shared goals, shared knowledge, and mutual respect. We also learned that relational coordination accounts for a great deal of Southwest's performance advantage. Does relational coordination boost performance in other service delivery settings? This chapter demonstrates the power of relational coordination in the health-care industry.

The Challenge of Coordinating Patient Care

Effective coordination is lacking in many service settings, but particularly in the delivery of health care.[1] Patients are often left to find their own way through the system, receiving diagnoses and treatments from a loosely connected set of providers. Even within the hospital setting, where coordination would seem to be more readily achieved, it often falls to patients and their families to coordinate their own care. According to Anselm Strauss and his team of medical sociologists:

> Coordination of care, for which personnel are constantly striving but know they are not often attaining, is something of a mirage except for the most standardized of trajectories. Its attainment is something of a miracle when it actually does occur.[2]

Similar to the flight departure process, some of the biggest challenges in patient-care coordination occur at the point of departure—or discharge—from the hospital. Michael Hubner, an administrator at one of the Harvard teaching hospitals, explained:

> Patient discharge is an interesting nexus. That's where all the failures are. That's where you can blow it. That's also where all the drama is. There is a letting go of safety into the unknown.

Her colleague, Mary McDonough, explained how these failures in coordination can occur:

> There's a moment in time when the patient is identified as perhaps needing extended care after discharge. . . . It's time-sensitive because you can't be too late or too early for the window. The window is determined by patient functioning, based on lab tests, their temperature, whether they are ambulatory, etc. This is a time when people are stepping over each other with overlapping responsibilities for the patient.
> Everyone is waiting for the next person to do something but it hasn't always been clear they were waiting. The social worker is waiting for the resident to get back to her about the next task. One or two people get to be seen as the person who is watching the discharge plan. But everybody needs to be on the same playing field.

There is a great deal of evidence that both the quality and efficiency of patient care are negatively affected by poor coordination among providers,[3] and some evidence that relationships play a critical role in the coordination of care.[4] Coordination failures occur during handoffs among hospital-based staff. Failure to coordinate can lead to errors in medication and errors in treatment.[5] Recent research suggests that errors in patient care stemming from coordination failures are more likely than other errors to result in costly malpractice claims.[6] Poor coordination also results in scheduling problems such as delays in testing or treatment. Finally, poor coordination results in conflicting information to the patient and his or her family, and can lead to a loss of confidence in the provider.[7] It can also produce confused, misinformed patients who may not be able or willing to cooperate with treatment. Even if all medical outcomes are achieved, patients who were dissatisfied with how they were treated can have a negative impact on hospitals in a competitive environment by generating negative word of mouth and reducing referrals.

Performance Effects of Relational Coordination

A nine-hospital study of patient care was conducted to measure relational coordination and its effects on patient outcomes. The study focused on joint replacement surgery because it is an increasingly common type of surgery performed on the elderly, and yet very costly, so hospitals have strong interests in improving both the quality and efficiency with which it is performed. Nine hospitals with orthopedic departments that perform high volumes of joint replacements were chosen to participate, including four Boston hospitals: Massachusetts General Hospital, Brigham and Women's Hospital, Beth Israel Deaconess Medical Center, and New England Baptist Hospital; three New York City hospitals: Beth Israel Hospital, Hospital for Joint Diseases, and Hospital for Special Surgery; and two Dallas-area hospitals: Baylor University Medical Center and Presbyterian Plano Hospital.

Relational Coordination

As in the flight departure study described in the previous chapter, relational coordination was measured using an employee survey, asking physicians, nurses, physical therapists, social workers, and case managers about their communication and relationships with each other regarding the care of joint replacement patients. Participants were asked to answer the same six questions as in the study of flight departures, concerning the frequency, timeliness, and problem-solving orientation of communication; and the degree of shared goals, shared knowledge, and mutual respect experienced with each other participant in the patient-care process. However, one new question was added—regarding the accuracy of communication—recognizing the importance of *accuracy* for effective coordination of patient care.[8]

Performance Measures

As in the flight departure study, performance was measured along two dimensions—the quality of care and the efficiency with which it was delivered. Patients assessed the quality of care in a survey they received after hospitalization. Patient-assessed quality has not traditionally been considered to be a relevant outcome in health-care settings. However, "as the orientation to health care began shifting from scientific mandates and medical techniques to markets and the more human side of health care—a service delivery system—patient satisfaction has become an important dimension of the quality of care."[9] The importance of patient assessment of quality became evident through clinical work on patient-centered care[10] and has continued to grow in importance as a dimension of health-care quality.[11] In addition, patients were asked to assess the quality of their surgical outcomes. The two primary outcomes patients expect from joint replacement surgery are freedom from joint pain and greater functional abilities (walking, climbing stairs, and so on). Patients were asked to report their levels of joint pain and functional abilities before and after surgery. The efficiency of care delivery was measured as the number of days spent in acute care.

As in the case of flight departures, other variables are known to affect performance in this setting, including patient age, health conditions, type of surgery (hip versus knee), psychological well-being, race, gender, marital status, and the volume of joint replacements performed by the hospital in the past six months.[12]

Findings

As in the flight departure study, all of the communication and relationship components of relational coordination were strongly interrelated with each other.[13] In addition, there were significant differences between hospitals in the strength of relational coordination among their care providers,[14] and in all aspects of patient-care performance.[15]

Accounting for differences in patient and hospital characteristics, relational coordination significantly improves performance of the patient-care process. Relational coordination among care providers enables shorter hospital stays, higher levels of patient-perceived quality of care, and improved clinical outcomes. To illustrate, a 100 percent increase in relational coordination among care providers enables a 31 percent reduction in the length of hospital stays and a 22 percent increase in the quality of service that patients receive. That same increase in relational coordination contributes to a 7 percent increase in postoperative freedom from pain and a 5 percent increase in postoperative mobility (the two key clinical outcomes of joint replacement surgery).[17]

Some of these performance effects of relational coordination are quite large and statistically significant. This means that you can be quite certain of achieving improved performance results if you can achieve an increase in relational coordination.[18]

There is a simpler, more graphic way to observe the overall performance effects of relational coordination. Efficiency and quality measures were adjusted for differences in patient and hospital characteristics, then combined into a single measure of performance. Overall performance was plotted for each of the nine hospitals against relational coordination. Exhibit 4–1 shows a clear positive impact of relational coordination on patient-care performance.

When Relational Coordination Matters Most for Performance

These data show that relational coordination contributes to important performance outcomes for patient care, a work setting that is dramatically different from the airline industry. Relational coordination has significant positive effects on several important outcomes for surgical patients: improved quality of care, improved clinical outcomes, and shorter hospital lengths of stay. As in the case of flight departures, it is important to note that increases in efficiency (shorter lengths of stay) were not achieved at the expense of either clinical outcomes or the quality of care. Indeed, as in the case of flight departures, relational coordination enabled hospitals to achieve simultaneous improvements in the quality and efficiency of patient care. In a very different service delivery

Exhibit 4–1 Impact of Relational Coordination on Patient-Care Performance*

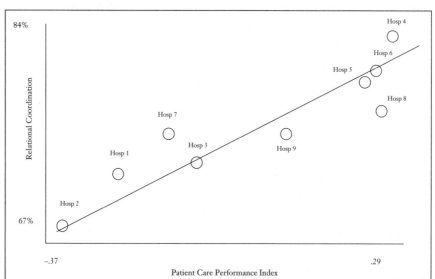

* Each circle denotes one of the nine hospitals included in the study. Relational coordination, coordination carried out through relationships of shared goals, shared knowledge, and mutual respect, is measured as the percent of cross-functional ties that are strong or very strong, based on an employee survey. Patient-care performance is an index of quality: quality of care, postoperative freedom from pain, and postoperative functioning, as well as efficiency: number of days in acute care. Each performance measure was adjusted for differences in patient and hospital characteristics and combined into a single performance index.

context from the one in which Southwest Airlines is operating, we find concrete evidence that relationships have a powerful effect on organizational performance.

What is it about flight departures and patient care that make relational coordination so important? What other kinds of settings should benefit most from relational coordination? Relational coordination is most valuable for performance in settings with three characteristics.

Task Interdependence

First, relational coordination boosts performance when tasks are reciprocally interdependent;[19] in other words, when each action taken by any participant has a potential influence on multiple other participants. In patient care, due to reciprocal interdependence, care providers do not have the luxury of simple, sequential handoffs that are found on production lines. Instead the handoffs are iterative, requiring feedback among providers as new information emerges about the patient. Likewise in the flight departure process, reciprocal task interdependence results in the need for feedback among the tasks that are performed by the 12 functions involved in flight departures, as new information arises during preparation for departure.

Uncertainty

Second, relational coordination boosts performance when there are high levels of uncertainty, requiring continuous updates of information and adjustments in plans.[20] In health care, uncertainty surrounds a given patient's reaction to interventions and the speed of his or her recovery. Uncertainty is also endemic to the flight departure process, with multiple sources of uncertainty: the timing of incoming flight arrivals, the possibility of mechanical difficulties, the weather conditions to be encountered by departing flights, the timing and number of passengers and bags arriving for departing flights, and the timing and quantity of freight to be shipped on departing flights. These multiple sources of uncertainty create the need for continuous updates of information and adjustments in plans, and often interact with each other in unforeseeable ways.

Time Constraints

Third, relational coordination boosts performance in settings that are time-constrained. Time constraints limit an organization's ability to use time buffers to reduce the effects of interdependence and uncertainty.[21] With strict time constraints, one cannot simply add time between tasks to reduce reciprocal interdependence and produce a more orderly, sequential work process. Similarly, one cannot reduce the effects of uncertainty by responding in a more leisurely way to new information. Time constraints play a critical role in the delivery of patient care due to clinical requirements to assess the patient for possible negative reactions and to mobilize the patient in a timely fashion after surgery. Pressures from managed care for timely patient discharge further intensify time constraints. There is no longer the luxury of allowing delays to occur due to poor coordination; the new payment structure imposes the costs of delays on the hospital rather than the payer. Time constraints also play a critical role in flight departures due to the need for all passengers, baggage, freight, fuel, and meals or refreshments—and the correct information pertaining to each of the above—to be on board at the time of departure. Time constraints have been further heightened in the airline industry as fare competition increases the pressure to schedule quick turnarounds at the gate to maximize utilization of costly aircraft.

Summing Up

The three conditions that increase the need for relational coordination—reciprocal interdependence, uncertainty, and time constraints—are increasingly common in the service economy of today. As advanced economies have shifted from a manufacturing to a service focus, work settings that require relational coordination have become increasingly common. Many service operations are characterized by reciprocal interdependence, requiring iterative interactions among service providers rather than the sequential handoffs performed by workers on production lines. Many service operations also have high levels of uncertainty relative to manufacturing due to the difficulty of buffering service operations from the external environment and from differences in customers themselves. Finally, most service settings are highly time-constrained; they are designed to provide a service to customers, real time, simultaneous with the demand, without imposing excessive waiting times on customers. Even the manufacturing sector, with its shift to service orientation and just-in-time production, is increasingly taking on the challenging characteristics of the service sector. This means that relational coordination is increasingly relevant for organizations of today, including possibly your own organization.

We now turn in Part 2 to the central questions in this book: how does Southwest Airlines achieve such high levels of relational coordination, and how can your organization do the same?

2

Ten Southwest Practices for Building High Performance Relationships

How does Southwest Airlines build strong relationships, generating high levels of coordination and therefore high levels of quality and efficiency performance? As you might expect, there is no magic bullet. Rather, Southwest has developed an innovative set of 10 organizational practices, each one designed to reinforce the others so that the total is greater than the sum of the parts. See Exhibit P2-1. These practices build and sustain relationships in multiple ways—through leadership at the top and at the front line, through hiring and training, resolving conflicts, managing work/family issues, creating special boundary roles, measuring performance broadly, negotiating flexible job descriptions, and partnering with the external parties that are critical for Southwest's success. These practices can be adapted to your own organization's needs to create high levels of relational coordination and outstanding performance.

The idea that high performance depends on bundles of organizational practices—rather than individual practices—is a powerful one that extends to other industry settings. Evidence from the auto industry,[1] the apparel industry,[2] the steel industry,[3] and the telecommunications industry[4] shows that bundles of practices can have powerful, positive effects on performance. This book is part of a series of studies that shows how bundles of mutually reinforcing organizational practices can launch organizations onto a high performance trajectory.[5]

Not just any organizational practice goes into these high performance bundles. Indeed, there is increasing evidence, as documented in Chaps. 3 and 4, that strong relationships are at the heart of high performance. Whether these relationships are conceived as social capital, teamwork, or relational coordination, the common thread is that they are critical for achieving high performance. The guiding principle behind organizational practices that create high performance is that they need somehow to build and sustain relationships among the organization's key participants.

The following 10 chapters show how Southwest's organizational practices do just this.

Exhibit P2–1 Ten Southwest Practices for Building High Performance Relationships

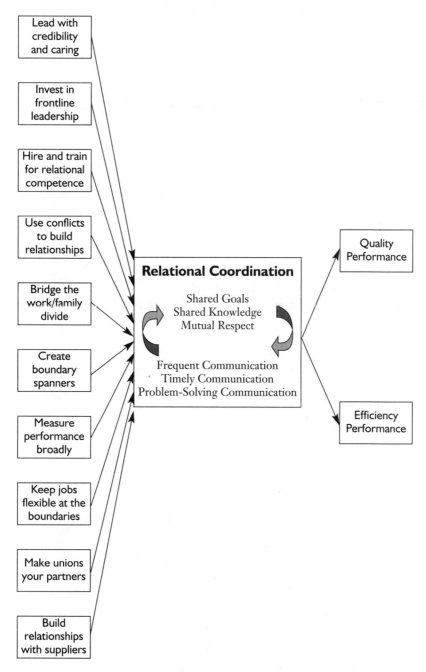

CHAPTER

Lead with Credibility and Caring

[Herb Kelleher and Colleen Barrett] have both got credibility. It's taken them a while to get to that point. They've created this level of honesty with us. If it's bad, they tell you it's bad.

—Ramp Manager, Southwest Airlines

[Herb] is one of the inspirations for this company. He's the guiding light. He listens to everybody. He's unbelievable when it comes to personal etiquette. If you've got a problem, he cares.

—Pilot, Southwest Airlines

I am not all that special. It is not like we have some formula here like "E equals MC squared." It is a tremendous mosaic made up of thousands of people.

—Herb Kelleher, Chairman of the Board, Southwest Airlines[1]

SOUTHWEST IS SO often congratulated on its outstanding leadership that this chapter hardly seemed necessary. Though the importance of leadership should not be overestimated relative to other organizational practices, neither should it be underestimated. But what *is* leadership? Leadership expert Ralph Stogdill once quipped that "there are almost as many definitions of leadership as there are persons who have attempted to define the concept."[2] These definitions range from the mundane—"the behavior of an individual directing the activities of an organized group toward goal achievement"[3]—to the esoteric—"articulating visions, embodying values and creating the environment within which things can be accomplished."[4] In this chapter we will attempt to understand better the effectiveness of Southwest's leadership by contrasting it to the leadership of American, United, and Continental Airlines. We will see that credibility and caring are two critical ingredients of leadership effectiveness at Southwest, and will conclude by describing the leadership transition at Southwest when Herb Kelleher stepped down, and the ongoing role that is played by Southwest's top management team.

Leadership at Southwest Airlines

CEO Herb Kelleher and his top management team have excelled at gaining the trust of managers in the field and frontline employees. They have built trust over time by being up front and consistent in their message. A ramp manager at Southwest explained how trust between frontline employees and top management facilitates the work of managers throughout the company:

> It helps you as a manager when Herb gives it to the employees without sugar coating. Something about Herb, if he says it, it's law. Colleen is a very, very big part of this puzzle too. The programs we try to get across have her name on it. And we know it. Herb's the showman but she's a very, very, very big force. Colleen in many ways is just as big as Herb to us. When she speaks we all listen. They've both got credibility. It's taken them a while to get to that point. They've created this level of honesty with us. If it's bad, they tell you it's bad.

An operations agent in the Phoenix station explained the importance to her of being able to trust top management:

> If I didn't work at Southwest, I would not work in this industry. At the other carriers, they don't trust the managers. I have friends who work for other carriers and the whole attitude is just completely different. The CEO says something, and they don't believe what he says. Herb is so obtainable.

Southwest's top managers have also made themselves available to frontline employees, demonstrating a level of caring that is beyond the norm in large companies. This accessibility was mentioned time and again as a building block of the relationship between frontline employees and top management at Southwest. A pilot explained:

> I can call Herb today. You don't just call and say there's a problem. He'll say, "think about it and tell me the solution that you think will work." He has an open door policy. I can call him almost 24 hours a day. If it's an emergency, he will call back in 15 minutes. He is one of the inspirations for this company. He's the guiding light. He listens to everybody. He's unbelievable when it comes to personal etiquette. If you've got a problem, he cares.

Another pilot concurred:

> Herb is a true charismatic leader. He's not your average CEO. He really cares to let people know he cares. When he talks to you, he is really focused on what you are saying. No one can pry him loose. I've seen this. He sets the example of respect for everyone. All are important. Treat each other with the same respect as our customers. So people are happy.

Colleen Barrett, president and chief operating officer of Southwest, is also mentioned time and again as an important leadership figure at Southwest. A station manager explained the role that Colleen Barrett plays at Southwest:

> Colleen remembers everyone and everything—if you have a birthday you'll get a card from her. She's up there with Jesus Christ, in our eyes.

A flight attendant base manager had similar praise for Barrett:

> I had the opportunity to be on the culture committee last year, and I got to know her firsthand. She and Herb are genuinely interested in creating jobs for people.

A customer service agent in Los Angeles gave Colleen similar praise, after experiencing firsthand the impact that Colleen had on turning around Southwest's troubled Los Angeles station in the early 1990s:

> Colleen is the greatest. She spreads the Southwest spirit. She's adamant about it.

One of Southwest's chief pilots offered his perspective on Colleen:

> Colleen Barrett has an amazing ability to work simply with a lot of issues. She and Herb must write letters all day and all night. They communicate with customers and employees on every little issue. Their philosophy is to take care of the small problems. When someone has a problem here, even if it might seem small, I have to take care of it. It is a necessary element in the development of trust.

In effect, Herb and Colleen set an example through their own actions to the rest of the company regarding the importance of relationships. To demonstrate caring, the top leadership of Southwest Airlines has held to a no-layoff policy throughout its 31-year history (more about this in Chap. 17).

Kelleher's belief in treating people with respect has infused relationships throughout Southwest Airlines. He explains how he came to have this belief:

> My mother taught me that. She was an extraordinary person. When I was very young—11 or 12—she used to sit up talking to me till three, four in the morning. She talked a lot about how you should treat people with respect. She said that positions and titles signify absolutely nothing. They're just adornments; they don't represent the substance of anybody.
>
> I was kind of her disciple. I learned firsthand that what she was telling me was correct, because there was a very dignified gentleman in our neighborhood, the president of a savings and loan, who used to stroll along in a very regal way up until he was indicted and convicted of embezzlement. She taught me that every person and every job is worth just as much as any other person and any other job.[5]

Leadership at Continental Airlines

Living in the shadow of Frank Lorenzo's legacy, subsequent leaders of Continental Airlines faced an uphill battle in winning the trust of frontline employees. Gordon Bethune was selected as Continental's new CEO in October 1994, based in part on his reputation in the industry for credibility with employees. Bethune's reputation was illustrated by the fact that he was one of the top candidates considered by United's unions in their selection of a new CEO after the employee buyout, though ultimately Gerald Greenwald was chosen instead. Bethune described his experience of coming to Continental:

> It was the most difficult place I've ever come in my life. . . . It's the value system that was in place, the over kind of focus on lowest cost is the way to win, when it certainly hadn't won in ten years. Obviously, it had the makings of a good company, but it was what you'd have to characterize as dysfunctional.[6]

Bethune brought with him a team of like-minded executives, including Greg Brenneman as chief operating officer and Mike Campbell as vice president of employee relations. Brenneman characterized the state of the airline when the new management team arrived:

> People were focused on pitting the pilots against the mechanics and the gate agents against the flight attendants to see if you could beat down labor costs by getting them fighting with one another. And, of course, this is the biggest team sport in the world. You have to get everybody working together.[7]

Prior to Bethune's arrival, managers felt they had to work against the dominant Continental culture to minimize these boundaries so that work could get done. From the perspective of the Cleveland station manager:

> I see *my* job as breaking down those invisible boundaries. This is not Continental culture more generally. . . . The chair of the board sets the tone. He is watching his investment. He is grounded in investment rather than operations.

Early in his leadership Bethune began to send strong signals that he would encourage openness, to win the trust of Continental's workforce. Within two weeks of his arrival, he declared Fridays to be casual dress days and announced that all offices in the company's Houston headquarters would be open to all Continental employees without requiring a special access card. He increased the employee newsletter to a monthly frequency, introduced a new publication for employees called the *Continental Quarterly*, and generated a daily "Message from Senior Management" available through voicemail to the entire Continental workforce. He took the approach of being open and frank with frontline employees regarding the strategy shift Continental was engaged in at the time he took on leadership of the company. A Boston customer service agent explained to me:

> Our strategy is changing constantly. No one knows what's going on. . . . Senior managers just walk into training sessions and say things that no one has ever heard. [But] there has been some attempt at informing us. Bethune made a videotape that we just viewed here in the station. He says that senior management screwed up for the past year. . . . Now we are doing a reversal. We have to make money by hook or crook. We will do whatever we have to do. . . . That's it, plain and simple.

Bethune's frankness was a dramatic change from the secrecy and hedging to which Continental employees had become accustomed, and went a long way toward winning the trust of frontline employees.

Bethune also made it his job to start breaking down the boundaries between functions to get people talking to each other. The Cleveland station manager described Bethune's approach:

> When Continental Lite was developed, schedulers were never involved. Neither was flight, maintenance, or the stations. Now Gordon is getting them to talk together. Putting people in a room and closing the door for five days.

In addition, Bethune became well known for his belief in using incentives to get employees to work together—paying each Continental employee $65 every month that Continental was ranked in the top 5 for on-time performance. According to Bethune, the money was simply a way to teach the lesson that working together pays off:

> Sixty-five bucks was a nice way of saying thank you to a bunch of people who learned that the only way to get the 65 bucks is when they all work together. And it's been working for us ever since. It's not a lot, but it doesn't sometimes take a lot to show that this is like an appreciative change in the way we behave.[8]

The challenge for Bethune's leadership would come with September 11, 2001, when employees would find out whether the new approach to leadership at Continental was for real, and whether the airline had built up enough resources after 10 lean years under Lorenzo to make

Bethune's commitment to Continental employees a reality (more on this in Chap. 17).

Leadership at United Airlines

When Gerald Greenwald was first brought in as CEO in 1994 as part of United's employee buyout, he worked hard to build relationships with both employees and their unions. United's unions had criticized his predecessor, Steven Wolf, for having a view of cooperation that meant "I decide and you agree." Gerald Greenwald enjoyed the support of the pilots and other employee groups partly on the grounds that he was perceived to respect them and their union representatives. Greenwald's background suggested that he would have the skills to bring together labor, management, and shareholders in an employee-owned company.[9] Greenwald had provided the financial expertise for Lee Iaccoca's bailout of Chrysler, and in so doing had gained the respect of both Wall Street and the United Auto Workers' union. Furthermore, Greenwald had worked as a labor organizer while a student at Princeton, and he had wanted to lead an employee-owned company since 1990, when United's pilots were first planning a buyout of the airline and approached him to lead it. Indeed, Greenwald placed great hopes on employee ownership as a solution for United's troubles. As he said in an interview with *Air Transport World*, "We're banking on ownership to be our edge in a competition we've simply got to win."[10]

Greenwald announced that he planned to spend half of his time with employees, empowering them to make decisions.[11] He traveled throughout the United system early in his leadership to learn from employees about the company. In one 10-day stretch, he held 37 meetings. In interviews with frontline employees in the mid-1990s, they expressed a belief that Greenwald cared about them and was interested in their work. They expressed hopefulness and outright enthusiasm about his leadership. One ramp agent in Los Angeles was strongly influenced by Greenwald's leadership:

> There are a lot of radicals here, but they are starting to change. I had the privilege of meeting Greenwald. He was incredibly supportive. I never knew that those kind of people cared. Everybody just wanted to be involved. Next thing you know, you had 300 people. I used to raise hell around here for

minor little things. But I was thrilled with the ESOP. Even the serious problem children were thrilled. . . . People are coming around.

The Los Angeles station manager was also impressed with Greenwald's
approach:

Steve [Wolf] had more of a controlling style than Gerry Greenwald. They
want the same thing, but have different ways of getting it. It may have helped
Gerry to be coming from outside the industry. . . . Greenwald's done it per-
fectly. He came in with no answers, but with an end result he wants. Others
come in and say I want to control this and this. Greenwald just says, make
yourself understand why you do what you do.

Given his lack of industry knowledge, one of Greenwald's first challenges was to choose a knowledgeable second-in-command who would
inevitably play a major role in leading the company. According to the
president of United's flight attendant union:

It is very difficult to have a conversation with [Greenwald] on substantial
issues, because he's just not conversant with the terms of the industry.[12]

Greenwald chose John Edwardson, former chief financial officer and executive vice president of Northwest Airlines, to serve as president of United Airlines and to run the day-to-day operations of the company. According to
Edwardson, "Gerry called me and said, 'Get to work,' so I drove in and
did."[13] As we will see in Chap. 13, however, Greenwald and Edwardson were
ultimately challenged and perhaps overwhelmed by the complexity of
labor/management relations in an employee-owned company.

Leadership at American Airlines

Long-time American Airlines leader Robert Crandall had a difficult time
winning the trust of American's frontline employees, because of the
approach he often took in his efforts to align American's frontline
employees with his goals. In one particularly critical incident, Crandall
announced publicly in 1993 that the only unprofitable piece of American's parent company, AMR Corporation, was the airline itself. AMR
Corporation's management consulting services and information systems

businesses were making money, Crandall pointed out, while the airline itself was losing money. Crandall proposed a Transition Plan, in which American would continue to fly in those markets where it could still compete, exit the markets where American could no longer compete, while American's parent company would continue to grow its profitable nonairline businesses. American would in effect become more of a back-office operation for other airlines.

In his President's Conference with employees in Boston that spring, Crandall presented for about 20 minutes on the challenges ahead for the airline and introduced his Transition Plan as a response to those challenges:

> We have labor cost problems, but we have decided not to ask for changes. Every time we talk about pay, we get in a big fight. We can't afford to get in a fight now. When we fight, we lose the ability to work together to deliver quality service, which, as I've explained, is something we absolutely must do. Still, it's important for everyone to understand that as low-cost carriers enter more and more markets, there will be more and more places where American cannot compete.

Crandall then took questions on the Transition Plan from employees for a 30- to 40-minute period. One employee asked, "You say that you are tired of fighting. So what are you going to do?" Crandall responded: "We will talk quietly. If they fight, we'll sell more routes and aircraft." Employees asked about potential solutions to the challenges he had posed, asking Crandall whether he had considered the possibility of forming international alliances, competing through subsidiaries, what would happen to American's smaller hubs, whether NAFTA would offer any new competitive opportunities for American, whether American could contract out to UPS to do some of its night flying, and so on.

Crandall's response to each query was masterful and informative, seemingly in command of every conceivable detail. But many of the questions were being posed in the form of suggestions and potential solutions, and Crandall did not seem to hear them that way. When the questions ended, Crandall concluded, "Well, I guess we've exhausted everybody's curiosity." To refer to this uprising of interest from employees and downright concern for their futures as "curiosity" seemed highly disrespectful and dismissive. It became clear that Crandall had come to inform, not to learn from the interaction.

A manager later explained why everyone had been so polite, asking questions rather than taking positions and engaging Crandall in debate. "Nobody likes to get their head knocked around," he answered. "Crandall can be very militant and scary." Another manager who had attended the conference shared his thoughts:

> Crandall's transition plan—to pull out where we're not making money, and increase investment where we are—is being well received in the investor community, it seems. Rose Anne Tortora of Donaldson, Lufkin and Jenrette has just written a very positive report on the plan, and is recommending investors to buy American stock. But the plan won't have the intended effect on the unions. People won't believe it until it hits. It's a loser. Crandall won't get what he wants from it.

The Transition Plan was clearly intended to pressure the unions into concessions, but it also led American's employees, from the front line to the executive level, to question Crandall's commitment to the business that provided their livelihood and that many of them loved. The exchange in Boston also suggested that Crandall's leadership style was characterized by little willingness to learn from others, and a tendency to inspire fear in those under his authority.

These aspects of Crandall's leadership style were apparent in his internal dealings with headquarters staff as well. One former rising star at American Airlines explained:

> Crandall's initial philosophy when he came in was to make individuals accountable for their actions, to help turn the system around. But it's gone too far. People are afraid to speak up because they might get zapped, or might cause other people to get zapped.

She described a meeting in which she unexpectedly took a controversial point of view. She knew she was taking a big risk and had not planned to say anything, but felt she had to. Crandall was angry and was criticizing the employees of American Airlines for being incompetent and lazy. Others present were either silent or were agreeing with Crandall. She suggested, however, that perhaps it was American's systems and not the employees that were at fault. The reaction was dramatic:

To suggest the system is wrong was interpreted by Crandall as suggesting that no one is accountable. Or perhaps that the people at the top are accountable, since they are responsible at least in part for keeping the system in place. My statement was not well formulated. I was immediately attacked from many sides. Everybody wanted to hear examples of what I meant. I didn't have any. My boss was mortified. Crandall said get some examples and get back to me.

The outcome of the incident was a demotion for the young executive who had spoken up. She was taken off the fast track and given a "special assignment" that seemed like a part-time job relative to her previous responsibilities. She never fully recovered from the demoralization of that experience, and later left the company.

Clearly Crandall's style was to lead by fear. In addition, Crandall's trustworthiness as a leader was consistently called into question. According to one senior pilot:

There is no trust for Crandall. He is nasty, mean. He's irascible, he points his finger, he's boiling inside. Crandall is not loyal to his employees. He has no respect for employees. We're not going to be loyal to the company or each other. When there is no love for the company, it translates to how you treat each other. . . . People do what they can get away with.

A young pilot for American Airlines in the Los Angeles station showed a full-page ad taken out by Southwest employees to recognize CEO Herb Kelleher on Boss's Day. "It really makes you sad when you read it," he said.

Another widely held view was that Crandall was smart and extremely knowledgeable about the industry. That was generally not perceived to be sufficient, however. A long-time ramp agent explained:

Crandall knows more than any other CEO in the world. He was the right person for American Airlines because he knew so much. He would always tell you the answer or get it for you. But he's too isolated now. He gets the wrong information.

A pilot leader concurred, and pointed out other flaws:

American's management is top shelf, and Crandall is brilliant. But he always plays right into our hands. This is why we don't have to worry about [the Transition Plan]. When it comes down to the wire, Crandall says something really inflammatory and everybody pulls together. He's trying to be noncon-frontational, but he still says things that get people upset. He can't help it.

A few weeks ago, he told the press that American was getting out of the airline business. Bob Baker [senior VP of operations] and Don Carty [senior VP of finance] had to cover for him and explain to the press that he really didn't mean it. Then he went out and said the same thing again.

After the failed Transition Plan, Crandall made several subsequent efforts to rebuild trust in his leadership. Although his efforts first appeared to be geared toward placating the investor community, it became apparent that the investor community needed reassurance that he had the trust of his employees. In 1995, he invited a broad range of American's employees to a summer retreat in Seattle called Council on American's Future. He also established a cross-functional team for front-line employees called the Customer Satisfaction Council. According to a Crandall supporter in the Boston station:

> Pilots, flight attendants, and everybody else participates. He showed the pilots the books. He asked each station to put cross-functional teams together.

Still, the damage had been done over the years, and it seemed to have culminated in the Transition Plan. American's board recognized the dif-ficulty Crandall had in winning the trust of his employees, and ultimately even the trust of the analysts. One observer noted:

> The credibility of a CEO to the analysts is a dominant consideration in CEO longevity. Bob [Crandall] has a complex relationship with the analysts. They think he's very capable. But do they believe him? One thing for sure, the rank and file doesn't believe him. They think he's painting a dark picture to gain a bargaining advantage.

Partly in recognition of these difficulties, American's board of directors handed over the leadership of the airline to Don Carty, executive vice pres-ident of finance, in 1995, while Crandall remained as CEO of the AMR Corporation. Carty was reputed to be more of a people person than Cran-dall, and also appeared to have the trust of the pilots. He had demonstrated during the time of the Transition Plan a stronger commitment to the airline business and therefore was able to start his leadership without the stigma of the Transition Plan. Although the Crandall legacy, particularly the distrust, would not be quickly left behind, American Airlines appears to have become more unified under Don Carty's leadership. One thing that still remained, and on which Carty has drawn, was the desire of many American employees to feel pride and loyalty toward their company.

Southwest's Leadership Transition

The importance of the relationship between top management and frontline employees to Southwest's success should not be underestimated. It is one reason why many observers wondered whether there would be a Southwest without Kelleher. Kelleher had said for years that he would step down as CEO when he reached the age of 70. Given the central role he plays at Southwest Airlines, this prospect generated a great deal of anxiety on the part of Wall Street analysts and other industry observers. Some Southwest employees themselves wondered how Southwest would fare after Herb's departure, given his visibility in the company. One operations agent who had been with Southwest for 20 years said:

> We used to say when Herb retires we're leaving—he's been the force behind Southwest's success. When he leaves it will all go down the tubes. We used to say that 6 years ago. No one says that anymore. You wouldn't know that he left—it's not any different.

Others closer to the top leaders themselves, however, including one of Southwest's chief pilots, expressed confidence as early as 1994 that Southwest would continue to thrive without Herb.

> Herb is so important to what Southwest is. But it will continue without him. He has done a very good job of selecting people. He has a good group around him. He picks sharp individuals to fill various roles then entrusts them to make decisions. There never will be another Herb Kelleher, but the spirit will carry on.

Indeed, Herb confirms that he selected his successors with great care:

I thought about who would be my successor very seriously for quite some time. My biggest concern was that I wanted someone who would be respectful of Southwest's culture and would be the sort of person who was altruistic in nature. I think Jim [Parker] and Colleen [Barrett] fit that.[14]

Kelleher chose long-time colleague Jim Parker to succeed him as CEO and long-time colleague Colleen Barrett to succeed him as president and chief operating officer.

In selecting Barrett, Kelleher also left Southwest with the legacy of having the first top woman executive in the U.S. airline industry. About breaking this barrier, Barrett says with characteristic humility:

It's not anything I ever aspired to. . . . All I ever really wanted to do all my life was enjoy what I do, and I obviously do that. But since all the coverage on this transition has come out, I have been amazed at how many women I have heard from that I don't know. So obviously it's a bigger thing than I would have thought.

First of all, the airline industry really isn't known for its women. That is a fact. But the glass ceiling has never been an issue for me at Southwest Airlines, so I've never particularly thought of that. But I have heard really big-dog people saying how great this is. It makes me feel great for women. It's kind of humbling. And I wish my mother was alive, because she'd love it.[15]

Southwest's Top Management Team

The other key factor for the successful transition was the existence of a very cohesive, well functioning top management team, giving Kelleher multiple strong leaders from whom to select, and giving Southwest's new leaders a cohesive, well functioning team with which to lead. Southwest's current top management team is shown in Exhibit 5–1.

It was evident at a March 2001 top management team meeting that Southwest's leadership extended well beyond Kelleher.[16] It appeared to be a group that would not allow itself to be torn apart by jealousies related to succession. Kelleher had not yet stepped down or announced his successors, but he was absent from the meeting, preparing his annual "Message to the Field." There was ample opportunity to observe the team on its own, without the charismatic leader who has garnered such enthusiastic attention in the press and in the investment community.

Exhibit 5-1 Southwest's Current Top Management Team

Herb Kelleher	Chairman of the Board and Chairman of the Executive Committee
James Parker	Vice Chair and Chief Executive Officer
Colleen Barrett	President and Chief Operating Officer
Deborah Ackerman	Vice President, General Counsel
Beverly Carmichael	Vice President, People
Donna Conover	Executive Vice President, Customer Service
Greg Crum	Vice President, Flight Operations
Alan Davis	Vice President, Internal Audit and Special Projects
Ginger Hardage	Vice President, Corporate Communications
Robert Jordan	Vice President, Purchasing
Camille Keith	Vice President, Special Marketing
Gary Kelly	Executive Vice President and Chief Financial Officer
Daryl Kraus	Vice President, Provisioning
Kevin Krone	Vice President, Interactive Marketing
Pete McGlade	Vice President, Schedule Planning
Bob Montgomery	Vice President, Properties and Facilities
Ron Ricks	Vice President, Governmental Affairs
David Ridley	Vice President, Ground Operations
Joyce Rogge	Senior Vice President, Marketing
Jim Ruppel	Vice President, Customer Relations and Rapid Rewards
Keith Taylor	Vice President, Revenue Management
Ellen Torbert	Vice President, Reservations
Tammy Walker-Jones	Vice President, Inflight
Greg Wells	Vice President, Safety, Security, and Flight Dispatch
Steve Whaley	Controller
Jim Wimberly	Executive Vice President and Chief of Operations
Laura Wright	Vice President, Finance and Treasurer
Mike Van de Ven	Vice President, Financial Planning and Analysis

There was clearly a well functioning, remarkably well integrated top management team in place at Southwest Airlines. The meeting reflected Southwest's approach to decision making. Managers from different business areas spoke knowledgeably about issues beyond the expertise suggested by their titles, and they repeatedly built upon one another's thoughts. It was like stepping into an ongoing conversation in which these managers had been engaged for many years. As Colleen Barrett pointed out at the start of the meeting:

> Titles mean very little here. Most people overlap in functionality. You would not get an accurate impression of Southwest from interviewing us individually about our areas of functional expertise.

Not only does Southwest invest a great deal of time and energy in building relationships between top management and frontline employees and among frontline employees. In addition, members of Southwest's top management team also invest their own valuable time in building relationships with one another. This ongoing conversation among senior managers at Southwest is one important way that this organization achieves shared goals, shared knowledge, and mutual respect across functional divisions.

Scholars have explored decision-making processes among members of top management teams.[17] The value of real-time communication is clear. However, long meetings can be an enormous expenditure of valuable time. How can Southwest, with its focus on efficiency, justify such an expenditure of time? There are two reasons why Southwest's lengthy top management team meetings may be worthwhile. First, the time invested in developing shared goals, shared knowledge, and mutual respect among senior managers may actually save time in the long run by resolving early on the functional disputes that can slow down implementation and blunt the effectiveness of policies even after they are implemented. Second, the coordination achieved at the top of the company translates into coordination on the front line, where customer service is delivered. Coordination on the front line in turn helps Southwest deliver reliable service while achieving efficient utilization of both its aircraft and its people, as we saw in Chap 3.

Summing Up

Herb Kelleher has often been described as a charismatic leader. According to leadership expert Robert House, a charismatic leader has the ability to relate the mission of the organization to deeply rooted values, ideals, and aspirations shared among followers, thus giving the work of the organization more meaning than it would otherwise have.[18] Kelleher has certainly provided Southwest Airlines employees with a sense of mission that connects to their own values, ideals, and aspirations. That sense of mission, if strong, will remain with the organization as a legacy. Not every leader of a successful organization must be charismatic. What successful organizations do need from each of their leaders, however, is credibility—the ability to inspire trust; and caring—the ability to inspire a belief by employees that their leaders care deeply about their well-being.

Invest in Frontline Leadership

The most influential leaders in our company—aside from Herb—are the frontline supervisors.

—Donna Conover, Executive Vice President of Customers, Southwest Airlines

IRONICALLY, ALTHOUGH SOUTHWEST Airlines is known as a flat, team-based company, it has more supervisors per frontline employee than any other airline in the industry. This directly contradicts many contemporary management thinkers, who have argued that the purpose of supervisors is to perpetuate bureaucracy by controlling and monitoring workers who might otherwise act irresponsibly.[1] Many organizations believe that teamwork and coordination are needed among frontline employees, and that supervisors tend to get in the way. Flat organizations with few supervisors should therefore perform better than more bureaucratic organizations.[2] Despite this, data on the U.S. workforce show that managers and supervisors have *increased* rather than decreased as a proportion of the workforce consistently since the 1950s, and have continued to do so in the 1980s and 1990s despite the downsizing and delayering reported in the business press.[3] These trends hardly suggest that supervision is becoming irrelevant.

This chapter will show why supervision continues to be relevant, despite predictions to the contrary. As we will see, at Southwest Airlines, leadership is not only relevant at the top of the organization. Leadership is better understood as a process that can take place at any level of the organization.[4] Indeed, leadership at the front line can play a critical role in organizational success. Rather than undermining coordination among frontline employees, supervisors play a valuable role in strengthening coordination through day-to-day coaching and counseling.[5]

Supervision at Southwest Airlines

At Southwest, each supervisor is responsible for 10 to 12 frontline workers, the highest supervisor-to-employee ratio in the industry. The job of the supervisor goes far beyond a focus on measuring performance and disciplining the "bad apples." Southwest supervisors are "player coaches," having managerial authority but also performing the work of frontline workers. Supervisors take part in frontline work on a regular basis, even highly physical work such as baggage handling. A Southwest supervisor explained:

> A supervisor fills in spots when people are on breaks, or when we are short on a zone. We make sure all the gates are [staffed] and that everything is running smoothly, working in a timely manner. When agents see the supervisor working consistently, they give more in a crunch. Also, you get their respect by working with them.

Working side by side with frontline employees is conducive to building shared goals with them, and to developing the credibility and knowledge needed for effective coaching.

Southwest supervisors also spend more time than their counterparts in other airlines engaged in coaching frontline employees. Coaching takes the form of problem solving and advising. The Chicago station manager explained:

> If there's a delay, supervisors find out why it happened. We get ideas on how to do it better next time. If you've got that kind of relationship then they're not going to be afraid. Say there was a ten-minute delay because freight was excessive. If we're screaming, we won't know why it was late.

The Chicago ramp manager confirmed this approach:

We work real hard to remove that barrier so that agents can come in and talk to a supervisor or manager. There's an open door policy so when employees have a problem, they know we can work on it together. It's a totally different environment here. We sit and listen. When that person walks away, he'll have self-esteem.

I learned this when I came to work the ramp [here]. Even when you did something wrong, they'll ask what happened. You know you screwed up. They'll tell you what you can do so it doesn't happen again. You walk away so upbeat that you work even harder.

There was some supervisory monitoring, but the supervisory role was not focused on discipline. A Los Angeles supervisor explained:

If there is a problem like one person taking a three-hour lunch, they take care of that themselves for the most part. Peer pressure works well.

Southwest supervisors told me that the people who reported to them were their internal customers and that their job was to help them do their jobs better. A supervisor in Phoenix described her job:

We are accountable for what the agents do. It is very difficult sometimes, because it's such a family-oriented company. You might feel like a sister to one of the agents, then you have to bring discipline. You have to step back and put the friendship aside and say, I don't agree with what you just did. But the agents are our customers. We are here to help them do their jobs.

One supervisor explained how he had been chosen and trained to take on the supervisory role at Southwest. (He had been a firefighter in Chicago, and had joined Southwest as a frontline agent 8 years ago.)

You let it be known that you are trying to pursue a new position, preferably before the position opens up. Then that person will say, let me take you through the job performance standards, the attendance and other knowledge. The manager of ramp and ops might be the one to train you. You let it be known that you are grooming yourself for it. After you are chosen, you take the core courses in leadership training. This is the class that all brand new supervisors take.

The supervisory training left an impression on him:

> I wanted to change after taking the course. We learn that not everyone is the same as you or each other. You develop your best qualities and treat everyone as a human being. Every year or 18 months, there is more management training. It's the same thing—a lot of focus on interaction between departments. Everyone on the team is working toward a common goal.

One recent training session for Southwest supervisors included a lesson in the importance of coaching. Three groups of supervisors-in-training were formed.

> One member of each team was blindfolded and asked to throw a ball into a trashcan. Unknown to the throwers, one team could say nothing, the second was instructed to say only "good job" or "keep trying," and the third could give detailed information about where the bucket was.
>
> Not surprisingly, the third group had the most success. The person who had received the best instructions said: "I couldn't wait for it to be my turn again." "Wow!" said facilitator Chris Robbins. "How does that relate to work? How many agents do you think we have out there who are told nothing or just 'good job' instead of people really listening to them?"[6]

In sum, supervision at Southwest was hands-on and intended to be informative and supportive in nature. It was not arm's-length supervision—interactions were intense and performance measures were not used as a substitute for these interactions.

Benefits of High Supervisory Staffing Levels

The supervisory role at Southwest Airlines, with its emphasis on coaching, counseling, and working side by side with frontline employees, required high levels of supervisory staffing. Relative to the other airlines included in this study (United, Continental, and American), Southwest had very high levels of supervisory staffing.[7] In a study that included two American Airlines sites, two Continental Airlines sites, two Southwest Airlines sites, and three United Airlines sites, a statistical analysis suggested that high levels of supervisory staffing contribute to higher levels of relational coordination. Supervisory staffing levels also contribute to improved flight departure performance, particularly faster turnaround times, greater staffing productivity, fewer customer complaints, and fewer lost bags.[8] To observe the effects of supervisory staffing on relational coordination, we can plot supervisory staffing for each of the nine sites against relational coordination. Exhibit 6–1 suggests a clear impact of supervisory staffing levels on relational coordination.

Supervision at Continental Airlines

Continental Airlines intended for its supervisors to have a strong coaching and counseling role, but supervisory staffing levels were too low to do justice to the role. Their job description included coaching and counseling, but a good deal of their time was spent completing paperwork regarding wages and scheduling. Nonmanagement "lead agents" played a role in directing the operations, but played only a minor role in coaching and counseling. Still, station managers in Boston placed high priorities on coaching and counseling and encouraged supervisors to do it despite their limited numbers.

In the interests of increasing productivity, supervisory levels were cut again in the mid-1990s. At the same time, the role of supervisors was expanded even further to include working side by side with frontline employees. One obvious problem, which had yet to be resolved, was how supervisors with lower staffing levels and increased numbers of direct reports would be able to perform this frontline leadership role effectively.

Exhibit 6–1 shows Continental's moderate staffing levels for its supervisors, relative to Southwest Airlines, and its correspondingly lower levels of relational coordination.

Supervision at United Airlines

Supervisory staffing levels at United were reduced in the 1980s with the intent of improving productivity and empowering frontline employees. Supervisors at United had both administrative and operational responsibilities and were stretched quite thin. As a result, frontline employees spent little time interacting with supervisors, and the coaching and counseling role of supervisors had become relatively neglected. A Los Angeles customer service manager voiced his concerns:

Exhibit 6–1 Impact of Supervisory Staffing on Relational Coordination*

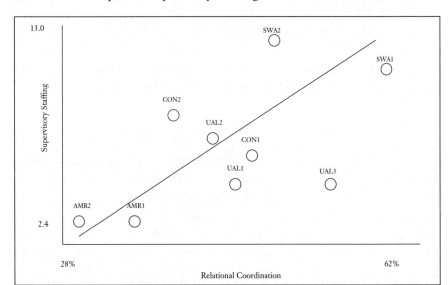

* Each circle denotes one of the nine sites included in the study. Supervisory staffing is measured as the number of supervisors per hundred frontline employees. Relational coordination, coordination carried out through relationships of shared goals, shared knowledge, and mutual respect, is measured as the percentage of cross-functional ties that are strong or very strong, based on an employee survey. Relational coordination in turn has a positive impact on quality and efficiency performance, as illustrated in Exhibit 3-4.

> [Frontline employees] only get to see supervisors two or three times a day. [Supervisors] make sure that people are there at the start of the flight, then go off to the next. They deal with crises only. As a result, customer service reps aren't getting the attention they need on critiquing their work. Also there is no help with their career plans. The operation takes precedence. There is no softer side. On the coordination of the departure, yes, you get feedback. But critique without the benefit of analysis. . . . We haven't developed our talent.

In the mid-1990s, United's top management team redefined the role of supervisors to include a specific focus on coaching and mentoring. According to the Los Angeles ramp supervisor:

> Supervisors are to become coaches, to support team members. We will use our clout and ability to support the people who are closest to doing the job.

Formal training in leadership and team building was offered to help supervisors take on this new, expanded role. However, their role would have to expand without an increase in supervisory staffing. The customer service manager explained:

> The word supervisors does not exist in the CEO's nomenclature. . . . Supervisors and managers will not grow.

The United Shuttle was designed with a philosophy of using even less supervision than the rest of United. The initial design teams decided that supervisors were not needed at all. In the implementation, however, it was decided that Shuttle employees needed supervisors in an advisory role. The Shuttle supervisors were called team advisors, and were supplemented by supervisors in the non-Shuttle operations who also had some responsibility for Shuttle employees. The supervisors' job was not conceived to involve monitoring, per se, since Shuttle employees were expected to be self-monitoring. But given their staffing levels, supervisors had a hard time playing even the advisory role that their job description called for. Ramp employees built a self-monitoring group with lead agents in charge, and wanted to have nothing to do with management. Customer service agents complained that supervisors were never available when needed. Neither frontline group had a strong relationship with either their supervisors or higher levels of management.

As we will see in subsequent chapters, the United Shuttle differed in many of its organizational practices from those of United Airlines, and had correspondingly higher levels of relational coordination and performance. However, supervisory staffing was one of the few ways that the Shuttle remained exactly like the rest of United. After a brief experiment with lower levels of supervision, the United Shuttle ended up with nearly the same supervisory staffing levels as the rest of United. Exhibit 6–1 shows United's low staffing levels for its supervisors, relative to Southwest Airlines, and its correspondingly lower levels of relational coordination.

Supervision at American Airlines

Supervisors at American Airlines were staffed very leanly, with responsibility for more than 40 employees each. Supervisory staffing at American had been reduced as part of a companywide effort to create a leaner, flatter organization with greater employee empowerment. However, due to their lean staffing levels, supervisors had little time to carry out supportive functions. Instead of building shared goals with frontline employees, working side by side with them and providing them with coaching and feedback, supervisors spent their limited time communicating performance standards to employees and measuring their performance.

One typical comment from frontline employees at American was that supervisors "only care about delays. Otherwise the little report card won't look good that week." The concern with delays did not appear to be reflected in supervisory efforts to analyze and engage in problem solving, however. Instead, the focus was on allocating blame for the delay to the function responsible for causing it so as to comply with reporting requirements from headquarters, and to pressure frontline employees to improve performance. The reliance on performance measurement allowed for a largely hands-off relationship between supervisors and frontline employees, consistent with the low levels of supervisory staffing and the large numbers of direct reports for which each supervisor was responsible. To the limited extent that supervisors could focus on individual employees, their approach tended to focus on monitoring compliance with directives. According to one supervisor in Boston, "we only have time to focus on the bad apples."

To assist supervisors, nonmanagement "lead agents" were appointed from among the frontline employees to help carry out supervisory functions. Their job was to help supervisors direct the operations. However, they were not responsible for providing discipline, leadership, coaching, or feedback to frontline employees. Because leads were clearly nonmanagement, and did not see themselves as management representatives, they were not well positioned to align frontline employee goals with those of the organization.

Meanwhile, supervisors themselves had little opportunity to bridge the management/nonmanagement divide or to participate in frontline work. They had few opportunities to observe the work process directly and to provide coaching and feedback to frontline employees. They had little contact with any given employee, and little opportunity to build the relationships and know-how that would allow them to play a supportive role. In sum, supervision at American Airlines was primarily arm's-length in the sense that supervisory interactions with frontline employees were quite limited, and tended to focus on performance measurement.

Exhibit 6–1 shows American's extremely low levels of supervisory staffing, relative to Southwest Airlines, and its correspondingly low levels of relational coordination.

The Southwest Difference

Interaction between supervisors and frontline employees ranged from infrequent and arm's-length in American Airlines, to frequent and intensive in Southwest. These differences were consistent with levels of supervisory staffing. Higher levels of supervisory staffing at Southwest gave supervisors fewer direct reports, enabling them to engage in more frequent and intensive interaction with their direct reports, while supervisors at American, United, and Continental, with more direct reports, engaged in less frequent and more arm's-length interaction with their direct reports.

With fewer direct reports, Southwest supervisors also had greater opportunities for working side by side with the frontline employees they were responsible for supervising. Working together appeared to reduce informational and social distance between supervisors and the supervised, and to support the creation of shared goals. Shared goals in turn made frontline employees more receptive to supervisory coaching and feedback, and reduced the role of supervisory monitoring even further as employees began to monitor each other. With fewer social and informational boundaries between themselves and their direct reports, supervisors were also able to perform their coaching and feedback functions more effectively.

In sites with low levels of supervisory staffing, a different story emerged. Supervision had been reduced to economize on staffing and, ironically, to increase participation by frontline employees. Supervisors had arm's-length relationships with their direct reports and played a largely bureaucratic role, relying on impersonal rules to allocate responsibility for late departures and other errors. Their role was primarily to monitor compliance with performance targets set by headquarters, and with basic rules of behavior such as being on duty at the scheduled times.

The Case for Reduced Supervisory Staffing

Some organizational scholars acknowledge that supervisors can play an important role in supporting coordination and teamwork, but they claim that this supportive role requires less supervisory involvement, not *more*.[9] According to team theorists Richard Hackman and Gregory Oldham:

> When a group is first formed . . . it may be necessary to help members get off to a good start by inviting them to participate in some "team-building" activities intended to establish the boundaries and identity of the group and to assist members in coming to grips with their shared authority for managing internal group processes. Then, as the group gains a sense of its identity and begins to develop its own ways of dealing with task and organizational issues, the manager or consultant can gradually withdraw from prominence in group activities.[10]

The gradual reduction of supervisory involvement is argued to be a win/win proposition for frontline employees and for the organization. Employees can have more autonomy and the organization can achieve better performance once supervisors have handed off their responsibilities to frontline employees.[11]

Consistent with this view, an empirical study in the 1980s found that the elimination of supervisory positions was associated with improved productivity in a manufacturing setting.[12] An analysis of multiple studies conducted in the 1980s concluded that work teams without supervisors performed better than work teams with supervisors.[13]

The Case for Increased Supervisory Staffing

But because effective leadership is both time-consuming and relationship-intensive, *more* time rather than less may be required to perform the job effectively. According to Douglas McGregor, founder of the "human relations" approach to management:

> Roles cannot be clarified, mutual agreement concerning the responsibilities of a subordinate's job cannot be reached in a few minutes, nor can appropriate targets be established without a good deal of discussion. It is far quicker to hand a subordinate a position description and to inform him of his objectives for the coming period.[14]

Higher supervisory staffing levels increase the time a supervisor can spend with each employee, increasing the opportunities for working side by side, building shared goals, and providing coaching and feedback.[15] Even Frederick Winslow Taylor, the founder of "scientific management," agreed with this reasoning:

> More than all other causes, the close, intimate cooperation, the constant personal contact between the two sides, will tend to diminish friction and discontent. It is difficult for two people whose interests are the same, and who work side by side in accomplishing the same object all day long, to keep up a quarrel.[16]

With higher staffing levels, supervisors can add value by building strong relationships with frontline employees. They are more available for coaching and feedback,[17] have more opportunity to interact with individual subordinates,[18] and have more time to provide support, encouragement and recognition to individual subordinates.[19] With lower staffing levels, by contrast, supervisors are more likely to make autocratic decisions[20] and to handle problems with subordinates in a more formalized, impersonal manner, using warnings and punishments instead of coaching and feedback.[21]

Summing Up

Higher levels of supervisory staffing lead to improved performance in many settings other than the airline industry. In new product development, groups in which frontline supervisors play a significant role have been found to perform better than groups with greater autonomy from supervisors.[22] Even in manufacturing, higher supervisory staffing levels permit "more intimate and informal" relationships to develop between supervisors and frontline workers, setting the context within which shared goals can be developed.[23]

With insufficient staffing, supervisors are forced to focus on the "bad apples" and to play an arm's-length, oversight role. With higher staffing levels, as we saw at Southwest Airlines, supervisors can work side by side with frontline employees, gaining their respect and becoming sufficiently familiar with the work so that they can provide meaningful coaching and feedback to their direct reports. They can be more available for conversations with their direct reports, thereby reducing the barriers between themselves and frontline employees, and creating a richer flow of information between frontline employees and those at higher levels of the organization. In addition, supervisors with sufficient staffing levels can facilitate the development of strong relationships *among* frontline employees.

Top managers at Southwest have repeatedly touted the important role that supervisors play in their organization. According to Libby Sartain, former vice president of people:

> We're only as strong as [our supervisors]. That's where most organizations break down. [Now] we are putting even more time and effort into internal recruitment and training for frontline supervisors.

Executive Vice President of Customers Donna Conover concluded:

> While other airlines are cutting supervisors, we have a large number of supervisors to encourage, guide, and give structure to people. It lends to the family atmosphere here.

Hire and Train for Relational Competence

*It's mutual respect. We get it partly from the selection process. We really try to select peo-
ple with the right attitude. We evaluate the impact they will have on internal and external customers.*

—Chief Pilot, Southwest Airlines

BECAUSE DIFFERENT JOBS require different abilities, one of
the most important objectives of the hiring process is to find people who
best fit the requirements of the job. The critical skills to be identified in
the hiring process go *beyond* the technical and cognitive realm to include
personality traits.[1] Service management experts Leonard Schlesinger and
James Heskett have made the case that service companies in particular
should hire for "soft skills" such as customer orientation and teamwork
ability.[2] In a survey of employees conducted by Peter Cappelli, teamwork
ability is the single trait that employees most frequently identify as being
necessary to accomplish their work successfully.[3]

Teamwork ability can be understood more specifically as relational
competence—the ability to relate effectively with others. Relational
competence is a critical ingredient of organizational success,[4] though it
tends to be undervalued in the world of work.[5] Particularly when hiring
people for jobs that require high levels of expertise, organizations tend to

underestimate the importance of relational competence. Yet even people who perform highly skilled jobs—e.g., engineers, doctors, pilots—need relational competence to integrate their work effectively with the work of their fellow employees. When relational competence is overlooked, the result is the hiring of excellent individual performers who cannot contribute fully to the organization's goals and who often undermine those goals.

This chapter shows how Southwest Airlines builds high performance relationships by hiring and training for relational competence, then compares Southwest's approach to that of its competitors.

Hiring and Training at Southwest Airlines

Southwest places a great deal of importance on the hiring process to identify people with relational competence. Southwest's assessment of how a job candidate will affect the "overall operation" of the airline goes beyond the typical search for appropriate skills and experience. According to the former head of Southwest's People Department, Ann Rhoades, one of the important unwritten rules at Southwest is that "you can't be an elitist."[6] According to a Southwest ramp manager:

> One thing we cannot teach is attitudes toward peers or other groups. There's a code, a way you respond to every individual who works for Southwest. The easiest way to get in trouble at Southwest is to offend another employee. We need people to respond favorably. It promotes good working relationships. . . . You find an individual with an upbeat and positive attitude—and you'll find that everything that needs to be done, will get done. It's very contagious.

Unlike other airlines where supervisors hire frontline airport employees with little support from management, at Southwest employees are selected with the participation of station management and the People Department, using a time-consuming process to identify the desired characteristics. According to a ramp manager:

> Something we look at is people who are very team oriented from prior work experiences. . . . [We say], "take an incident from your prior work and walk us through it." Do they limit themselves to the job, or go above and beyond?

We don't just look at work history. We've turned away people with 15–16 years of airline experience in favor of people with none. The concept of teamwork is tough. You really don't know if a person will be able to cross over from his or her primary responsibility and do other things. We get a feel for people who will go above and beyond.

According to Libby Sartain, former vice president of people:

We spend more money to recruit and train than any of the other airlines do. We take the time to find the right people to hire, at all levels within our organization, and we spend time training them.

We really believe in the notion of "one bad apple." It's like a religion here. As a result, our turnover is far less than it is at other airlines.

Even when hiring pilots, Southwest explicitly seeks people who lack an attitude of superiority and who seem likely to treat coworkers with respect, in addition to being highly skilled in their profession. A story circulated around industry pilot circles that a pilot came to interview at Southwest and treated an administrative assistant with disrespect—and didn't get the job as a result.

Even for mechanics, who are typically hired strictly for their technical skills, and who are known at other airlines for being insular and not interacting well with nonmechanics, Southwest's hiring goals were the same—to find team players who would relate well with the other functional groups. A Southwest personnel manager explained, "We're looking for experience but also for someone who is going to be able to work with other groups in a good environment."

Training New Hires

In addition to the hiring, an important related task is training and acculturating the newly hired people, most of whom have come from other, more functionally divided companies. Southwest watches newcomers carefully at the outset, to identify and correct potential hiring mistakes. Colleen Barrett, Southwest's president and chief operating officer, said:

We bring someone in, and it is fascinating to watch. We say, we don't make decisions based on what is good for me or my department. It is collective. It's not treated as a single decision. We do what's best for Southwest as a whole.

If new hires do not catch on to the Southwest way of taking a holistic, collective perspective on work, they stand out as misfits, and are fired or counseled out. Barrett explained:

> We've got to be pretty darn religious watching that person's performance during the probationary period. That sounds strange for a family-oriented company, but if we see a misfit with teamwork or an attitude, we will counsel once or twice and we will be harsh.[7]

Often people who do not fit at Southwest realize it early on, sometimes even during the early stages of training, and they opt to leave. Barrett is sympathetic in these cases:

> They stick out like sore thumbs, they really do, and they feel it even before others notice it.

Training at Southwest is geared toward building functional expertise as well as relational competence. Each newly hired employee receives both classroom training (from 1 to 2 weeks depending on the job) and on-the-job training (from 2 to 3 weeks depending on the job). A training coordinator is assigned to each newly hired employee to guide his or her on-the-job training. This on-the-job training takes the form of explaining to the newly hired employee both what to do and why. For example, a training coordinator explained to a new trainee:

> . . . and then we write down the number of bags that we've put in each bin and hang it on the clip, so the operations agent can do the final weight and balance check, and determine how much fuel this plane is going to need.

As a result, in the course of being trained for a specific job, the employee learns about the jobs of each other functional group that interfaces with the job for which he or she is training. The training is therefore geared toward fostering relational competence. By learning about the overall work process, employees understand where they fit and how their job relates to and supports that of their colleagues.

Later in their tenure at Southwest, employees learn more about each other's jobs through job exchanges. Through programs called a "Day in the Field" or "Walk a Mile," Southwest employees periodically spend a day working in another department to become familiar with other aspects of the work process related to their own jobs, or jobs they aspire to move into. A customer service agent in Phoenix explained:

> If we want, we have an opportunity to spend a day in operations to see how they do it. Or with a ramp agent. We do it to gain more knowledge. It's an optional thing. Still, everybody knows what's involved because you have to interact with them. If a bag is mis-tagged, we will call down to the ramp supervisor. [Classroom] training doesn't cover it—but we get it on the job.

Promotion from Within

Most positions at Southwest are filled through internal promotion and through lateral moves across departmental lines, creating a great deal of internal job mobility and therefore opportunities for learning about other parts of the operation. A Southwest station manager explained:

> The only jobs we really hire off the street are the frontline jobs—ramp agent, customer service agent, operations agent, provisioning agent, pilot, and flight attendant. Most move up. We look for people who want to move up in the company.
>
> People move across departments a lot here. That helps break down status barriers between departments. It also helps people understand the whole process. They also have a lot of opportunity to move up in the company. Most of our managers started in frontline positions. I started as a cabin cleaner at Eastern. Neil [my assistant manager] started on the ramp. This helps to break down the status barriers. People at Southwest don't forget where they came from.

A flight attendant articulated the same perspective:

> The tremendous job mobility at Southwest means that people have more respect for the other jobs.

In effect, Southwest employees learn about each other's jobs through initial on-the-job training led by a training coordinator, through on-the-job experience, through the training that occurs during a Day in the Field, and through cross-departmental job mobility. The end result of these hiring and training activities is high levels of relational competence in Southwest's workforce.

Stresses and Strains of Rapid Growth

At one of Southwest's rapidly growing stations in Los Angeles in the early 1990s, hiring and training for relational competence began to break down. Southern California was one of the first locations to which Southwest moved outside Texas. In Los Angeles in the early 1990s, the People Department had difficulty finding enough people who met Southwest's hiring criteria, resulting in high levels of turnover. This turnover snowballed due to the failure to hire quickly enough. The more seasoned Southwest employees who had transferred to the Los Angeles station experienced heavy workloads and burnout from the need to constantly train new employees, and began to seek transfers to other, more established Southwest locations.

Part of the problem was a culture clash between employees coming from Texas, the company's home base, and employees who originated in Southern California. An operations supervisor explained:

> People in California are totally different from Texans. People here feel they have to know you to talk to you.

A customer service agent reported a similar experience:

> I'm from Texas and coming here was a real rude awakening. I said HI! People would say "hi, do I KNOW you?" A lot of people here are prideful, not warm and friendly.

Southwest's top management team addressed these problems by infusing the Los Angeles station with a high level of resources to break the cycle of failure.[8] The People Department set up shop right in the station itself, next door to the station manager, and interviewed new applicants intensively to overcome the staffing deficit while maintaining Southwest's hiring standards for relational competence and team spirit. Managers who were known and respected for their work in other successful Southwest stations, including the manager of ramp and operations from Phoenix, came to Los Angeles for several months to give their input into the hiring process, and to help support the training of new hires.

These efforts at turning around the Los Angeles station through intensive focus on hiring and training were ultimately successful. Southwest faced a similar challenge in the late 1990s with the Baltimore station, another place where outsiders believed it would not be possible to find "the Southwest type of person." Just as in Los Angeles in the early 1990s, Southwest's top leadership responded with additional resources for hiring and training: establishing a local branch of Southwest's People Department, bringing in highly successful managers from other stations, and overseeing the development of a local Culture Committee.

Southwest managers have heard the argument that the "Southwest type" can only be found in Texas, or in the southwestern region of the United States, but they claim it is misguided. Colleen Barrett notes:

> The naysayers said we could never fly to the Northeast because we wouldn't be able to find employees there who were nice. But we can do it, and we do. Someday, we may go international. And even internationally, we can maintain our culture if we go after people's hearts and grow our community.

Benefits of Hiring for Relational Competence

Relative to the other airlines included in this study (United, Continental, and American), Southwest placed far greater attention on hiring for relational competence.[9] This study, which was outlined in detail in Chap. 3, included two American Airlines sites, two Continental Airlines sites, two Southwest Airlines sites, and three United Airlines sites. A statistical analysis of hiring practices suggested that hiring for relational competence contributes to higher levels of relational coordination. Hiring for relational competence also contributes to improved flight departure performance, particularly faster turnaround times, greater staffing productivity, fewer customer complaints, fewer lost bags, and better on-time performance.[10] To observe the effects of hiring practices on relational coordination, we can plot hiring practices for each of the nine sites against relational coordination. Exhibit 7–1 suggests a clear impact of hiring practices on relational coordination.

Exhibit 7–1 Impact of Hiring for Relational Competence on Relational Coordination*

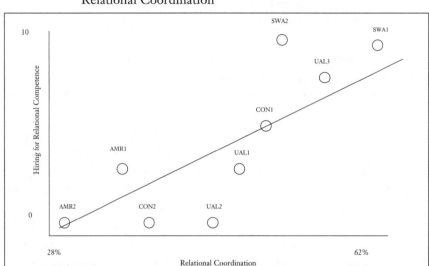

* Each circle denotes one of the nine sites included in the study. Hiring for relational competence is measured as the number of functional groups for which relational competence is an important hiring criterion. Relational coordination, coordination carried out through relationships of shared goals, shared knowledge, and mutual respect, is measured as the percentage of cross-functional ties that are strong or very strong, based on an employee survey. Relational coordination in turn has a positive impact on quality and efficiency performance, as illustrated in Exhibit 3-4.

Hiring and Training at United Airlines

The United Shuttle was the one other site in this study where employees with teamwork ability had been deliberately attracted in large numbers, but here it happened primarily through self-selection, rather than through deliberate selection by the organization. Shuttle employees came largely from United's traditional operations, by electing to bid for Shuttle jobs. Because the Shuttle was publicly premised on cross-functional teamwork, "people only came here if they weren't snobs," said a customer service agent. Employees from United's non-Shuttle operations who were adamantly opposed to the cultural changes at the Shuttle, particularly to the interactions with lower-status functional groups, chose not to bid for Shuttle jobs. Signals about the importance of teamwork on the Shuttle were received loudly and clearly and were understood to be a condition of entry.

Shuttle employees received initial training for teamwork when they first started working the Shuttle, further bolstering their relational competence. They also learned about each other's jobs through participation on cross-functional design teams and quality improvement teams. Through these design teams, said a customer service manager:

> People are learning what others do. It is good for them. They ask, how does that affect you?

One of the top managers who helped to implement the Shuttle concept argued that participation in the design of the Shuttle trained Shuttle employees in process thinking.

> People in the Shuttle tend to look at process because that's the way the Shuttle was designed. People were trained to that point of view through the design of the Shuttle. We took this perspective from the start. We integrated all the people. We used smaller teams to develop solutions, then communicated that to larger teams. They were all cross-functional, which also reinforced the process mindset. It's gotten the flight attendants much more involved in the turnaround.
>
> At work, people physically touch someone who was involved in the design process. We are not trying to formalize it. We are taking the commonsense view that people are the best communicators. They sit down beside each other and get the ideas. Six thousand employees participated in the design and implementation of the Shuttle. There were 100 people on the teams that made the recommendations for the changes. Everybody has a kernel of the idea.

These training opportunities helped the United Shuttle achieve strong relationships between functions in a very short time, even though the Shuttle had emerged out of a hierarchical culture with deep divisions between functions.

Another change was in uniforms. All Shuttle station employees wore the same uniform—even maintenance started wearing the Shuttle polo shirt in the Los Angeles station after about 6 months. Finally, Shuttle station employees shared a common break room, where they sat around the same table before shifts and during breaks.

As a result of the Shuttle's hiring and training practices (and other practices that will be highlighted in the chapters that follow), the United Shuttle achieved significantly higher levels of relational coordination compared to United's non-Shuttle sites (55 percent versus 42 percent of cross-functional ties that were strong or very strong). Exhibit 7–1 shows how these higher levels of relational coordination are related to the Shuttle's hiring practices. The United Shuttle, denoted by UAL3 in Exhibit 7–1, has higher levels of relational coordination than its non-Shuttle counterparts (UAL1 and UAL2), corresponding to its greater focus on hiring for relational competence. Accordingly, the Shuttle outperformed its non-Shuttle counterparts at United, with higher on-time performance (86.5 percent versus 79.6 percent), fewer customer complaints (20.7 versus 24.4 per 100,000 passengers enplaned), faster gate turnarounds (32.6 versus 64.3 minutes), and higher labor productivity (42.1 versus 86.1 employees per 1000 daily passengers enplaned). When these performance measures were adjusted for differences in product characteristics, the Shuttle still showed higher performance, due in part to higher levels of relational coordination that were achieved in the Shuttle operations.[11]

The United Shuttle benefited from having employees who had self-selected into an operation that was clearly advertised as based on teamwork, and from cross-functional design teams that helped to build relational competence. However, the rest of United Airlines did not have this advantage. United's hiring practices did not put a great deal of emphasis on hiring frontline employees for relational competence. Instead, they followed the more traditional approach of looking for skills specific to the particular job being filled. According to a United station manager:

> Hiring for teamwork is not something we've paid attention to in the past. It's something we need to do in the future. It's not just work experience and background, but communication skills.

Additional training experiences at United came through efforts to imitate the cross-functional problem-solving teams of the United Shuttle, and the intensive learning experiences these problem-solving teams had provided for Shuttle employees. These problem-solving teams, called max-mix teams, seemed to result in broader knowledge and changed attitudes. According to a long-time ramp agent in Los Angeles:

> There's an incredible benefit in overall attitudes. I call it the Shuttle attitude because it started there. There are a lot of radicals here but they are starting

to turn. People still ask, have you been Shuttle-ized? Like brainwashed. It's changing though. Not such a negativity any more. It's becoming contagious.

A ramp supervisor commented on these early efforts:

Everyone says it's a big help because now they know a face, it's not just anonymous. . . . You can run up and ask, need any help?

However, many of these early lessons from the Shuttle were confined to cities like Los Angeles, where there was a major Shuttle presence. More recently, United has tried to spread these problem-solving teams more broadly throughout the United system. At Chicago O'Hare and San Francisco, cross-functional "Timeline Teams" began to document flight departure procedures, much as the original Shuttle teams had done. Meanwhile in Denver and Washington Dulles, United experimented with a program called "Team Based Organization," a partnership of local management and union leadership responsible for day-to-day problem solving. It was hoped that these problem-solving teams would serve as a form of training throughout United's system, much as they had in the early years of the Shuttle, providing frontline employees with broader knowledge of the flight departure process and higher levels of relational competence.

Hiring and Training at Continental Airlines

At Continental Airlines, there was nothing in place like the selection process used by Southwest to identify relational competence, or like the self-selection process at the United Shuttle that initially yielded similar results. At Continental, supervisors were in charge of hiring frontline employees, guided only by a checklist. However, some aspects of relational competence were considered. One key item on this checklist was the ability to get along with others. Still, when pressed, it was clear that the larger station at Continental was not actively seeking relational competence in its frontline employees, but rather was focused on functional skills. However, at the smaller Continental station, there was an effort to look for relational competence, particularly when hiring for gate and ramp positions.

Likewise, at Continental's smaller stations, some training for teamwork occurred through cross-utilization of station jobs. There was a great deal of rotation within the ramp, for example, between cabin cleaning and loading. "We like to do that here in Boston—cross-training, cross-utilization," said a ramp supervisor. "There is a lot of switching between ticketing and the gate in Boston too," said a customer service supervisor.

Like the United Shuttle, Continental's own experiment with a quick-turnaround operation—Continental Lite—had provided employees with some training in relational competence. Frontline employees were involved in timing gate turnarounds and mapping the work process to understand what each function was doing to support the turnaround, even specifying the communication that was supposed to take place. Interfaces between groups became better understood. Even when Continental Lite was dropped in 1995 in favor of Continental's high-fare model, some of the learning from Lite was retained by those who had experienced it.[12]

Exhibit 7–1 shows Continental's moderate attention to hiring for relational competence relative to Southwest Airlines, and its correspondingly lower levels of relational coordination. In addition, we see substantial variation between the two Continental sites, with CON1 showing considerably higher levels of attention to hiring for relational competence, and correspondingly higher levels of relational coordination, relative to CON2. These results suggest that local managers can make a difference.

Hiring and Training at American Airlines

At American Airlines, the hiring process deliberately did not seek to identify frontline employees with relational competence. In part, it was a reflection of how the work itself was organized. According to a supervisor:

> The work groups are so well-defined that they are not allowed to help out, so we don't look for that. It would cause problems.

According to a human resource manager:

> We would not ask how this person would interface with other groups. I'm not sure interfacing isn't a better way, but what we have is a chain process.

Because the work was understood to be a chain process, as in a production line, rather than an iterative, interactive process, the hiring process at American put very little emphasis on relational competence.

The criteria for ramp, baggage transfer, and cabin cleaning personnel did not seem to be particularly ambitious. In addition to looking for people who were capable of the physically demanding work involved in loading and unloading an aircraft, and who had a history of showing up on time for work, "we look for people who speak clearly and distinctly," said a supervisor. For mechanics, American Airlines sought people who also had the requisite licensing. For gate and ticketing agents, American looked for people who were comfortable with the computer interface and, if possible, for people who were already familiar with the information systems in place. In addition, as the notion of customer service made its way into organizational objectives, there was increasing attention to hiring gate and ticketing agents who would interact well with customers. However, there was no systematic attention to how these employees would interact with their colleagues in other functional areas. One exception existed, however. At American's smaller stations, gate and ticketing agents were cross-utilized, and as a result they tended to be hired with a view to how well they would work together cross-functionally.

For pilots, American's hiring practices were notable not just for overlooking relational competence but for running counter to it. In addition to flight training and experience, American Airlines looked for pilots with qualities that they felt would be conducive to the leadership responsibilities of a pilot. In the opinion of an employee relations manager:

> We look for command presence, the most self-assured arrogant people we can possibly find. Then we teach them to be even more arrogant, so to speak.

The results of this hiring process were problematic, according to this manager:

> There is a certain amount of hostility that pilots face from the other employee groups. The personality of the pilot generates that hostility.

This personality was not inherent to pilots, however, but rather was an artifact of the hiring process. And as we will see in Chap. 11, this hiring process for pilots clearly contributed to the failure of efforts at American Airlines to move toward shared accountability for delays.

There were some efforts to move pilots in the direction of greater teamwork through training programs. Along with other airlines, American invested tremendous resources into crew resource management training, to encourage pilots to be team players on board the aircraft, and to listen to others. These programs were adopted in response to evidence that some accidents had occurred because the captain was not receptive to information from other crew members, and because other crew members hesitated to communicate even potentially critical information to the captain because of respect for the "line of command." However, crew resource management programs did not extend teamwork beyond the cockpit to the flight departure process, where it was seemingly so critical and so underdeveloped. Even flight attendants, for whom such training was available, typically did not take advantage of it, according to a flight attendant manager:

> It's important, but . . . [our] flight attendants do not seek it out. They typically do not like training of any kind. Their mind set is that their time off is their time off. Even though the training time is paid, that's how they look at it. . . . They complain so much that sometimes it's just not worth it.

Other training programs were designed to encourage shared goals, shared knowledge, and mutual respect across functional boundaries. American's Human Resource Department implemented a program called "Walk a Mile" that encouraged employees to trade jobs across functional lines, to understand better the work that was done by their colleagues in other functions. This job training program was also designed to give employees an opportunity to try out other positions for the purpose of job transfers and promotions. In addition, the Human Resource Department designed training programs to address particular breakdowns that occurred in the coordination of the flight departure process. For example, a half-day program called "Commitment to Courtesy" was offered systemwide at American to improve communication between flight attendants and gate agents. A flight attendant manager explained the origin and expected outcome of the training program:

> Some places have bad relations between the flight attendants and the gate agents. The gate agents sometimes make decisions unilaterally, and tell passengers to start boarding 40 minutes before departure even though there may only be 50 passengers. It is ridiculous. So we just stand there and politely refuse to let the passengers board. It is not good for customer service. It's probably confusing for the passenger. But they can't tell us what to do. We are independent.

I don't know how successful the training program will be. It is designed to open up communication, and allows an hour open discussion at the end of the seminar. But the flight attendants at some stations have objected and have said they will not participate.

Clearly, a training program cannot proceed without the cooperation of the participants. In the case of American Airlines, employees had been selected through the hiring process for their ability to perform their own jobs, not for their ability to relate to others who were engaged in performing other related jobs. It is difficult to use training to make up for mistakes in the hiring process, though—as we saw at United and Continental—experiential learning through problem-solving teams can be helpful in building new relational skills.

Exhibit 7–1 shows American's lack of attention to hiring for relational competence relative to Southwest Airlines, and its correspondingly weak levels of relational coordination. In addition, we see some variation between the two American sites, with AMR1 showing considerably higher levels of attention to hiring for relational competence, and correspondingly higher levels of relational coordination, relative to AMR2. As we also saw at Continental, local managers can indeed make a difference.

Summing Up

In this chapter, we have seen how hiring for relational competence helps organizations achieve higher levels of relational coordination. As we learned in Chap. 3, relational coordination in turn has a dramatic effect on both quality and efficiency performance. The benefits of hiring for relational competence extend beyond the airline industry. In the study of patient-care coordination described in Chap. 4, hospitals differed in the importance they attached to relational competence when hiring nurses, social workers, therapists, and physicians. Some hospitals invested heavily in developing techniques to identify relational competence in the hiring process. In other hospitals, administrators put little to no emphasis on hiring for relational competence, looking instead for the most qualified individual performers. The tendency to neglect relational competence was most pronounced in physician hiring. One result was that hospitals often ended up with physicians who had the kind of "command presence" that may have been effective and necessary in some aspects of the physician's job, but that also tended to undermine working relationships that were critical for achieving efficient, high-quality patient care. Some hospitals in the study had departed from the norm and had begun to use relational competence as a criterion for hiring physicians. Those hospitals interviewed coworkers from previous jobs to assess a physician's likelihood of working well with others, particularly nurses with whom they would have to work closely. In that study, as in this one, hiring for relational competence resulted in higher levels of relational coordination, and in more efficient, higher-quality outcomes.

Increasingly, jobs require not only functional expertise but also relational competence—the ability to interact with others to accomplish common goals. Indeed, people who perform jobs that require high levels of functional expertise also tend to need high levels of relational competence to integrate their work with the work of fellow employees. Organizations like Southwest Airlines that recognize the importance of relational competence, look diligently for employees who have it, then develop it to even higher levels through training, will have a distinct performance advantage over organizations that do not.

CHAPTER

Use Conflicts to Build Relationships

What's unique about Southwest is that we're real proactive about conflict. We work very hard at destroying any turf battle once one crops up—and they do. Normally they are not malicious or ill intentioned. Sometimes it's a personality conflict. Sometimes it's bureaucracy.

—Station Manager, Southwest Airlines

CONFLICTS ARE A fact of life in highly interdependent work processes that span multiple functions.[1] People in different functions occupy different "thought worlds" that make shared understanding difficult.[2] Not only are conflicts more likely to occur in highly interdependent processes, those conflicts are also more likely to have intensified effects.[3] In flight departures, for example, conflict is a common occurrence. There is tremendous pressure to get the plane out on time, and at the same time there are multiple functions involved, each of which tends not to understand very well the perspective of the others. From pilots to cabin cleaners, the functions whose coordination is essential to achieving performance outcomes in the departure process tend to be divided by the lack of shared goals, shared knowledge, and mutual respect. The resulting friction between these functions often contributes to poor performance.

To many people, conflicts appear to be destructive, and are to be avoided at all costs. However, there are potentially constructive aspects to conflict as well. Conflict expert Karen Jehn demonstrated that task-related conflict can improve performance when it takes place in a setting where it is valued.[4] But what does it mean to value conflict? How does an organization make conflict a constructive rather than a destructive force? This chapter shows that proactively identifying and resolving conflicts is a way to strengthen the relationships that underlie effective coordination. Conflict resolution is an often-overlooked opportunity to build a shared understanding of the work process among participants who do not fully understand each other's perspectives. As we will see, Southwest Airlines invests a great deal of time and effort in doing just this.

Conflict Resolution at Southwest Airlines

At Southwest, managers are expected to take an active role in resolving cross-functional conflicts. A customer service manager explained her approach to conflict resolution:

> You're going to have conflict. You try to get them to talk it out. They can bring it up to the supervisors and myself. Hopefully they'll do it in a positive tone. Maybe a wrong call was made in the heat of the moment. You give them the other side of it. It [sometimes] works to bring them together. . . . You just shed light on why they did what they did.

When conflicts arise at Southwest and are not resolved by the parties themselves, a conflict resolution process is used. A customer service agent in Phoenix explained:

> Some flight attendants have a "better than thou" attitude but they are by far the exception. We try to minimize that attitude. . . . You can turn people around, even if they have an attitude, by the way you treat them. Most people can be turned around.
>
> If it's a real conflict, we bring the people together and we don't leave here until it's resolved. If it's a conflict across groups, we might have an information-gathering meeting where we all sit down.

These information-gathering meetings were quite common at Southwest for resolving conflicts across functions and in some locations were called "Come to Jesus" meetings, suggesting that conflicting parties were expected to bare their souls if necessary to achieve reconciliation. According to an assistant station manager: '

> When there's really a problem, we have a "Come to Jesus" meeting and work it out. Whereas it's warfare at other airlines, here the goal is to maintain the esteem of everybody.

An administrative assistant for the pilots gave her perspective:

> When something really serious happens and you can't work things out, the two managers involved call a "Come to Jesus" meeting, a face-to-face between the people who have the problem. You take the day off and bring everyone together. It doesn't happen much, but it happens. It's a matter of mutual respect. You are part of the company first. If a person can't work it out. . . .

One of Southwest's chief pilots explained his approach to conflict resolution:

> Because we are moving at a fast pace, miscommunication and misunder-standings happen sometimes. We take great pride in squaring it away as quickly as possible. Pilots and flight attendants—sometimes an interaction didn't go right between them. They are upset, then we get them together and work it out, in a teamwork approach. If you have a problem, the best thing is to deal with it yourself. If you can't, then we take it to the next step—we call a meeting of all the parties.

A flight attendant base manager explained his experiences with conflict resolution and the positive outcomes that can result:

> We are encouraged to intervene if there is a problem between employees. If a problem emerges between a flight attendant and a provisioner, for example, we will have a team building meeting. We investigate the problem, but it's not a whodunit. Just get the two to sit down and face each other. Each will give their perception of what happened.
>
> This happened recently with a flight attendant and a pilot. I get chills on my neck because of how wonderfully this worked out. Almost gag me with a spoon—it was such a blessing. Each one said—"that's not what I meant." We came away so enriched.

The flight attendant had gotten a question from a customer about an unusual movement the plane made. The flight attendant asked, and the pilot did not respond. He felt she was questioning his judgment. She was asking because the customers are our most prized possession and the customer wanted to know. That pilot will have a different sense with every other flight attendant he sees. The meeting will have a ripple effect. The idea here is to pay a lot of attention to little things because they are so important.

Of course, it is not easy to engage in conflict resolution, and it is not always effective. President and Chief Operating Officer Colleen Barrett pointed out:

It's not easy to pull these meetings off if the flight attendant is based in Baltimore and the gate agent is on the West Coast. Every now and then one will blow up. Sometimes the problem is magnified by bringing them together, rather than resolved. But I think when that happens, the bottom line is that both don't belong here.

Executive Vice President of Operations Jim Wimberly agreed:

Some people don't get it. We'll normally encourage them to pursue opportunities elsewhere.

The Southwest philosophy is that individual conflicts should be dealt with on an interpersonal basis, and should serve as a learning experience. However, the success of this philosophy depends a great deal on its implementation. At Southwest's Los Angeles station, which was struggling to stabilize staffing in the mid-1990s, conflict resolution was not being actively pursued. The Southwest philosophy regarding conflict resolution would have been helpful during this period, but rather than being actively surfaced, conflicts appeared to be suppressed, due in part to the station manager's anxiety about his performance.

Southwest's top leadership played a critical role in getting conflict resolution back on track at the troubled Los Angeles station. One of headquarters' first moves in responding to the need for help was to encourage a dialogue between parties that were in conflict, particularly between the pilots who flew out of Los Angeles and the ramp agents there. Pilots agreed to work on the Los Angeles ramp for a week to increase understanding between the two functions. The effects were reportedly quite positive. A Southwest pilot who participated in the initiative explained how it worked.

> I was part of the Cutting Edge team [the name given to the initiative]. After working a week here with people on their jobs, I see what they're up against. Out of it we got some goodwill, and a lot more understanding.

A ramp agent concurred:

> It's true. Especially here with certain flights with the heavy on-load and off-load. Pilots really learned what the delays were. The other day we took a 20-minute delay on an originator. The pilot came down calmly to talk—it made all the difference in the world.

Benefits of Conflict Resolution

Relative to the other airlines included in this study (United, Continental, and American), Southwest took a far more proactive approach to conflict resolution.[5] This study, which was outlined in detail in Chap. 3, included two American Airlines sites, two Continental Airlines sites, two Southwest Airlines sites, and three United Airlines sites. A statistical analysis of these approaches to conflict resolution suggested that proactive conflict resolution contributes to higher levels of relational coordination. Proactive conflict resolution also contributes to improved flight departure performance, particularly faster turnaround times, greater staffing productivity, fewer customer complaints, and better on-time performance.[6] To observe the effects of conflict resolution on relational coordination, we can plot conflict resolution for each of the nine sites against relational coordination. Exhibit 8–1 suggests a clear impact of proactive conflict resolution on relational coordination.

Conflict Resolution at United Airlines

United Airlines took a traditional approach to conflict resolution: submerging conflicts between functions and focusing instead on labor/management conflicts. However, the United Shuttle was far more proac-

Exhibit 8–1 Impact of Proactive Conflict Resolution on Relational Coordination*

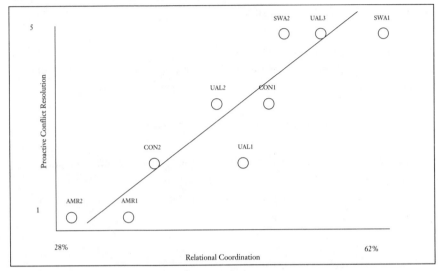

* Each circle denotes one of the nine sites included in the study. Proactive conflict resolution is assessed on a 1-to-5 scale. Relational coordination, coordination carried out through relationships of shared goals, shared knowledge, and mutual respect, is measured as the percentage of cross-functional ties that are strong or very strong, based on an employee survey. Relational coordination in turn has a positive impact on quality and efficiency performance, as illustrated in Exhibit 3-4.

tive toward resolving cross-functional conflicts. The cross-functional teams that were used to design the Shuttle were also used to surface and resolve conflicts among functional groups. Cross-functional briefings before and after shifts were used to resolve more immediate and interpersonal conflicts among members of different functional groups. Partly as a result of these opportunities for conflict resolution, relationships between functional groups at the Shuttle were more accepting and respectful than the relationships normally observed among United employees. A United customer service agent who went to work in the Shuttle explained to me:

> Over there [in the mainline United operation] they say, "Oooooh, how can you hang out with someone who cleans the toilets?" Here they say, "Need a ride?"

As a result of the Shuttle's approach to conflict resolution (and other practices highlighted in this book), the United Shuttle achieved significantly higher levels of relational coordination compared to United's non-Shuttle sites (55 percent versus 42 percent of cross-functional ties were rated by employees as strong or very strong). Exhibit 8–1 shows how these higher levels of relational coordination are related to the Shuttle's conflict-resolution practices. The United Shuttle, denoted by UAL3 in Exhibit 8–1, has higher levels of relational coordination than its non-Shuttle counterparts (UAL1 and UAL2), corresponding to its more proactive approach to conflict resolution. In addition, as we saw in the previous chapter, the Shuttle outperformed its non-Shuttle counterparts at United on both quality and efficiency dimensions.

After the employee buyout, managers for both the Shuttle and mainline United received training in conflict resolution, and all United employees were scheduled to receive such training. Soon after the buyout, conflict resolution began to occur in United's mainline operation in Los Angeles. The ramp and freight departments were engaged in ongoing conflict over their interface in the departure process. According to the ramp manager:

> At first, we would blame them and they would blame us. So we started having joint meetings, twice monthly. At first they were bitch sessions. Now they've evolved into—"I can take that on, I can do that."

One meeting was the turning point, the manager recalled.

> The meetings started out first with attacks on management, then attacks on each other. Terry [a ramp manager] came in with flip charts and thought it was chaotic. But Charlie [a ramp lead] said, it's the best meeting we ever had. Everyone spoke their minds, and people were behind the scenes saying "here's what we're going to do."

There was still a hesitance by supervisors to address conflicts openly, according to a Los Angeles ramp manager.

> Supervisors don't like to deal with conflict. . . . We need to be convincing people, teaching them how to have conflicting conversations.

From another manager's point of view, however, United had come a long way.

> We're always dealing with conflict now. It's movement for our company.

Conflict Resolution at Continental Airlines

At Continental, management evaluation during the study period was reported by station managers to focus almost exclusively on bottom-line results. The airline was still recovering from the legacy of Frank Lorenzo, a leader who paid little attention to employee relations and who led the airline into bankruptcy twice before leaving in 1990. According to a flight attendant who worked for Continental during that period:

> When you went to work for Frank Lorenzo, there was no compassion. The employees, they were a commodity like a file cabinet, like a desk or a chair. They just moved the pieces around, and you weren't to have any feelings, or they didn't care if you liked the job.[7]

However, station managers reported a change in the mid-1990s, with the arrival of a popular new CEO, Gordon Bethune, who spoke extensively and with credibility about teamwork. Despite the lack of formal mechanisms for conflict resolution across functional groups, Continental's Boston station management was quite attentive to resolving these conflicts. Supervisors were expected to mediate between employees. A customer service supervisor explained:

> Ultimately a supervisor will hear both sides and act as the referee. We get people to work it out. No hard feelings. It's a very important part of the supervisor's job. It's all a part of coaching and counseling, part of the training that supervisors get. Supervisors are valued because they can identify and solve problems in communication.

One of the potential high-conflict areas at Continental was between pilots and flight attendants about pay and authority differentials. According to the Director of Inflight Service:

There is some animosity because of the money. The pilots make so much. Also due to "I say it because I'm the captain." There are some flight attendants who don't mind letting men make decisions. . . . But we are not immune from pilot/flight attendant conflicts. To be respected, you have to behave a certain way, I tell them. I show them through my relationship with the chief pilot. My message is that certainly I respect you as the leader on the aircraft. I want respect as an individual fellow employee.

In addition to addressing conflict through these individual behavior strategies, Continental developed a new training program for addressing conflict between pilots and flight attendants, focused on communication and leadership skills.

Exhibit 8–1 shows Continental's moderate attention to proactive conflict resolution, relative to Southwest Airlines, and its correspondingly lower levels of relational coordination. In addition, we see substantial variation between the two Continental sites, with CON1 showing considerably greater attention to proactive conflict resolution, and correspondingly higher levels of relational coordination, relative to CON2. Again, local managers can make a difference.

Conflict Resolution at American Airlines

As at the other airlines, conflict at American Airlines often occurred around the flight departure process. At the same time, American Airlines as an organization failed to send a clear, consistent message to its managers about the importance of identifying and resolving cross-functional conflicts. Instead, managers in the field perceived that headquarters cared only about bottom-line performance. In the early 1990s, the managerial report card for stations was changed to include a score for "leadership" along with scores for operating performance. Unlike the other categories, however, leadership received zero weight. A customer service manager gave his perspective:

They look at individual traits like leadership skills. Conflict resolution is implicit in that. But if the department's numbers aren't good, I'll get canned anyway.

This belief was confirmed by an employee relations manager at American headquarters:

> Some of our station managers use the carrot and others use the stick. But they [headquarters] don't care how the station managers get the results— they just want to see the results.

The conflict resolution processes that did exist at American were largely designed to address union/management conflicts rather than conflicts among peers in different departments. Still, there were some exceptions. Though only a half-day program, the Commitment to Courtesy was a clear example. A flight attendant manager described the reason for the program:

> We wanted to improve the interaction between flight attendants and gate agents, since it's been pretty contentious around departures. . . . We needed this because the boarding process is the most stressful and chaotic part of any flight. Gate agents and flight attendants have typically worked against each other rather than together. We wanted them to have a chance to sit down and find new ways to interact. . . . But we are getting a lot of complaints from flight attendants and some have refused to do it.

Another example was Crew Resource Management, an ongoing training program for pilots that American expanded to include its flight attendants. The new version encompassed not only technical skills but also periodic training in interpersonal relations and dispute resolution. However, flight attendant participation was voluntary, and most refused to participate, not seeing the value. Though aimed at the right target, these efforts appeared to be too isolated to have a strong effect on the relationships between functions.

Exhibit 8–1 shows American's lack of attention to conflict resolution relative to Southwest Airlines, and its correspondingly low levels of relational coordination.

How Conflict Resolution Evolved at Southwest

Although many assume that Southwest's success has come relatively easily, its leaders point out that many years of effort have been required to develop the practices, such as proactive conflict resolution, that support high performance relationships. As Jim Wimberly testified, "We have worked for years to get to this point." Around 1990, Southwest leaders promoted the idea of "internal customers" to get people to respond to each other. "We were trying to improve communication across functional boundaries," Colleen Barrett explained. To reinforce the idea of internal customers, she and Wimberly revised the old irregularity report and made it into a device for conflict resolution among employees. Wimberly explained:

> We have a very heated, potentially dangerous, operation on the ramp. There is a lot of stress when the plane is on the ground. Inevitably some conflict will arise. If something happens out of the ordinary, if you feel someone didn't handle something correctly, you fill out a report.

Under the old system, these reports would go from frontline employees to senior managers of their department, and on to the CEO. According to Wimberly:

> So if there was a conflict between a flight attendant and a gate agent, or a ramp worker and a pilot, me and Flight Ops and Kelleher would get reports from everybody involved. . . . Employees were taking the time to fill them out, and department heads were reading them—but usually not with high priority. And they were not getting back to the employee.

As a result, top managers began trying to push resolution of these conflicts and problems down to where they actually occur. Barrett explained:

> We got so many reports after awhile, we changed the form. We added a line. "If it involved a Southwest employee, have you discussed it with him or her?" If we got a form where the answer was no, we would call and say, why don't you all have a little chat?

The meetings themselves were relatively straightforward:

> The local managers . . . will help get the people together. When the senior managers get the final report, we decide if a "Come to Jesus" meeting is needed, if it looks like they haven't resolved it. We tell them this is not a dis-

ciplinary meeting, nobody needs union representation, we'll leave the room if you like. We are just moderators, the focus is between employees and on how important teamwork is.

At these meetings, said Barrett, "it is wonderful to see the lights go on in people's eyes when they understand the other person's point of view."

Summing Up

As we noted at the start of this chapter, conflicts can be expected to erupt in processes that span multiple functions, particularly when those processes are highly interdependent. In health care, as in many other industries, functional boundaries are reinforced by professional identities, specialized knowledge, and status differentials, undermining relationships and making communication more difficult.[8] Status differences between doctors, nurses, therapists, social workers, and others create divisions among the parties who are involved in caring for the same patients. Managed-care pressures and the resulting speed-up of care delivery have put additional pressure on care-provider relationships, increasing the incidence of conflict.[9] Case managers are typically expected to take a hard line on limiting resource utilization, for example, while doctors and nurses are expected to push back to assure high-quality care for their patients. In addition, a nurse explained:

> Miscommunication between the physician and the nurse is common because so many things are happening so quickly. But because patients are in and out so quickly, it's even more important to communicate well.

However, processes for resolving conflicts are not always well developed. In some hospitals, no formal processes of any sort exist for cross-functional conflict resolution. Other hospitals take advantage of multidisciplinary meetings that were convened regularly for other purposes to work out conflicts about patient care, while others developed cross-functional councils or protocols dedicated to the resolution of cross-functional conflict. In one hospital, all staff members were required to take a pledge that they would seek to resolve conflicts by following a series of agreed-upon steps, and would seek help if unsuccessful. Statistical analyses showed that the hospitals with formalized conflict-resolution processes in place enjoyed higher levels of relational coordination among their doctors, nurses, physical therapists, social workers, and case managers, as well as higher-quality, more efficient outcomes for patients.

Management theorist Louis Pondy noted that one way to prevent conflict is to reduce interdependence by "1) reducing dependence on common resources; 2) loosening up schedules or introducing buffers, such as inventories or contingency funds; and 3) reducing pressures for consensus." He also noted, however, that "these techniques of preventing conflict may be costly in both direct and indirect costs," and that ultimately, "interpersonal friction is one of the costs of 'running a tight ship.'"[10]

Rather than reducing cross-functional conflict by introducing costly buffers, and rather than simply accepting it as a cost of running a tight ship, this chapter shows that organizations can approach conflict as an opportunity to build relationships. Organizational theorist Andrew Van de Ven argued that conflicts are necessary to process the uncertainty and information that is present in highly interdependent processes.[11] In addition, he argued, conflicts among interdependent parties can serve as an occasion for learning about the process and for developing a clear understanding about goals, expectations, and behaviors.[12] This perspective on conflict resolution is consistent with Karen Jehn's finding that conflict leads to improved performance when it takes place in a context that values task-related conflict.[13]

Organizations should proactively seek out conflicts rather than allowing them to fester. Then managers should bring the parties together to better understand each other's perspective. If organizations do not identify and resolve cross-functional conflicts, those conflicts will weaken critical relationships of shared goals, shared knowledge, and mutual respect. When managers treat cross-functional conflict as an occasion for learning, they strengthen relationships between employees and boost performance of the work processes in which those employees are engaged.

CHAPTER

Bridge the Work/ Family Divide

People at Southwest care about one another's families. We recognize deaths and births. We help in times of tragedy. You do not see these things at other airlines. We hire people who have worked for other airlines who say they never received anything at home from their former employers, that they were never acknowledged in a personal way.

—Libby Sartain, former Vice President of People, Southwest Airlines

RELATIONSHIPS AT SOUTHWEST—characterized by shared goals, shared knowledge, and mutual respect—are critical for getting work done effectively, yet these relationships extend beyond the work itself, spilling over into friendships and even taking on some characteristics of family ties. A Southwest station manager commented:

> We're kind of a big family here, and families have fun together. The passengers are part of the family too, so we have fun with them.[1]

Employees regularly referred to their work relationships as ties of family and friendship, and management encouraged this view. The vice president of people explained:

> With family structures as they are these days, we often help our young employees to grow up. . . . It lends to the family atmosphere here.

Hugs were observed to be a common form of greeting, whether in the original Southwest station at Love Field, or at Southwest's big East Coast station in Baltimore. Indeed, family was more than a metaphor at Southwest: many employees reported family ties with other Southwest employees, something the company encouraged as long as those involved were not also in a reporting relationship.

There seem to be powerful benefits to blurring the boundaries between work and nonwork aspects of life, for both organizations and their employees. Traditional organizational practices often demand that individuals disconnect themselves from nonwork aspects of their identity—such as those related to family and spirituality,[2] personal pain and tragedy,[3] and racial or ethnic identity[4]—while at work. As a result, individual attitudes and performance often suffer. Erving Goffman's classic study of self-presentation chronicles the efforts to which people go to present the correct self for the given context, and the stresses and strains that are involved in doing so.[5] Arlie Hochschild's work on the "managed heart" reports the stress these self-presentation requirements can place on service workers, and the falseness sometimes perceived by customers.[6] There is some evidence that people cooperate with an organization and give their best efforts to the extent that they *identify* with the organization.[7] However, as many of us can attest, it is difficult to identify deeply with an organization in which one is encouraged or required to present a false self. To create healthier and more productive employees, organizations should strive to create more harmony between work and nonwork aspects of life.[8]

On the other hand, clear boundaries may be *needed* to protect family time from the ever-encroaching grasp of paternalistic companies that seek to bring their employees' lives into the service of the companies' own goals.[9] Hochschild describes how work has become the safe haven that family used to represent, while family has come to seem more and more like work. It is a vicious cycle, she explains. When people spend too much time at work, they shortchange their family relationships. Their family relationships weaken, and become more a source of stress than comfort as children and spouses act up to get the attention they need. As a result, employees may use work as a source of community and as a refuge from their dysfunctional family relationships.[10]

Both sides seem to agree, however, that for better or worse, this blurring of the boundaries between work and family can serve as a powerful force for building commitment to organizations. Southwest leverages the strength of its employees' external relationships to build strong internal relationships. However, Southwest also recognizes the hazards of blurring the boundaries between work and life—the organization can encompass so much of a person's time and loyalty that family and community ties suffer from neglect, thereby becoming useless as a source of strength for the employee or the organization. We will see how Southwest managers blur the boundary between work and life, and how they strive to do so by *enhancing* rather than undermining their employees' family and community ties.

Encouraging Employees to Be Themselves at Work

At Southwest, employees are encouraged to be themselves at work. As Herb Kelleher once explained:

> We try to allow our people to be themselves and not have to surrender their personality when they arrive at Southwest.[11]

You are not expected to park your personality and true identity at the door. Some of Southwest's reputation for being funky and fun comes from this expectation. Southwest customers are familiar with flight attendants who go beyond the written script for take-off instructions to passengers, and inject their own personalities into the role.

Though being oneself is a concept normally associated with leisure time and not with work, it is an important concept at Southwest, and seems to contribute to easing tensions between individuals and between functions. A ramp agent in Phoenix explained:

> If the captain thinks he's better, he'll make you say everything in detail. You get to know some of the pilots after awhile. The whole concept is to be yourself and to have fun in your job. The relaxed atmosphere around here helps to ease the tension between departments.

A gate agent offered her thoughts on the side effects of having fun at work:

> We sing and laugh and play games. Let everyone enjoy their job so they'll work and make the company profitable, and give the customer what they want at the same time. No one department is any more important than another.

A customer service supervisor in Phoenix explained why she liked to work at Southwest:

> The main thing is that everybody cares. We work in so many different areas but it doesn't matter. It's true from the top to the last one hired. People tell me—now I know why everyone is smiling here.

The assistant station manager had a similar perspective:

> You have to laugh. Weather affects everything, and puts things beyond your control. We always ask people in an evaluation if they are having fun in their job. If they are, there's a good chance they are doing well.

Not only does being oneself at work help to reduce stress—some argued that it also fosters employee loyalty and commitment.

> Senior people don't get jaded here. . . . Employees are able to be their own person. This stimulates hard work and loyalty. It really seems to build loyalty. People just don't quit here. People who do leave will go to other departments.

This personal identification with Southwest sometimes occurs through a personal transformation experienced at work. A flight attendant base manager described his experience:

> This may be a cult, but I believe I never had a job where I wanted to go to work. This company is geared for families. We dress up on Halloween and Christmas. My life has changed 180 degrees from what it was 8 years ago. I have a career mindset. I have learned to set goals. I met my wife here. I could get real mushy.
>
> This company has offered me something completely different from what I had—honesty, openness, sharing of information. I take it for granted. Only when we're here talking do I realize how fortunate we are.

From the perspective of an operations agent:

> There is an opportunity to find yourself in this company.

On a similar note, a customer service agent credited Southwest with a personal transformation in her life:

Southwest has helped me make a wonderful contribution in my world. . . .
We *belong* to this company.

Recognizing Personal Pain and Triumph

One way Southwest encourages employees to be themselves at work is by
openly recognizing major events in the lives of employees and their families. According to Libby Sartain, former vice president of people:

> People at Southwest care about one another's families. We recognize deaths
> and births. We help in times of tragedy. You do not see these things at other
> airlines. We hire people who have worked for other airlines who say they
> never received anything at home from their former employers, that they
> were never acknowledged in a personal way.

To help in times of personal catastrophe, Southwest has a Catastrophic Fund. During a meeting with the Phoenix station manager, he
received a phone call from Southwest's Catastrophic Fund. On the
other end of the phone were the Director of Special Projects, the Director of Inflight (flight attendants), and several others from Southwest's
headquarters. They had received a request for help from one of Southwest's Phoenix employees. The station manager told them what he
knew of the employee's history, and they talked at length about what
kind of help would be needed. Then they said good-bye and the station
manager resumed his meeting. The station manager acted as though
making arrangements for the care of an employee in need was an unremarkable part of his workday. Similarly, Southwest President and Chief
Operating Officer Colleen Barrett once discovered that a long-time
employee whose work performance had inexplicably declined was facing $1800 in legal bills due to divorce and custody proceedings. Barrett
immediately sent the needed sum of money from her own account,
recalling her own experience as a single mom.[12]

Through the recognition of its employees' personal tragedies and triumphs, Southwest brings the organization into the personal realm, and
the personal realm into the organization. When people disguise the pain
they are experiencing in their personal life from their colleagues, they
can experience a lack of internal connectedness.[13] Recognition of their

pain allows individuals to have more holistic identities at work, facilitating both their own personal health and their productivity.

Employee and Family Identification with the Organization

As a result of being themselves at work, employees identified strongly with Southwest Airlines and talked about the organization as though it were an extension of their own families. A ramp supervisor in Phoenix explained his responsibilities:

> I have a responsibility for a family, a house, and for this company. The idea is to keep customers coming back. The goal is for you to come back and fly on Southwest.

Likewise, the families of Southwest employees also tend to identify strongly with Southwest Airlines. Libby Sartain, former vice president of people, explained:

> Kids and spouses feel the same way we do when they see a Southwest airplane. When we talk at company events, family members talk about Southwest as "we." If you get involved, you have to make sure family members become part of that or they get jealous. We encourage people to bring their kids to work to show them what work is.

The Culture Committee

The Culture Committees, started by President and Chief Operating Officer Colleen Barrett in the early 1990s to ensure that Southwest's rapid growth would not result in barriers between functions, also helped to blur the boundaries between work and life. The systemwide Culture Committee included frontline and management employees from all over the Southwest system. It included members from each of the functions, including pilots, flight attendants, gate and ticketing agents, mechanics, and so forth. Members met quarterly at headquarters with Barrett to brainstorm ideas for maintaining and strengthening Southwest's culture. In addition to the systemwide Culture Committee, each individual station had its own Culture Committee that met monthly to plan social and charitable events. An operations agent from Baltimore explained:

> Each station has its own Culture Committee. The station manager puts out a letter asking who wants to be on it. They organize fund-raisers and parties. We usually have a spring party, a summer party, a fall party, and a Christmas party. We raise money doing other things so the parties are free, or maybe $10 to get in.

Local committee members planned social events such as summer barbecues, Christmas formals, Casino Nights, and carnivals that included employees and their families. The Baltimore station's summer event, organized by its Culture Committee, has typically been a moonlight cruise on Chesapeake Bay. The walls of Southwest stations and headquarters are then adorned with candid photographs of Southwest employees and their families taken at these social events, bringing family and other personal relationships into the workplace in a highly visual way.

Giving to the Community

The local Culture Committees also plan ways for Southwest employees to give back to the community; for example, by preparing and delivering meals to the local Ronald McDonald House, a residence provided to families while their children are undergoing treatment for cancer. Southwest's relationship with the Ronald McDonald House has been central for Southwest and its employees for many years. The Ronald McDonald House was supported by each of Southwest's local Culture Committees as well as by the pilots' union. As one gate agent told me with pride:

> Did you know about Southwest and Ronald McDonald House? We *are* the Ronald McDonald House.

In a meeting of the Baltimore Culture Committee, a serious discussion ensued among committee members regarding how to serve the next monthly meal to Ronald McDonald House residents without disrupting the quiet needed by the families in residence. At the Phoenix station, an administrator regularly made popcorn, sold it for 50 cents a bag to employees throughout the station, and sent the proceeds to the Ronald McDonald House.

Efforts to Bridge the Work/Family Divide

Southwest does not just encourage its employees to give back to the community. Southwest also has a long tradition of seeking to accommodate the needs of families, so as not to burn out this important source of employee commitment. Southwest's biggest contribution to strengthening the family ties of its employees is the flexibility of scheduling the company offers to employees. According to Libby Sartain:

> We are a work- and family-friendly place. We're very flexible with scheduling, for example. But it's more of a flexible attitude here than formal policies. For instance, we don't officially have flextime and other family programs, but there is a lot of leeway for employees to trade shifts and so on.

Indeed, Southwest has been recognized for its innovations in achieving scheduling flexibility for frontline employees through shift trading. In effect, this approach to achieving scheduling flexibility requires employees to use their workplace relationships to negotiate flexibility with each other, further integrating workplace relationships with family ties. Southwest's shift-trading approach to achieving flexibility also reduces the administrative burden associated with flexibility and instead places it in the hands of employees to negotiate with one another.

Southwest recognizes this scheduling flexibility as a major benefit for both the organization and its employees, enabling employees to meet their family commitments without neglecting their work commitments. As a result, Southwest has foregone workplace innovations that may have helped performance in principle but that would have reduced employees' ability to schedule their work around family obligations. For example, some airlines have attempted to schedule the same employees to work together on particular flights over the course of an extended period, hoping to build more permanent teams. But Southwest decided against such scheduling practices, not wanting to reduce the scheduling flexibility enjoyed by Southwest employees. In effect, Southwest did not want to sacrifice the family relationships of its employees to build stronger working relationships. Southwest looks for synergies between family and work relationships and tries to avoid trading off one for the other.

Pilots and flight attendants have unique challenges staying in touch with their families when they are away on trips for multiple days. An administrator for the pilots at Southwest explained her role in keeping them connected:

> Part of my job is to take calls from them and from their families. Let them know what's going on. We help keep them connected.

Preventing Work from Overwhelming Family and Community

Southwest recognizes the strength of the working relationships and the potential for these relationships and commitments to overwhelm family and community relationships. Particularly for top managers, who have no contractual limits to their time at work, this has been a challenge. According to Jim Wimberly, executive vice president of operations:

> It is an intoxicating business. We love the business and this company. We all need to make sure it stays intoxicating and not addictive.

Managers attempt to use peer pressure with each other to keep their family commitments as well as their work commitments. For example, Libby Sartain revealed:

> Joyce, our head of marketing, told us how much she appreciated that we encourage her to be a good mother, as much as a good employee. We make her take a vacation.

Summing Up

Southwest's approach to work/family issues is to recognize and encourage the energy that good family and community relationships bring to the workplace, and the energy that good working relationships bring to family and community life. In addition to energy, organizations that encourage their employees to care for others at home and in the community will ultimately benefit from higher levels of relational competence in the workplace, as employees exercise their relational skills both at home and at work. Indeed, as work/family expert Joyce Fletcher has argued:

> Organizations intent on developing relational skills in their workers might do so through the systematic encouragement of all individuals to be involved in some sort of care-taking experience. . . . [There are] organizational benefits of relaxing the boundary between work and family and/or community as a way of developing relational competence in workers.[14]

The energy and learning that employees gain from building strong family and community ties can be brought into the workplace and leveraged to achieve stronger working relationships and better organizational performance. Organizations should therefore be vigilant to ensure that relationships at work do not overwhelm and undermine the family and community relationships that are needed to sustain strong working relationships.

Create Boundary Spanners

One thing this job will do for you is form a personality. You've got to talk to so many people. If you don't like people, you'll either be miserable or get out of the job real fast.

—Operations Agent, Southwest Airlines

M ANY DIFFERENT EMPLOYEES play a critical role in coordinating flight departures at Southwest Airlines—pilots, flight attendants, gate agents, ticket agents, baggage handlers, mechanics, and so forth. One role, however, is particularly central for coordinating flight departures—the operations agent. In the airline industry, the operations agent is at the center of communication among the various functional groups that are working to get the plane unloaded, serviced, reloaded, and on its way. The tasks of the operations agent include collecting information about the passengers, bags, freight, mail, and fuel going out on a particular flight, making calculations about how much of each can be loaded and where they should be loaded, consistent with weather and route information. Before the plane arrives, during its time at the gate, and after its departure, operations agents gather and process the needed information from each of the other functions, make adjustments as needed, and communicate those adjustments back to each of the functions. In so doing, operations agents bring together and reconcile sometimes conflicting perspectives among the various departments regarding passenger needs, commitments to freight and mail customers, and the requirements of flight safety.

Operations agents in effect serve as "boundary spanners," managing the flow of information across functional boundaries. Organization design theorists tell us that boundary spanners are particularly important for coordinating work when employees perform very different tasks and as a result have very different perspectives about what needs to be done.[1] The boundary spanner has traditionally been seen as a mechanism for collecting, filtering, translating, interpreting, and disseminating knowledge across organizational boundaries.[2] However, we learn in this chapter that an effective boundary spanner does *more* than process information. An effective boundary spanner is also engaged in relationship building, developing relationships of shared goals, shared knowledge, and mutual respect among fellow employees to facilitate the coordination of work.

Still, boundary spanners are costly because they require an entire workgroup whose primary task is coordination.[3] One way to reduce the cost of boundary spanners is to reduce their staffing levels—and increase the number of projects or flight departures they are assigned to coordinate. Since the mid-1980s, many airlines have been doing just this—attempting to make operations agents more efficient by relying more and more on computer interfaces to bring together the information required to dispatch a flight. And indeed, these new systems allow operations agents to be more efficient. With information technology, operations agents can be located centrally and can coordinate up to 15 departures at a time. Operations agents read a computer file into which each function has input the relevant information, make contacts when there is a discrepancy or need for further information, then make the necessary judgments and decisions before dispatching the flight. However, the quality and detail of communication is not very high in this arrangement. The operations agent is remotely located and is forced by workload to rely almost exclusively on the computer interface.

Operations agents had traditionally served as a source of social cohesion across functions in the stations. Operations agents used to be well-known personalities because they came into face-to-face contact with each function during the preplanning or implementation phase of each departure. The on-site operations centers where they worked used to serve as "watering holes," as one of the few locations where members of diverse functions, such as pilots, fuelers, baggage handlers, mechanics, and customer service agents, could congregate comfortably. In their efforts to reduce the staffing levels of operations agents, airlines lost the personal interactions that built strong relationships across functional boundaries. Only Southwest Airlines has recognized this unique role of the operations agent, and staffs the job generously to permit it to be done well.

Boundary Spanning at Southwest Airlines

Moving in the opposite direction of the rest of the industry, Southwest increased the staffing of the operations agent to even higher levels than the other airlines had traditionally used, allowing the operations agent to play an even greater role in the flight departure process. Each individual *flight* was assigned its own dedicated on-site operations agent, who engaged in face-to-face contact with each function before, during, or after the turnaround of that flight—then went on to concentrate on another incoming flight.

As noted above, the job of an operations agent involves a great deal of information processing. A Southwest supervisor explained the basic tasks:

> A couple hours before the flight arrives an operations agent is assigned to the flight. The agent gets a release from dispatch in Dallas. [The release] tells if the plane needs anything, how much fuel due to weather conditions and time of year. The ops agent writes that down and computes the total amount of weight that plane can take. The ops agent tells the ramp and freight agents what's going out, and they say what they have to put in. The gate and ticket agents take the information, and decide [how many passengers] can go.
>
> The ops agent is dealing with the ticket agents, is phoning everybody. There is constant communication between the groups. There are passengers who need special care, for example. We interact with pilots and flight attendants about the weather, information from the families, anything.
>
> Then when the plane arrives, the ops agent sets up the jet way, gets everybody out and everybody boarded. He gets the cargo slip which says how much stuff has been put on board and where, then computes the weight and balance and hands that information off to the pilot. After the door is closed, the ops agent pulls back the jet way.

The information processing tasks in this example are not very distinctive and could certainly be more highly automated, as they have been at other airlines, allowing for a far greater workload than one flight at a time per operations agent. And yet the boundary spanning role at Southwest is highly regarded, and it is often credited for playing a critical role in achieving reliable flight departures. According to Donna Conover, Southwest's executive vice president of customers:

> The operations agent's job is important. It's their responsibility to coordinate the flight. You need someone quarterbacking the flight departure. We are unique in that our operations agents are assigned to lead only one departure at a time. It's a good investment.

According to a Southwest pilot:

> Dispatch doesn't have the time to dedicate to each individual departure. The operations agent is the team leader when the airplane is on the ground.

And, according to a customer service agent:

> The operations room is the heartbeat of the airline. It's totally the heartbeat. They are real selective about who they put there. They want people with smarts. That's a part of our overall coordination—what makes it work.

The centrality of the operations agent role at Southwest Airlines is supported by Southwest's promotion policies. Employees typically come into this job after serving on the ramp and in customer service, bringing the perspective of both key areas to the job. The operations agent job is also considered to be a necessary step before becoming a ramp or customer service manager, because of the broad, cross-functional perspective one gains from being an operations agent.

But why? What is so important about this role that Southwest staffs it at one flight departure per agent, while other airlines staff it at three to fifteen flight departures per agent? Upon closer observation, it became clear that the operations agents at Southwest play a critical social role as well, helping to build relationships across functional boundaries. At Southwest, unlike at the other airlines, the boundary spanner role involves face-to-face interactions with every party involved in the flight departure process. It is not coordination from a distance, conducted primarily through a computer interface, as other airlines have tried to achieve. It is coordination with a human face.

Benefits of the Boundary Spanner Role

Relative to the other airlines included in this study (United, Continental, and American), Southwest employs far higher levels of staffing for its boundary spanner role.[4] This study, which was outlined in detail in Chap. 3, included two American Airlines sites, two Continental Airlines sites, two Southwest Airlines sites, and three United Airlines sites. A statistical analysis of boundary spanner staffing showed that dedicating boundary spanners to a small number of flights is associated with higher levels of relational coordination. Dedicated boundary spanners also contribute to improved flight departure performance, particularly faster turnaround times, greater staffing productivity, fewer customer complaints, and better on-time performance.[5] To observe the effects of boundary spanners on relational coordination, we can plot boundary spanner staffing for each of the nine sites against relational coordination. Exhibit 10–1 suggests a clear impact of boundary spanner staffing on relational coordination.

Exhibit 10–1 Impact of Boundary Spanner Staffing on Relational Coordination*

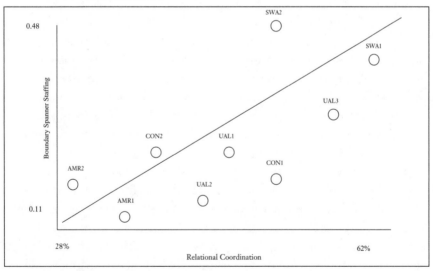

* Each circle denotes one of the nine sites included in the study. Boundary spanner staffing is measured as the number of boundary spanners on staff per daily flight departure. Relational coordination—coordination carried out through relationships of shared goals, shared knowledge, and mutual respect—is measured as the percentage of cross-functional ties that are strong or very strong, based on an employee survey. Relational coordination in turn has a positive impact on quality and efficiency performance, as illustrated in Exhibit 3–4.

Boundary Spanning at United Airlines

At United Airlines as at Southwest, operations agents play a boundary spanner role, but at United they are not assigned to one flight at a time, nor are they expected to leave the operations center and go down to the ramp or the gate to interact with other employees. Rather, they are expected to stay at their computers and coordinate multiple flight departures simultaneously, using the computer interface and the telephone and PA system as needed. Some ops agents are equipped with cameras to watch the aircraft, and so have at least a partial view of what is happening on the ramp.

The United Shuttle's operations agents are organized in the same way, but they have somewhat higher staffing levels per flight than do United's non-Shuttle operations. Operations agents for the Shuttle are not equipped to play the same boundary spanner role that Southwest operations agents play, but they can approximate it more closely than their non-Shuttle counterparts at United, because of their more generous staffing levels. In effect, even though they are located at a distance from the ramp and gate, they have the staffing levels to devote more individualized attention to each flight departure.

Due in part to the Shuttle's boundary spanner staffing (and other practices highlighted in this book), the United Shuttle achieved significantly higher levels of relational coordination compared to United's non-Shuttle sites (55 percent versus 42 percent of cross-functional ties were rated by employees as strong or very strong). Exhibit 10–1 shows how these higher levels of relational coordination are related to boundary spanner staffing levels. The United Shuttle, denoted by UAL3 in Exhibit 10–1, has higher levels of relational coordination than its non-Shuttle counterparts (UAL1 and UAL2), corresponding to its higher levels of boundary spanner staffing. In addition, as we saw in Chap. 7, the Shuttle outperformed its non-Shuttle counterparts at United on both quality and efficiency dimensions.

Boundary Spanning at Continental Airlines

Continental's operations agents at the Boston station are equipped to play the role of boundary spanner to some extent—operations coordinators and load functions are located together in the operations room at each station. Their job does not involve a direct interface with every function, but their location as well as their active role in load planning produces a great deal of face-to-face contact with pilots, ramp agents, fuelers, and mechanics.

The boundary spanner role at Continental's Cleveland station is different from that at the Boston station. The Cleveland operations center has a greater division of labor. Operations coordinators maintain contact with pilots and central dispatch. Load planners organize information from central dispatch and the various departments to ensure that passengers, baggage, and freight are loaded properly. In addition, maintenance, ramp, and customer service representatives sit in the operations center to provide a link between operations and their departments. Load planners work in a separate room and do not have ongoing contact with the rest of the operations center staff.

Exhibit 10–1 shows Continental's moderate staffing levels for its boundary spanners, relative to Southwest Airlines, and its correspondingly lower levels of relational coordination.

Boundary Spanning at American Airlines

American Airlines traditionally had operations agents who played the boundary spanning role. An American pilot in Boston described an operations agent who had retired:

> Sal could identify a problem and he could solve a problem. Ops agents used to be this way. They used to have a leadership role. But their authority was changed. Nobody has that job now.

In addition to playing a central role in information flow and problem solving, operations agents at American traditionally had served a social function. Because of the central location of the operations center, where the operations agents worked, "The ops center used to be the watering hole, the place where everybody came together to hang out between flights." The operations center was one of the few locations at American that were regarded as neutral ground, where functions that were divided by status could share the same space, whether they were cabin cleaners, caterers, fuelers, mechanics, ramp agents, gate agents, flight attendants, or pilots.

However, American began to downsize its on-site operations centers starting in the mid-1980s and to move their staff to a central load house in Dallas, where load agents coordinated 10 to 15 flights simultaneously, with the use of a computer interface. By the mid-1990s, American Airlines had moved farther than any other airline toward reducing the staffing levels of operations agents. According to a load house manager:

> At any one time, a load agent is prereleasing up to four trips, about four trips are one hour from departure and quite active, about four are in the last five minutes, and three have just left. We utilize our people very well.

These off-site load agents have remained the center of communication for the flight departure process in some respects. However, given their off-site location, their low staffing levels per flight, and their reliance on a computer interface, they lack familiarity with the particular features of the flights they coordinate and lack time to dedicate to each individual flight. According to the same load house manager:

> Our biggest problem is communication—getting them [employees at the airports] to talk to us, tell us what's on the airplane.

From the standpoint of the stations, the problem is more basic: "We don't understand their process, and they don't understand ours," said the Los Angeles station manager. Reports of inadequate communication were common. A customer service supervisor complained about the lack of information from ops:

> Here you don't communicate. And sometimes you end up not knowing things. . . . Everyone says we need effective communication. But it's a low priority in action. On the gates I can't tell you the number of times you get the wrong information from ops. . . . We call it the creeping delay. The hardest thing at the gates with off-schedule operations is to get information. They are leery to say the magnitude of the problem.

As the boundary spanning role was taken from operations agents at American, the role fell upon the gate agents. Gate agents became responsible for communicating with the other functions, and were made to feel responsible for delays. However, gate agents found themselves in this role by default rather than by design, and without explicit recognition or support for that role. Gate agents received no training for the boundary spanning role, and were not selected with an eye to playing that role. According to a manager of gate agents:

> We find that a lot of the responsibility for communication with the flight attendants and the ramp falls on our gate agents. We have assumed the responsibility of coordination at the point of departure. It has just evolved that way. Certainly not because of the caliber of our employees.

As an American pilot pointed out:

> Nobody has the job now. The gate agents do it by default.

In addition, gate agents at American Airlines do not occupy a key position in the job ladder, unlike the boundary spanners we observed at Southwest Airlines.

Exhibit 10–1 shows American's low levels of boundary spanner staffing relative to Southwest Airlines, and its correspondingly low levels of relational coordination.

Southwest's Boundary Spanners in Action

Let's follow two of Southwest's operations agents as each coordinates a flight departure.

Steve Collins, Southwest in Baltimore

Steve Collins was busy making the preflight preparations for his incoming flight, Flight 110 to Manchester, tracking its progress on his computer screen, making calls and sending messages to various functions, asking for wheelchairs, extra help for certain passengers, and so on. Everything seemed quite technical and somewhat impersonal. Then, when he heard the announcement from the ops coordinator that Flight 110 was "in range," i.e., 10 minutes from landing, Steve gathered his materials and switched into another mode. He headed out to the tarmac, greeting ramp agents who were getting the baggage loading equipment in place, ready to service the incoming flight; greeting the fueler, who was preparing to refuel the incoming flight; greeting the provisioning crew, who would provide food and beverages for the next flight. He exchanged pleasantries with several of them, checking to see if they needed anything.

Steve then climbed up the stairs to the jet way and greeted the pilots and flight attendants who were waiting there to replace the incoming crew. He knew two of them, and engaged in an animated discussion for several minutes about where they had been and where they were headed. He then greeted the skycaps who were waiting with wheelchairs for two incoming elderly passengers and noted that one additional wheelchair would be needed. Steve then ran up the jet way to greet the gate agents, to ask how many passengers had checked in, and to ask whether there were any special needs or problems. He then ran back down the jet way to prepare for the arrival of the incoming flight. As he took his position at the steering control for the jet way and watched the aircraft pull up to its parking position, he turned and said: "That's what I love about this job—every flight is like a reunion!"

When the doors of the aircraft opened, there was yet another reunion. Steve greeted the flight attendants like old friends, exchanged some observations about weather delays and passenger loads, asked if there was anything they needed, then stepped into the cockpit to greet the pilots. Meanwhile, passengers began to disembark from the plane, and he returned to the gate area to greet the passengers who were lined up and waiting to board the outgoing flight.

Steve took his position at the entrance to the jet way, picked up a microphone and announced, "OK, we are now ready to board Southwest Airlines Flight 110 to Manchester, Flight 110 to Manchester. We'll start with our preboards. Please have your boarding passes ready!" Steve took boarding passes from a couple with two small children and let them board first. He took the boarding pass of an elderly man in a wheelchair, pushed him down the jet way to the aircraft, and handed him off to one of the flight attendants. He folded up the stroller and wheelchair, tagged them, and placed them in a position where the ramp agent could easily find them.

Jogging back up to the jet way door, Steve took the microphone and said, "Now I'll take everyone with boarding passes 1 through 30 please." He began gathering a green boarding pass from each passenger as they filed by. Steve finished with the first 30 passengers in about 2 minutes, then paused and sorted the green cards in numerical sequence. He then stepped into the jet way to check on the boarding progress of passengers 1 through 30. About a minute after having finished with passengers 1 through 30, he announced he was ready to board everyone with passes 31 through 60. Steve gave a quick smile or hello to passengers as he took their boarding passes, answering questions as he kept people moving.

After taking the last boarding pass and putting the cards in sequence, Steve handed them to Lisa and confirmed that 97 passengers had boarded. He returned to the end of the jet way and retrieved the clip attached to the end of the rope tied to the railing. The clip contained the fuel invoice, the cargo bin loading schedule with the actual number of bags in each bin, and a lavatory service record stating that the appropriate cleaning had taken place. Now he had all the information he needed. He made the final trim calculations based on actual passengers rather than reservations, the 18,000 pounds of fuel, and the actual baggage count and bin allocation. Steve handed one copy of the loading schedule to the captain and kept one for himself.

By this point in the boarding process, the window and aisle seats had all been taken and only the center seats remained. A flight attendant took the microphone. "This is a full flight and we want to get you home as soon as possible. Those of you sitting down who are avoiding the eyes of those standing, please make eye contact—they want that seat beside YOU!" As the last passenger took his seat, Steve picked up the cabin loudspeaker microphone and said, "On behalf of the Baltimore ground crew, I'd like to apologize for the delay this evening, and wish you a very good trip up to Manchester!" He replaced the microphone and said good-bye to the flight attendants and the pilots, then closed the door, and steered the jet way back from the aircraft. The plane started to push back 30 seconds later, and Steve gave the traditional salute to the captain through the window. It was 9:15, just 20 minutes since the aircraft had arrived at the gate.

After entering final data about the flight into a computer, he checked the screen to confirm that he had no more flights to work this evening. Steve and Jim, the lead ramp agent for Flight 110, walked down to the break room. Members of Southwest's People Department had been serving root beer floats in the station all evening in recognition of the station's hard work, and Steve had heard that some were still left.

Brook Smith, Southwest in Phoenix

After she steered the jet way into place, Brook Smith opened the door of the plane, said a warm hello to the flight attendants, then walked right into the cockpit. She gave the captain the weather packet for his next flight and the release that included all the information needed for take-off. Then she talked to the flight attendants to tell them what to expect on the next flight out—how many through customers, how many terminating customers, and so forth. "They need to know so they can plan luggage storage," she explained. She picked up some papers from the floor while she was talking, and the flight attendants were busy doing the same. Brook left the plane to let several waiting Southwest employees know whether there would be room on board for them. There was a mechanic whom she listed as a "must go"—because he was going somewhere to fix a plane. "He is a must go," she explained, "so we can utilize the other aircraft. It doesn't help to have them sitting on the ground."

Then Brook walked up the jet way to talk with the gate agents, and checked in with them to find out the number of passengers expected to board. She walked to the door of the jet way and announced that children and people who have difficulty boarding should move into the preboarding area. She allowed them to board first. Then she told passengers with boarding passes 1 through 30 to board. She took each plastic boarding pass, smiled at every single customer, and said thank you.

Almost all the passengers were smiling, though it was not apparent why. There was a general feeling of speed and efficiency rather than the usual feeling of "hurry up and wait" that one gets when boarding an airplane. These passengers seemed to feel confident that they were in good hands and that their hurrying would pay off. They seemed not to mind being hurried.

Brook got everybody through the gate, then walked the boarding passes back to the gate agent. She walked down through the jet way into the plane and spoke again with the flight attendants and the captain. She went to her station at the end of the jet way and pulled the freight, baggage, and fueling numbers up on a string, where the ramp agent and fueler had attached them to a clip. She began to fill out her master load form in pencil, doing rapid calculations of weight and balance. The total came out just about 20 pounds below the maximum allowed on this plane.

Passengers were still getting situated in the plane. The captain came out to stretch his legs and talk to Brook. The gate agent called down the jet way, saying a passenger from the last flight had left his book on board. Brook went on board to inform the flight attendants. The passenger was allowed to come down, reboard the plane, and claim his book. The mechanic who was flying to go fix another plane boarded and went into the cockpit to speak with the first officer. Brook showed the weight and load information to the captain, who then boarded the plane and helped the flight attendants stuff more luggage into the overheads. The flight attendants said thank you. Brook waved good-bye to everybody and a flight attendant announced over the speaker that it was time to push off. The passengers applauded. Brook closed the door and they were off—1 minute late.

After the plane pushed back, Brook put the boarding passes into order, from 1 through 137. She talked with the gate agents and then walked back to the ops room, where she prepared a dispatch report for the down-line city (the city to which the airplane was headed next) and explained what had gone on.

"The gate agent was checking in the flight all that time. She deals with the passengers. The up-line ticket agent puts the information in. Thirty-six people were standing by for this flight. The weight was close to the maximum, but if it went over a little, I could have called dispatch. They might change the ultimate weight. You would call them if you had to. But you do the preflight planning to avoid the problem.

"You could delay the freight if the load was too large. We have 72 hours to get the freight there, and we usually get it there the same day. If we had to pull something, we'd pull company materials first. I get this dispatch report out ASAP so I don't screw the down-line city, so they can plan. Because we appreciate getting ours on time."

One of Brook's coworkers, Robert, who was stationed at the coordinator's desk, was intent on communicating with the pilots on the incoming flights and assigning them to gates. A poster on the wall read: "Administrative thought of the week: If you have knowledge, let others light their candles off it." There was an open window between the operations room and the ramp agents' break room, where there always seemed to be people congregating, talking and asking questions. Rock 'n' roll was playing on the radio in the ops room; everybody was in khaki shorts, intent on their work but having a good time, it appeared. The supervisor, Bob Curbey, was at a computer terminal, keying in the information that appears on the airport monitors for customers to read. People from different functions walked freely around into each other's break rooms, and into the ops room. Brook finished sending her dispatch report, then checked in to see when her next flight would be arriving.

The Boundary Spanner as Relationship Builder

In this chapter we have gained a more holistic perspective on the boundary spanner. Boundary spanners act as gatekeepers of critical information, and as such are influential in determining how the environment is perceived.[6] Boundary spanners interpret and translate information for other organization members[7] in a variety of settings, including research and development,[8] new product development,[9] mergers and acquisitions,[10] and patient care.[11] However, we have seen that the boundary spanner works not only by sharing information but also by building relationships. By developing a web of relationships across boundaries, the boundary spanner constructs a broader sense of shared identity and vision among previously divided parties, creating opportunities for collective action among them. The actions of an effective boundary spanner can contribute to creating more permeable boundaries, which leads to enhanced coordination and improved performance. This relational role played by boundary spanners has also been demonstrated in a very different context from flight departures—mergers and acquisitions—where "building connective tissue"[12] and "forging social connections"[13] are seen as critical contributions that boundary spanners can make.

Summing Up

Boundary spanners play a critical role in coordinating work processes, but the boundary spanner is most effective when the position is conceived to be more than an automatable conduit for information exchange. When the boundary spanner role is generously staffed, the boundary spanner can develop a web of relationships of shared goals, shared knowledge, and mutual respect across functional boundaries. Coordination that occurs within this web of relationships is more effective and leads to improved performance of the flight departure process.

This new understanding of the boundary spanner as a builder of relationships suggests a different way of thinking about staffing levels for the position, and a more skeptical view of the possibility of using information technology to replace the boundary spanner. We have seen that reduced staffing levels result in less effective coordination of the flight departure process, due to weaker relationships of shared knowledge, shared goals, and mutual respect across functional boundaries. We have also seen that information technology has been used in some airlines to dramatically reduce staffing levels for the boundary spanning role. But the substitution of automated communication for boundary spanners may sacrifice the exchange of complex information and the development of shared understandings across functional boundaries, a loss that is not apparent from a purely technical point of view. Though information technology can be a facilitator, it is not expected to be an effective substitute. When a job is mediated largely through a computer or a telephone, an important element of social interaction is lost.[14] The loss of social interaction weakens relationships, and weakens critical performance parameters. These limitations on the effective use of information technology exist because coordination is not simply about the transfer of information. Instead, coordination requires the construction of shared meaning in order to facilitate collective action. As we see at Southwest Airlines, boundary spanners can play this role, building relationships of shared goals, shared knowledge, and mutual respect across functional boundaries.

CHAPTER

Avoid Finger Pointing— Measure Performance Broadly

You can get to the point where you saturate yourselves with information, and you get paralyzed. We have more interest in broader categories, rather than analyzing and assessing blame. It's easier to adjust with broader categories. Maintenance could come up with 50 categories of flight delays, if they wanted to. But you end up chasing your tail.

—Jim Wimberly, Executive Vice President of Operations, Southwest Airlines

LIKE MANY ORGANIZATIONS in other industries, airlines have traditionally relied on systems of functional accountability. Outcomes of the departure process are typically divided into departmental objectives, for which individual departments are held accountable. Each departure delay is traced to the department that is thought to have caused it. Then, on a daily, weekly, and monthly basis, the percentage of on-time departures is calculated for each department.

This system of accountability tends to generate a search for departmental failure. Yet because of the task interdependencies in the flight departure process, it is often difficult to determine which department caused a particular delay. One rule of thumb often used is "whoever was off the plane last." If the gate agent who was boarding passengers was last off the plane, it is presumed to be a customer service delay. If the ramp agents loading baggage were last off the plane, it is presumed to be a ramp delay. If the fueler was the last one off, it is presumed to be a fueling delay. Therefore the common pattern is a race to finish one's own assigned task before the other groups finish their tasks, even when cooperation between the groups would improve the speed and quality of the process. Worse, participants tend to hide information to avoid blame, thus undermining the potential for learning.

Through these unintended dynamics, functional accountability undermines relationships of shared goals, shared knowledge, and mutual respect among those who must coordinate their tasks in order to achieve high performance. To achieve quality outcomes in the face of weak coordination requires longer turnaround times and higher staffing levels, resulting in tremendous efficiency losses. This chapter shows that there are constructive alternatives to these systems of functional accountability. Cross-functional performance measures encourage participants to focus on learning rather than blaming when things go wrong, thereby bolstering relationships of shared goals, shared knowledge, and mutual respect. We will see how Southwest Airlines in particular has learned these lessons.[1]

Performance Measurement at Southwest Airlines

Determining the cause of a delay had once been a conflict-ridden process at Southwest, as it was at other airlines, and had often deteriorated from problem solving to finger pointing and blame avoidance. Southwest countered this tendency in the early 1990s by instituting a "team delay" which allowed less precise reporting of the cause of delays, with the goal of diffusing blame and encouraging learning. According to Jim Wimberly, executive vice president of operations:

> We had too many angry disagreements between flight attendants and gate agents about whose delay it was. It was too hard to determine whose fault it was.

One of Southwest's chief pilots explained:

> The team delay is used to point out problems between two or three different employee groups in working together. We used to do it [in the following way]: if people were still in the jet way at departure time, it was a station delay. If people were on board at departure time, it was a flight crew delay.

But now if you see everybody working as a team, and it's a team problem, you call it a team delay. It's been a very positive thing.

In addition to the team delay, Southwest has about 10 other delay categories, far fewer than at other major airlines. The reduced precision of performance measurement did not appear to concern Southwest leaders. How does Southwest motivate performance? A station manager explained:

> Through personal pride. Because we've always done it, I guess. Also, we track the source of delays. Usually it's a situation rather than a person who is at fault. We take a delay when the situation warrants it. Besides this, we have delay codes to identify which department caused the delay. We try to figure out what caused a delay, but we don't do much finger pointing. We find that the more you point fingers, the more problems go underground rather than getting solved.
>
> The only punitive measures are taken when there's a personnel delay. When someone just wasn't there to do their job. Supervisors often refer disciplinary problems upwards to the department manager, if they can't solve them.

Southwest also uses rewards to motivate performance, he explained:

> Customers send letters to headquarters, with compliments or complaints, about 5000 per month. These letters are sent to the relevant station, then when I get it I will put a smiley face sticker on it and frame it. People like to see their name up there.
>
> We have agent of the month awards in each department. The winners are chosen by their fellow employees. Then managers and supervisors pick agents of the quarter from among the agents of the month. All agents of the quarter come to an award lunch to receive their plaques.
>
> We also use $5 meal vouchers to reward people for good performance. Supervisors do this. And agents reward each other by sending Love Reports.

Benefits of Cross-Functional Performance Measurement

Relative to the other airlines included in this study (United, Continental, and American), Southwest took a cross-functional approach to performance measurement.[2] This study, outlined in detail in Chap. 3, included two American Airlines sites, two Continental Airlines sites, two Southwest Airlines sites, and three United Airlines sites. A statistical analysis

Exhibit 11–1 Impact of Performance Measurement on Relational
Coordination*

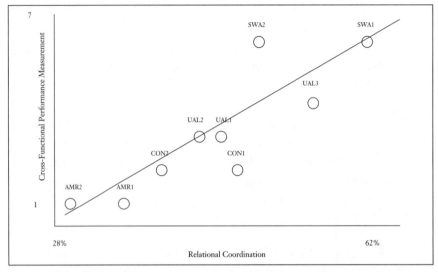

* Each circle denotes one of the nine sites included in the study. Cross-functional performance measurement is measured as the number of functions that could be held jointly
accountable for a delay. Relational coordination—coordination carried out through relationships of shared goals, shared knowledge, and mutual respect—is measured as the percentage of cross-functional ties that are strong or very strong, based on an employee
survey. Relational coordination in turn has a positive impact on quality and efficiency performance, as illustrated in Exhibit 3–4.

showed that a cross-functional approach to performance measurement is
associated with higher levels of relational coordination. Cross-functional
performance measurement also contributes to improved flight departure
performance, particularly faster turnaround times, greater staffing productivity, fewer lost bags, and fewer customer complaints.[3] To observe
the effects of performance measurement on relational coordination, we
can plot performance measurement for each of the nine sites against
relational coordination. Exhibit 11–1 suggests a clear impact of cross-
functional performance measurement on relational coordination.

Performance Measurement at United Airlines

Up through the mid-1990s, United had a system of functional accountability for delays, similar to the rest of the industry. As a result, a Boston
ramp manager explained:

At United—and I'm sure at others—there was always a lot of finger pointing at different departments and different divisions. All divisions had their own goals. They weren't interconnected. The attitude was, if they are taking a delay at least it's not mine, so you would sort of forget about it.

Under this system, assigning delays involved a great deal of conflict, according to the Los Angeles operations manager:

You used to need a titanium suit. We used to spend hours and hours figuring out whose delay it was.

Reinforcing these dynamics within each station was a Friday conference call with the regional director, nicknamed the "Friday Flogging." According to the Boston ramp manager:

Our regional vice president is from the old school of management. You hate to manage by intimidation. Our vice president is more along these lines than others. We're changing over.

On the theory that "if you're responsible for all delays, you might get more involved in the process and help them out," United introduced a new delay accounting system in the mid-1990s. According to a Los Angeles customer service manager:

Individual managers are not responsible for just their own department's delays because we have families of delays now. As a customer service manager, I may be responsible for delays that are partly caused by flight attendants. This means I'm supposed to communicate with that other group. Flight attendants and customer service agents interact a lot. This system makes them talk. It's a family of delays. There is no win or lose.

Under this new system of accountability, up to three departments can be held responsible for a given delay, and all are therefore expected to work on finding and resolving the underlying problems.

The new system also includes a focus on on-time arrivals rather than departures, in effect combining the goals of the station and the flight department. In keeping with this, a team delay code was added to allow the station and flight department to take joint responsibility for a delay. The team delay was to be used exclusively, however, for getting additional revenue on the flight—for example, additional passengers or freight. It is not supposed to be used to take joint responsibility for breakdowns in communication, as it was at Southwest.

The Shuttle took this team delay concept a bit further than the rest of United Airlines, however, in keeping with its focus on teamwork. Whereas three functions could be held jointly responsible for a delay in mainline United, up to four functions could take responsibility in the Shuttle operations.

Due in part, perhaps, to the Shuttle's approach to performance measurement (and other practices highlighted in this book), the United Shuttle achieved significantly higher levels of relational coordination compared to United's non-Shuttle sites (55 percent versus 42 percent of cross-functional ties were rated by employees as strong or very strong). Exhibit 11–1 shows how these higher levels of relational coordination are related to the Shuttle's performance measurement practices. The United Shuttle, denoted by UAL3 in Exhibit 11–1, has higher levels of relational coordination than its non-Shuttle counterparts (UAL1 and UAL2), corresponding to its more cross-functional approach to performance measurement. In addition, as we saw in Chap. 7, the Shuttle outperformed its non-Shuttle counterparts at United on both quality and efficiency dimensions.

Performance Measurement at Continental Airlines

Continental Airlines remained more specific in its delay reporting, allowing each delay to be charged to only two departments. An operations coordinator explained:

> We can split the delay into primary and secondary causes. We split the minutes and charge them to different departments.

The possibility at Continental of charging two departments rather than one raised the level of shared responsibility somewhat, but still the measurement system was perceived to be an obstacle to coordination and teamwork. According to the Cleveland station manager:

> We might take one delay and take one or two hours to find the root cause of the problem. Instead of punitive action, we use a positive constructive approach.

However, interviews with supervisors and frontline employees revealed that this "positive constructive" approach was counterproductive in certain respects. It encouraged them to pay excessive attention to documenting who did what at what time, rather than looking ahead to figure out together what should be done to get the next plane out.

Also, despite the efforts to focus on objective reporting of what happened, fear reportedly continued to play a major role. According to an operations coordinator:

> There's this fear over taking a delay—everybody fears they'll be chastised for it. You spend so much time filling out delay forms and fighting over a delay—just think what we could be doing. We had a two-minute delay that no one would take responsibility for.

According to the station manager:

> Barriers between groups—it all comes down to the delay coding system. Upper management just wants to have a tracking system. If you have a lot of code 31s (maintenance delays), and then the maintenance guy is gone, you know it is punitive. That is the bottom line.
>
> You come in front of a tribunal. Headquarters doesn't have time to look at the details. They just see code 10s and then passenger services has a lot of explaining to do. . . . It's a punitive system, but if you're a good station manager, you buffer it, don't allow it to cascade down to the frontline employees.

Comments from frontline employees, however, suggested that this attempt to buffer them from headquarters' punitive approach to accountability had not fully succeeded.

Exhibit 11–1 shows Continental's functional approach to performance measurement, relative to Southwest Airlines, and its correspondingly lower levels of relational coordination. We see little variation between the two Continental sites in their approaches to performance measurement. Headquarters often resists local variations in performance measurement, as we will see in the case of American Airlines, leaving local managers to buffer employees as much as possible from their potential negative effects.

Performance Measurement at American Airlines

American Airlines exemplifies the attempt to achieve accountability through a strictly functional approach to performance measurement. One field manager explained the company's philosophy, as he understood it:

> It helps a lot just to keep score. People are naturally competitive. They absolutely need to know the score. Once they know, they will do something about it. Every delay comes to my attention and gets a full investigation. . . . The last thing most of them want is the spotlight on them. I just increased the amount they had to do to keep the spotlight off of themselves.

Each time a delay occurred, managers on duty were responsible for figuring out which function caused it. Immediate penalties accompanied delays, in the form of having to explain what happened. If a delay occurred on a flight scheduled to make connections elsewhere, "Crandall wants to see the corpse," said a ramp manager in Boston. "It is management by intimidation."

This system had the unintended effect of encouraging employees to look out for themselves and avoid recrimination, rather than focusing on their shared goals of achieving high-quality outcomes efficiently. A ramp supervisor explained how goal displacement occurred:

> If you ask anyone here, what's the last thing you think of when there's a problem, I bet your bottom dollar it's the customer. And these are guys who bust their butts every day. But they're thinking, how do I keep my ass out of the sling.

American's system of accountability also resulted in a great deal of time spent trying to sort out the cause of delays. According to an operations manager:

> There is so much internal debate and reports and meetings. This is time that we could be focusing on the passengers.

Another result was frequent misidentification of the problem. A ramp supervisor told me, only half in jest:

We have delay codes for when the Pope visits, or if there are beetles in the cockpit, but sometimes a problem occurs routinely and we have no code for it. What usually happens is a communication breakdown, but we have no code for that. So we tag it on the last group off the plane.

Sometimes there is a failure to identify the problem altogether, due to outright distortion of information. Due to the perceived harshness of consequences for delays, cheating sometimes occurs—for example, the practice of releasing the aircraft brake early to prevent a delay from being registered electronically. According to a pilot:

Gate agents are so much under the gun. They are scared of disciplinary action. Some of us will tell the gate agent—take all the time you need to load this plane. I'll take care of it. Captains have authority. We can use it well. If you use your authority as a captain to take the fear away from the gate agent, they can relax and do their job. It's informal, behind the scenes. We were distorting the data to keep the gate agent from getting in trouble.

In this example, employees collaborated across functional boundaries to mitigate the perceived harshness of the performance measurement system. Most often, however, this system of functional accountability undermined relationships across functional boundaries. A ramp supervisor in Los Angeles complained:

It seems like it should be very easy to sit down and develop a plan for everyone to work as a family. It's because of all the report cards, the cover your ass stats, the cover your boss. You'll do whatever you can. . . . How can everyone work together, striving to be perfect, when it's going to be on *your* report card, reflect on *your* performance?

Station managers at American were intimately aware of these problems, and attempted to solve them through changes in the system of performance measurement. According to American's station manager at Boston, rather than hold people individually accountable for their contribution to outcomes, the company should hold people collectively accountable for outcomes.

> In a company that depends so heavily on cross-functional teamwork, how useful is a diagnostic system that focuses on individual efforts exclusively and does not effectively measure the ability of the team to work together?

She eventually tried to implement cross-functional teams and cross-functional measures of performance at her station. She received no support from the company for this initiative, however, and quit in discouragement after 14 years of service to the company.

Soon afterwards, ironically, American Airlines launched a different initiative to move toward a more cross-functional approach to performance measurement. Departure teams were formed wherein pilots could determine, in conjunction with gate agents and other employees, whether to delay a flight up to 5 minutes to accommodate passengers or their baggage. This was called a "discretionary delay" program. Some pilots agreed they had much insight to offer based on their trips from station to station. "The captain sees all," one pilot told me, "and can make a lot of recommendations for making things work better."

However, pilots were limited in their ability to work as part of a team with other employee groups. Rather than deciding in conjunction with the other employee groups, pilots reportedly insisted on being the first among equals. According to the vice president of flight operations:

> There are real problems with the way that program is working right now. The pilot thinks he is in total control and that the ground workers don't know as much. The gate agents are getting around the pilots by cheating, saying they already got approval from the pilots when they didn't.

The senior vice president of operations concurred, claiming:

> The performance is dismal; dismal. We are doing the customers a disservice. The lesson is that captains without the right knowledge base cannot make decisions properly.

Pilots were limited in the decisions they could make, according to these managers, because they did not understand the perspectives of the other groups well enough to make the relevant trade-offs. The initiative was considered a failure and dropped.

Other local innovations were also tried, with little success. Consistent with the thinking of the Boston station manager, the Los Angeles station manager initiated a system of cross-functional accountability for delays, in which up to three functions could take joint responsibility for a delay. He explained:

> Delays are usually caused by a combination of factors—say a lack of communication between the gate and cabin cleaning. So we came up with a system for coding delays jointly to the groups that contributed.

However, the experiment fell apart when American's headquarters insisted the station would have to continue identifying and reporting to headquarters the one functional group that was responsible for the delay. According to this station manager:

> It undermined the credibility of our program here. People didn't believe anything had changed.

Like the Boston station manager, he left the company soon after.

Exhibit 11–1 shows American's highly functional approach to performance measurement relative to Southwest Airlines, and its correspondingly low levels of relational coordination.

Accountability versus Learning

As we have just seen, American and Southwest are on opposite ends of the spectrum with respect to performance measurement. At American, the purpose of performance measurement is accountability, often with a punitive twist. At Southwest, the purpose of performance measurement is to learn and improve over time. How did these airlines develop such different approaches?

American Airlines was designed at its inception to operate in a traditional military fashion, with managers given responsibility for performance, and frontline workers responsible only for following commands. When Robert Crandall became CEO in the 1980s, he tried to make American Airlines less bureaucratic by increasing the accountability of employees at every level of the company. Using new systems for measuring and attributing performance outcomes, Crandall fostered a culture of accountability in which managers at every level would be held strictly accountable for their performance. Along with increased managerial accountability, he introduced employee participation throughout the organization to push power and accountability down to frontline employees. According to a station manager:

> Under Crandall, we got the idea that everybody was accountable for results—not just top management. He started doing very tough reviews of budgets, for example, and increased the flow of company information to frontline workers by putting video machines in the ground workers' ready room and starting a company paper.
>
> People took on the idea of accountability. A lot of communication started to take place. . . . Crandall made these changes in response to deregulation, with an eye toward the competition.

Another station manager had a less positive perspective on this approach to accountability:

> When Crandall came in the early 1980s, accountability was so new for us that it had a dramatic impact even though it was based on functional goals. Then people figured out how to game it, and headquarters kept tightening the screws.

In her view, the new measures were not conducive to cross-functional coordination. Accountability was perceived to be punitive, which tended to make people focus on pleasing their superiors, and fear making mistakes or giving power to subordinates. Also, accountability at each level was pinned to individuals or functions rather than to the larger process, making people tend to look out for themselves and avoid recrimination, rather than focusing on their shared goals—on-time departures and satisfied customers. According to a Boston ramp manager:

> The hardest part about the restructuring has been changing the way I manage. I have grown a lot as a manager over this past year, but it has not been easy. . . . It is scary to delegate, especially at American, where there is a very strong company culture toward accountability. This is fine, but the penalties that go along with that accountability make people afraid to take risks—afraid to let go of their control.
>
> To push decision making and responsibility down, you have to be willing to let others make mistakes and learn from them. [But for this] you need the full support of your boss.

This support from one's boss did not seem to be present. Managers felt unable to play a supportive role for their direct reports because they were being judged critically by the managers above them, and so on. As part of the focus on accountability at American, station managers were given annual performance standards, called Minimum Acceptable Performance Standards (MAPS), for on-time departures, baggage handling, and customer complaints. A station manager complained:

> I am harassed on a daily basis. Headquarters has a performance analysis department that is looking at my MAPS every day, analyzing the station's performance.

A headquarters manager acknowledged the concern: "Failure to meet MAPS is perceived to result in punitive action."

Several managers interviewed at American Airlines commented that there was a split between the stations and headquarters, and that the information flow between them was based largely on the numbers. According to a manager of human resources:

> In this company, accountability is statistical. Managers are not judged on how well they delegate. They are judged by their results. The station manager is judged on the numbers and not on how he got them. He could have used a club for all it matters to his rewards.

An employee relations manager concurred:

> All that matters is the numbers; how you achieve them is secondary. This is part of the culture of fear.

The reaction to the split between field and headquarters on the part of some station managers was bitterness. "Better communication clearly matters at the station level, but it doesn't make a bit of difference what they do at headquarters," according to a station manager. Managers perceived that they were judged strictly on the numbers. Information in the form of numbers went from stations to headquarters for evaluation, but there was little discussion—and little learning. At the same time, managers transmitted to frontline workers the pressures they perceived from headquarters, and at times used methods to achieve goals that created resentment. Employees were well aware of their managers' performance evaluation system, and how it affected them. A customer service agent explained, with bitterness:

> Here you only care about delays. Otherwise the little report card won't look good that week. The ultimate goal is not the customers, it's the report card.

A Different Approach to Performance Measurement at Southwest

Like American, Southwest had adopted a formal hierarchical organizational structure at its inception. But given the airline's strategic focus on quick turnarounds, coordination of the flight departure process by frontline employees was emphasized from the start. Jim Wimberly, executive vice president of operations, explained:

> It's not, folks in Engineering do this, folks in Marketing do that. We recognized early on that it would only work if we worked as teams.

Southwest's approach to accountability can be seen not only at the front line, with the team delay, but also in the relationship between field and headquarters. In stark contrast to what was seen at other airlines, particularly American, there is a two-way flow of information between field and headquarters at Southwest and appears to be a great deal of learning. When station managers at Southwest were asked how their own performance was assessed, they were quite vague about it. "I don't know," was one typical response, given with a laugh. "I'll hear about it if I'm not doing a good job. I get free rein if I do OK." "It is watched, but there is no fear factor," said the Chicago station manager. "Everybody here is a self-motivator." According to the Phoenix station manager:

> I know what the relationship [between headquarters and the station] is usually like because I worked at Eastern for 20 years. It's usually an entrenched bureaucracy between the station manager and headquarters. It's nothing like that here.

His assistant station manager explained:

Each station is like an entrepreneur. We do what we think is right, and talk directly to our executive vice presidents and Herb. They are just a phone call away. If they question something we did today, they will call tomorrow.

In contrast to the oft-heard claim that American's system of performance measurement did not take into account *how* managers achieved their results, managers at Southwest claimed that they were judged by how they achieved their results. According to the Chicago station manager:

My director will look at overtime costs and on-time performance. But the biggest thing he'll look at is morale. He believes that morale affects the other things. If you are not treating people right, the other things will get you. They'll get you back in other ways.

At American, as we saw, the relationship was more hands-off, based on a much different flow of information. There was a perception by managers that they were judged strictly on the numbers. "Headquarters doesn't care how you get the numbers, just that you get them," was repeated time and again. Information in the form of numbers went from stations to headquarters for evaluation, but there was little discussion and little learning.

Summing Up

This chapter shows that cross-functional performance measurement improves coordination through its positive impact on relationships of shared goals, shared knowledge, and mutual respect, resulting in better performance. However, this approach to performance measurement flies in the face of classical organizational theory. Traditional management theorists including Max Weber and Chester Barnard believed that functional accountability was the most effective way to achieve control.[4] If you could clearly delineate someone's realm of responsibility, they believed, then you could clearly measure how they are doing, and reward or punish them for those results. Functional accountability was also a means to avoid overload. Herbert Simon argued that human beings have a limited scope of attention within which they can act in a rational way.[5] Simon recommended functional accountability as a way to focus employee attention on a limited set of responsibilities. He recognized the risks of functional accountability, particularly that employees would tend to focus on functional goals at the expense of organizational goals and might therefore fail to cooperate across functional boundaries. Still, he believed, the gains achieved from functional accountability outweighed these risks.

As we have just seen, however, trying to achieve control through functional accountability can seriously undermine information sharing and learning. Preoccupation with functional accountability leads to blaming, which in turn causes information to be distorted or to go underground.[6] Because organizations need to use mistakes as a basis for learning, they should not rely on functional performance evaluation. Traditional measurement systems are flawed because they orient employee attention toward functional rather than cross-functional outcomes and because they provide inadequate information for learning.[7] To orient employees toward cross-functional outcomes and to provide more useful feedback about what to do, cross-functional performance measures should be used to supplement traditional functional measurement systems. These insights are supported by much of the recent organizational literature.[8] What we learned in this chapter, in addition, is that traditional performance measurement systems undermine performance *because* they weaken relationships of shared goals, shared knowledge, and mutual respect among those whose cooperation is critical for achieving the organization's performance objectives.

CHAPTER

Keep Jobs Flexible at the Boundaries

At Southwest, anyone can do any function, even the supervisors. Some union contracts don't allow that—they have covered work. Our contracts here don't have covered work. The job descriptions all say at the end "and whatever you need to do to enhance the overall operation."

—Ramp Manager, Southwest Airlines

JOB DESCRIPTIONS THAT limit employees from doing each other's work can be found in many organizations. Traditionally, "managers have assumed that once a worker has been provided with a job description, the roles and tasks described represent the functional borders within which the employee must work. Encroaching on someone else's job territory has been considered a terrible offense."[1] But rigid, well-defined job responsibilities are no longer considered necessary or useful in many organizations, for several reasons. First, traditional job descriptions are considered to be too static in a dynamic economy. Such job descriptions assume that the same tasks and skills that are relevant at one point in time will continue to be relevant in the future.[2] Second, traditional job descriptions focus too much on specific tasks rather than on broader, more generic characteristics and behaviors that are needed to achieve organizational success.[3] Third, with greater job flexibility, it is possible to utilize people more fully, achieving higher labor productivity. However, there is another benefit to making jobs flexible at the boundaries, as we will see in this chapter. Flexible job boundaries help to build stronger relationships between functions, improving coordination between them.

In response to these perceived benefits, there has been an effort to broaden job descriptions to allow employees to take the actions they see as necessary to accomplish the organization's goals. However, broadening job descriptions is difficult to achieve because it threatens people's sense of security and introduces an element of the unknown into their jobs. These fears can prevent organizations from broadening job descriptions, particularly in unionized settings like the airline industry, where job descriptions are contractually negotiated through collective bargaining.

Throughout the 1980s and 1990s, job descriptions were a major subject of negotiation as airline management sought to reduce inefficiencies to compete better in a deregulated environment.[4] One way that a union can seek to protect the jobs of its members is by negotiating job descriptions or "work rules" that prevent employees in other workgroups from performing the work of its members. However, although these rigid job descriptions or work rules seem to boost job security, particularly in the face of potential downsizing, they also create boundaries that undermine working relationships.[5] Southwest Airlines has successfully negotiated flexible job descriptions in all of its union contracts. This chapter describes Southwest's approach toward job flexibility, compared to its competitors, then illustrates the impact of flexible jobs on relational coordination and performance.

Job Flexibility at Southwest Airlines

On the one hand, each person at Southwest has a very clear and specific job description. According to a Southwest station manager:

> We train people to do a specific function, and we train them very well. They are exposed to other functions in their training, but we don't cross-utilize.

On the other hand, a Southwest employee's job includes helping other colleagues with their work whenever necessary. A Southwest pilot explained:

This is not like People Express [an airline of the 1980s known for job descriptions that encompassed a wide range of functional responsibilities]. Each person has a specific job, but part of the job is to help the other person. Then it's easier to work in a more efficient manner.

According to a station manager:

> There are no work restrictions in our contracts. Most airlines have very restrictive work rules, will list in the contract very detailed job definitions. . . . We don't have the "it's not my job" mentality. We have very thin contracts.

With flexible job descriptions, Southwest employees are able to help each other as needed, often crossing functional boundaries to do so. A ramp manager explained:

> Maintenance has helped us load bags, push planes out. All we have to do is just call them. Not all of our rampers are technically inclined. We'll get help [from maintenance] disassembling a wheelchair [even though] it's not in their job description.
>
> What's really strange about the whole thing—these guys are represented by Teamsters. Teamsters seem to me to be a national labor organization that's the most traditional kind. Still, I've never seen one guy in maintenance hide behind a job responsibility issue. We've had cars break down and these guys will go help people out with their cars. This station is so much like a family.

A Southwest pilot had similar comments about the absence of restrictive job descriptions at Southwest, whether formal or informal.

> I'm not saying we're pristine or anything, but I've worked for other airlines and it's nothing like this. We had a lady pilot throwing bags the other day. You'll never see it somewhere else. Working for TWA, if you picked up a bag, the ramp filed a grievance. You'd have to write a letter saying "I'm so sorry."

"I can't believe they would file a grievance," said a young ramp worker who was sitting nearby.

An additional benefit of flexible job boundaries was that Southwest managers and supervisors were permitted to work side by side with frontline employees. Some made a point of doing so on a regular basis, while others pitched in primarily on busy days. The Los Angeles station manager gave an example:

> The Thanksgiving rush was very, very hectic. Supervisors were not giving up—managers were throwing bags.

A ramp supervisor claimed this was typical behavior at Southwest:

> Management will always pitch in at crunch time. This is true throughout Southwest. That's what's unique about this airline. . . . Whatever it takes to get the plane out.

Benefits of Job Flexibility

Southwest had higher levels of job flexibility than most other airlines included in this study.[6] This study, which was outlined in detail in Chap. 3, included two American Airlines sites, two Continental Airlines sites, two Southwest Airlines sites, and three United Airlines sites. A statistical analysis of boundary spanner staffing showed that job flexibility is associated with higher levels of relational coordination. Job flexibility also contributes to improved flight departure performance, particularly faster turnaround times, greater staffing productivity, and fewer customer complaints.[7] To observe the effects of flexible jobs on relational coordination, we can plot job flexibility for each of the nine sites against relational coordination. Exhibit 12–1 suggests a clear impact of job flexibility on relational coordination.

Job Flexibility at Continental Airlines

Because most workgroups were not organized at Continental after the Frank Lorenzo union-busting era, flexible jobs were thought to be one of Continental's competitive advantages. According to reports from Continental employees, there were no contractual job descriptions that excluded employees in one group from doing the work of another group, aside from those that were mandated by the Federal Aviation Administration. Even supervisors were not prevented from doing the work of frontline employees. Employees were hard-pressed to think of any exclusionary job descriptions at Continental. According to one employee:

Exhibit 12–1 Impact of Job Flexibility on Relational Coordination*

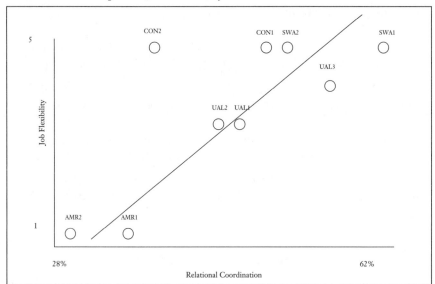

* Each circle denotes one of the nine sites included in the study. Job flexibility is assessed on a 1–5 scale. Relational coordination—coordination carried out through relationships of shared goals, shared knowledge, and mutual respect—is measured as the percentage of cross-functional ties that are strong or very strong, based on an employee survey. Relational coordination in turn has a positive impact on quality and efficiency performance, as illustrated in Exhibit 3-4.

> The only work rules that I can think of are that only flight attendants can do safety demos. But this is both the FAA and the contract. It's OK to help people get seated though.

The mechanics at Continental, though not unionized, did have job descriptions that were somewhat traditional:

> Company Policies and Procedures are the work rules for ops, customer service, and ramp. [But] maintenance has its own work rules. Completely different, more along the line of union rules. Their supervisors have to come through the ranks, for example. But people can help each other out. Even the maintenance guys will ask if they can help.

The relative absence of exclusionary job descriptions was useful for the implementation of the Continental Lite quick-turnaround operation, which had been designed to rely on cross-functional teamwork. The manager of customer service explained:

> In Lite, it can be really critical to do everything you can. We may run people down from the ticket counter to help clean the plane or do catering. Gate agents will also help to clean. There are certain flights that the flight attendants have to clean. But everyone helps—I'll even go and clean the planes.

Exhibit 12–1 shows Continental's high levels of job flexibility, comparable to those of Southwest Airlines, though its levels of relational coordination are substantially lower than Southwest's, suggesting that Continental's job flexibility is offset by other, less supportive organizational practices.

Job Flexibility at United Airlines

United Airlines shared in common with American a traditional attitude toward job boundaries that proved difficult to transform. A ramp agent explained:

> We try not to get out of our classifications because it can get grieved. . . . It's a silent type of thing. If they don't have enough manpower, that's for management to fix.

As a result of this attitude, it was perceived that "unions have always been an obstacle to productivity at United," according to a United manager. One result has been animosity between union and nonunion workgroups at United. A United ticket agent explained to me that "unions are disgusting." Another manager explained:

> Covered work is a big deal at United. It's very symbolic. We are trying to transcend those lines. Customer service reps will carry the bag down to the ramp when the bins are full on board. There have been no objections to that. But a union person would say no.
>
> Unions have always been an obstacle to productivity at United. Even within the International Association of Machinists [which represents mechanics, ramp agents, baggage transfer agents, cabin cleaners, and so forth], only mechanics can put in the chocks under the plane's wheels when the

plane comes to a stop at the gate. Everybody would sit and wait for the mechanic to arrive, if necessary.

Employees for the Shuttle belonged to the same unions as their counterparts in mainline United Airlines, but the success of the Shuttle was thought to depend on increasing the flexibility of jobs so employees could step over job boundaries to help each other out. A gate agent described the changes that had occurred in the Shuttle operation:

> On this side [the Shuttle side], there is an emphasis on teamwork. In mainline you have all the unions—ramp, cabin, maintenance. In the Shuttle, we were able to cross that line—I don't know how we did it. It's everybody's job. On the other side, you try not to offend anyone. You ask for their permission. Can you do this, can I do that? There's a different mentality in the interaction with other groups. . . . Here it's more informal. Flight attendants help cabin service clean the cabin. I wish it worked over there.

Consistent with these reports, a ramp employee for the Shuttle told me, "Here we can go up [on the jet way] and check for bags if it's a heavy flight." Much of the relaxation of rigid work boundaries on the Shuttle had been accomplished through tacit agreement among employees, rather than through formal union negotiations. Nonetheless, these changes had reportedly had a notable effect on cross-functional coordination. One Southwest pilot observed the job flexibility that had developed at the United Shuttle and took this change as evidence that United could become a serious competitor to Southwest over time:

> I've seen things at the Shuttle that amaze me. Interesting departures. Now you see the pilots helping out. You never saw that at United before. They're a formidable foe, don't get me wrong.

Inspired in part by the new employee ownership and in part by the Shuttle experience, United as a whole began working to increase job flexibility. According to the Los Angeles station manager, some progress was achieved. By late 1994 it was possible, for example, for a customer service representative to go into the bag room to help identify bags. The station manager explained:

As long as it's presented in a positive way, and not as trying to do your job, it's not been a problem. There has been no grieving it so far. We say someone's just trying to assist you—it's for a better product. Maintenance sometimes puts the jet way in place, to help customer service reps. We are trying to get more of it. There have been no grievances over this since I've been here [late 1993].

Similar reports were heard in United Airline's Boston station. Though the changes were still marginal, they carried great symbolic importance.

As a result of the Shuttle's greater job flexibility (and other practices highlighted in this book), the United Shuttle achieved significantly higher levels of relational coordination compared to United's non-Shuttle sites (55 percent versus 42 percent of cross-functional ties were rated by employees as strong or very strong). Exhibit 12–1 shows how these higher levels of relational coordination are related to job flexibility. The United Shuttle, denoted by UAL3 in Exhibit 12–1, has higher levels of relational coordination than its non-Shuttle counterparts (UAL1 and UAL2), corresponding to its higher levels of job flexibility. In addition, as we saw in Chap. 7, the Shuttle outperformed its non-Shuttle counterparts at United on both quality and efficiency dimensions.

Job Flexibility at American Airlines

American's management had worked hard over the years to achieve flexible job boundaries. In the 1983 contract with the Transport Workers Union, contractual changes allowed all jobs on the ramp, except mechanics, to be merged into one classification—ramp service worker. However, restrictive job boundaries between ramp employees and mechanics, and between ramp employees and customer service employees, still remained and appeared to undermine working relationships among frontline employees.

Customer service agents in the Boston station reported that, "If you want to help the cabin crews clean up because you're running late, you can't because that's their work." Also, when a passenger brings excess baggage to the gate, "union-wise, the ramp won't come up and get it. We send it back to the passenger, and they take it back to the ticket counter," even at the risk that the customer might miss his or her flight. Formal job descriptions also restricted the extent to which flight attendants could assist airport employees to achieve faster turnarounds. According to an American station manager:

> At Southwest, flight attendants collect trash on the plane. They go through the aisles and collect trash periodically throughout the flight. Our attendants do not. Our ground people have to do it. By the time the plane gets to the ground, it is full of trash. It creates extra work, unnecessarily. And it slows down our turnaround time.

Exhibit 12–1 shows American's low levels of job flexibility relative to Southwest Airlines, and its correspondingly low levels of relational coordination.

Why Flexible Boundaries Are So Uncommon

Given the performance benefits of flexible boundaries, why is encroaching on someone else's job territory so often considered "a terrible offense"?[8] Although rigid job descriptions are often blamed on unions, they were originally developed as part of a management system designed to *improve* workplace functioning.[9] They were seen as a way to rationalize the division of labor and prevent work overload.[10] Managers sought to establish formal job descriptions because they were considered to be the most effective way to manage a workforce in settings where there was little change and where environmental parameters were stable and predictable. Employees came to value job descriptions as a means of preventing work overload and as a means of protecting themselves against managers who might otherwise treat them arbitrarily. In addition, clear work boundaries may serve the interests of employees by permitting them to deepen their areas of expertise and therefore to take greater pride and ownership in their work.[11]

While specialization is clearly beneficial for all of these reasons, there is increasing evidence that *flexibility* at the boundaries of jobs is also beneficial, and that it can be achieved without losing the benefits of specialization. In particular, flexible job boundaries are conducive to coordination because they create more opportunities for communication across functional boundaries,[12] therefore enabling employees to develop stronger relationships of shared goals, shared knowledge, and mutual respect. Traditional job descriptions impede coordination by creating overspecialized knowledge and detracting from communication among parties who are engaged in interdependent tasks. Especially in settings that require a more spontaneous form of coordination, it is important that jobs be defined flexibly enough that people can come to understand the jobs of those with whom they must coordinate. Flexible job boundaries enable people to experience directly the work of those with whom their work most closely relates.

Summing Up

We have seen in this chapter the importance of flexible jobs for building strong relationships and high performance. Flexible jobs tend to get a lot of attention in the airline industry, relative to other organizational practices that are also important for achieving coordination. This attention is warranted not because flexible jobs are more important than the other practices, but rather because flexible jobs are one of the hardest to achieve, given the two-way negotiations and the high levels of trust required to achieve them. As Southwest's leaders pointed out on several occasions, flexible jobs are not simply achieved once and for all. Flexible jobs are an outcome of negotiations that occur repeatedly over time. Every time a contract is negotiated, the flexibility of Southwest's jobs is at stake. In Chap. 13, we will explore the labor/management partnerships that have made flexible jobs possible at Southwest Airlines.

Make Unions Your Partners, Not Adversaries

We treat all as family, including outside union representatives. We walk into the room not as adversaries but as working on something together. Our attitude is that we should both do what's good for the company. . . . [Unions] have their constituency, their customer base. We respect that. We have a great relationship with the Teamsters and they have a reputation for being tough negotiators. We try to stress with everybody that we really like partnerships.

—Colleen Barrett, President and Chief Operating Officer, Southwest Airlines

Southwest has helped me make a wonderful contribution in my world. I am not looking to abuse the company or take advantage. I just want the right thing. There are things we need to have represented. But there is no need to threaten the company. . . . It's fine to strike if you can't settle your differences any other way. But we don't need to strike. . . . We don't want to fight. We belong to this company. It's a system that works and that's been working for years.

—Marcie Means, Customer Service Agent and Union Activist, Southwest Airlines

BECAUSE OF ITS reputation for teamwork, most people assume that Southwest Airlines has no unions, or very few unionized employees relative to the rest of the airline industry. Indeed, a vice president of the United Auto Workers said in 1994 that Southwest's competitive advantage was its nonunion status. Similarly, a top airline industry analyst recently told a group of students at the Massachusetts Institute of Technology that "Southwest is not shackled by traditional unions." In fact,

Southwest is the most highly unionized airline in the U.S. airline industry, and since its founding has been one of the five most highly unionized airlines in the industry (see Exhibit 13–1). Because the airline industry is more unionized than almost any other industry in the United States, this means that Southwest is one of the most highly unionized companies in the United States. Southwest's employees are represented by several traditional unions, including the Transport Workers Union, the International Association of Machinists, and the International Brotherhood of Teamsters, as well as a pilots' union that is unique to Southwest (the Southwest Airlines Pilots' Association, similar to American Airline's company-specific pilots' union, the Allied Pilots Association) (see Exhibit 13–2). It is remarkable that Southwest, a well-recognized success story in the business world, has gained almost no recognition for its remarkable accomplishments in the realm of labor-management relations.

The airline industry is highly unionized, and managers in the industry often blame their unions for high costs and inefficiencies. But across the industry, there are important variations in the quality of labor relations, and in the strategies managers have used to work with or against their unions.[1] Union representation within an organization can give that

Exhibit 13–1 Percent of Employees Represented by Unions in
U.S. Major Airlines

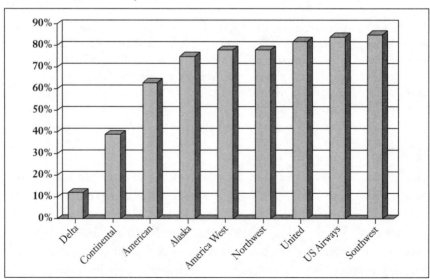

(*Source:* Airline Industrial Relations Conference)

Exhibit 13–2   The Unions That Represent Airline Employees*

| | | | | Mechanics and Related | | |
Airline	Pilots	Flight Attendants	Dispatchers	Mechanics	Ramp/Fleet Service	Clerical/ Agent
Alaska	ALPA	AFA	TWU	AMFA	IAM	IAM
American	APA	APFA	TWU	TWU	TWU	None
America West	ALPA	AFA	TWU	IBT	IBT	TWU
Continental	ALPA	IAM	TWU	IBT	None	None
Delta	ALPA	None	PAFCA	None	None	None
Northwest	ALPA	IBT	TWU	AMFA	IAM	IAM
Southwest	SWAPA	TWU	SAEA	IBT	TWU	IAM
United	ALPA	AFA	PAFCA	IAM	IAM	IAM
US Airways	ALPA	AFA	TWU	IAM	CWA	TWU

*AFA = Association of Flight Attendants
ALPA = Air Line Pilots Association
AMFA = Aircraft Mechanics Fraternal Association
APA = Allied Pilots Association
APFA = Association of Professional Flight Attendants
CWA = Communication Workers of America
IAM = International Association of Machinists
IBT = International Brotherhood of Teamsters
PAFCA = Professional Airline Flight Control Association
SAEA = Southwest Airlines Employee Association
SWAPA = Southwest Airlines Pilots' Association
TWU = Transport Workers Union

(*Source:* Airline Industrial Relations Conference)

organization increased legitimacy with its employees, and thus serve as a key element of a system of coordination and control[2] if employee representatives are respected and communication is open.[3] However, the leaders of some unionized organizations attempt to build trust with frontline employees by bypassing their selected representatives and communicating directly with them, while others pursue a dual strategy of both communicating directly with frontline employees and working in partnership with their union representatives. The risks and rewards of the two strategies are well established.[4] By attempting to compete with union representatives, managers risk losing the trust of employees who remain loyal to their representatives. Managers also risk dividing the group against itself, and groups against each other. This adversarialism undermines relationships among frontline employees and throughout the company, reducing the potential for high performance.

This chapter explores the effects of union representation on relationships, and on performance of the flight departure process. Southwest's experience as one of the most highly unionized airlines in the industry, with some of the most traditional unions representing its employees, yet with the lowest rates of labor conflict (see Exhibit 13–3) and the shortest time to contract (Exhibit 13–4), shows that union representation by itself is not an impediment to strong relationships or high performance.[5] In fact union leaders can be highly supportive of an organization's performance goals, as they have tended to be at Southwest Airlines and more recently at Continental Airlines, when they are cultivated as partners rather than adversaries of management.

Labor Relations at Southwest Airlines

Although Southwest is highly unionized, Southwest has experienced little labor conflict relative to its competitors. Looking more closely inside

Exhibit 13–3 Labor Conflict Index*

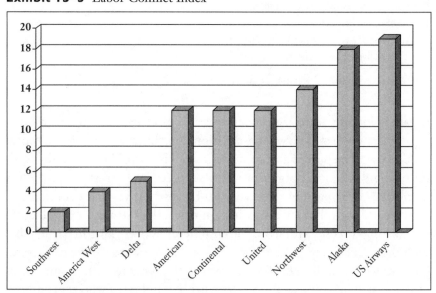

*Number of strikes, arbitrations, mediations, and releases since 1985.
(*Source:* National Mediation Board)

Exhibit 13–4 Length of Time Required to Reach Contract Agreement*

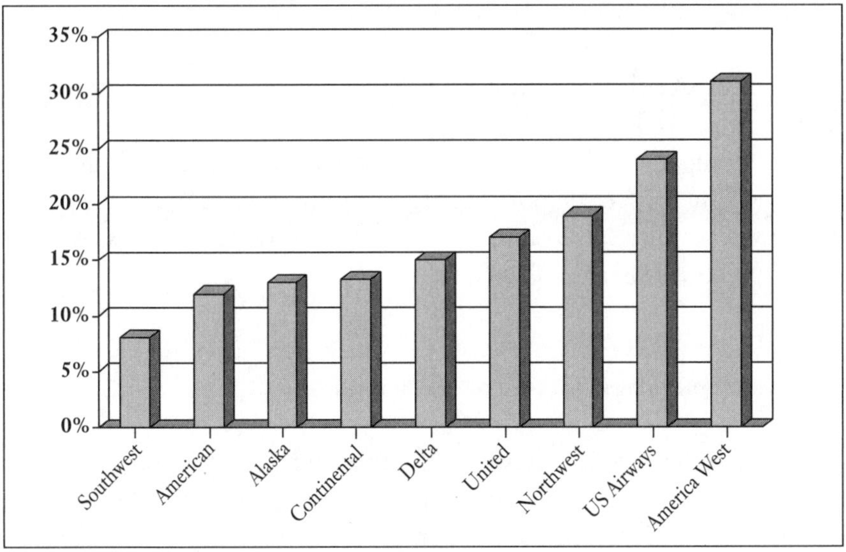

*Average months required to reach agreement, since 1985.
(*Source:* National Mediation Board)

the organization, one learns that Southwest has long emphasized the importance of labor/management partnerships. One of Southwest's chief pilots characterized Southwest's relationship with the pilots' union.

> We have an excellent relationship with SWAPA (Southwest Airlines Pilots' Association). Not a lot of finger pointing. I never see any, to tell you the truth. We share opinions openly. The groundwork for this was established a long time ago. We do not lose memories of where we've been, how it all started. We have a shared responsibility with the association. Some differences will occur. Sometimes there's the need for disciplinary action, but we always maintain respect for the person.

A Southwest flight attendant base manager described a similar relationship with the Transport Workers Union, which represents Southwest's flight attendants:

> The relationship is the best you'll ever see. The union representative is in my office three to five times a week. There is openness and communication. Our

general philosophy is the more knowledge you give the more they are equipped to do their job. We do that with the union too.

The respect that Southwest managers demonstrated for employees and their elected representatives reinforced frontline employees' trust for the company and their identification with the company's goals. In addition, the respect demonstrated by top management also helped to foster respectful relationships between the unions themselves. A long-time operations agent explained:

> At Southwest, everybody supports everybody else's union—in the whole aspect of the thing. That's just the way it is here.

This respectful attitude between unions stands in stark contrast to the other airlines, where derogatory comments were frequently heard about the unions that represented other employee groups.

The strong identification between frontline employees and top management in turn helps to keep union representatives in line. In the mid-1990s, one of the unions at Southwest was accused by its employee members of being "hard ass" in its relationship with the company, and unresponsive to legitimate employee needs. Discontent came to a head when the union proposed to set up a strike fund. According to Marcie Means, a customer service agent who helped lead the effort to replace that union with another:

> Unions can make or break a company. [This particular union] has been real stressful for Southwest . . . they want to fight. We don't want to fight. We belong to this company. It's a system that works and that's been working for years.

In the meantime, Colleen Barrett took the position that "we really want them to have whoever they want," suggesting that employee representatives are respected for the fact that they were chosen by employees, and that Southwest managers trust employees to make that choice.

In another case, Southwest's ramp and operations employees voted to replace their independent union—the Ramp, Operations and Provisioners Association (ROPA)—with a more established union—the Transport Workers Union (TWU)—which represents Southwest's flight attendants, as well as ramp and maintenance employees at American Airlines. Once the TWU was in place, its representatives took a more aggressive stance regarding wages for Southwest employees, leading to an impasse in contract negotiations and resulting in Southwest's first mediation in decades. While in mediation in the spring of 2001, Southwest employees conducted informational picketing at many of Southwest's stations. Despite the aggressive stance of the TWU regarding wages, Southwest managers spoke positively of the change employees had made in choosing the TWU to replace their own independent union. According to Baltimore station manager Mike Miller:

> The members felt they needed a more experienced union. We had become a major carrier. I think it's been easier to work with the TWU than with ROPA.

Miller also found that partnering with Southwest's unions was an effective way to think through and implement changes at the station level:

> We have a very positive relationship with the unions. . . . Union leadership here is good. I like those guys. They support the union perspective, we support the company perspective. Our conversations get heated, then we shake hands and move on. If we have a concept we want to kick around, we want to get the union involved, from a selling standpoint, and also to see if there are flaws.

There had been one strike in Southwest's history, however, and top management was willing to take another if necessary to maintain Southwest's basic commitments. Colleen Barrett explained:

> We've had one strike—a six-day strike with the mechanics in 1980. We got them temporary jobs with the census during the strike. We are very proud of our employee relationships. We treat people with respect. But we would take a strike if it got down to it—if the demands would hurt all employees. Especially if . . . we simply couldn't concede without hurting all employees by the decision. We are loving but very realistic and very pragmatic.

Jim Parker, Southwest's general counsel for years and recently chosen as Southwest's new CEO, explained Southwest's approach to contract negotiations:

> Our goal is to keep productivity high, keep the business model in place. I go to Herb [now chairman of the board] before the union negotiations, then I put as much money on the table as I can, right at the start. There is not

always harmony, but we know our employees at Southwest have realistic expectations. I would say there are different degrees of harmony.

Most labor disputes are not really about money. There is something else—respect. It comes down to personal contact between the company and its employees.

This personal contact between the company and its employees was achieved in part through the frontline supervisor, noted Donna Conover, Southwest's executive vice president of customers:

This is one reason our supervisors are so important. It is easier to walk out on people who do not give you respect than to walk out on a friend. You cannot make up for long-standing problems in the two months before a negotiation. Communication needs to be consistent.

Even members of the National Mediation Board, which oversees labor disputes in the airline industry, noticed the unique approach taken by Southwest in its labor relations. Maggie Jacobson, chair of the Mediation Board, described the Southwest difference:

In a service industry, your people are your most important thing. Companies have to treat their people with respect. They have to be open with information. Everybody knows anyway. You can't get away with it—the company telling unions we're doing poorly while telling the public we're doing great. The Southwests of the world use the process efficiently. What does it take? Day-to-day communication by CEOs. Be as honest as you can possibly be. . . . Credibility is a daily process.

Respectful relationships between management and frontline employee unions helped to set the tone for respectful relationships throughout Southwest Airlines.

Labor Relations at Continental Airlines

Thanks to Frank Lorenzo's successful union-busting efforts of the 1980s, Continental's workforce was largely nonunion in the early 1990s. Under Lorenzo, Continental had put in place an alternative form of employee representation in 1985. Customer service, ramp, and maintenance employees were represented by employee interest groups (EIGs), and supervisory employees had a parallel form of representation called management interest groups (MIGs). Customer service and ramp employees at the Boston station took these interest groups quite seriously, and reportedly the EIGs often formed alliances with the MIGs to pursue matters of mutual interest. According to a Boston supervisor:

> EIGs have been going on, in various forms, for the past 10 years. They've had different focuses and have organized under different titles, as the company has changed. Prior to 1987 and the merger of all the various companies, it was different. How much input they have has varied. Probably since 1990 there's been a far greater reliance and inclusion.
>
> As Lorenzo's power began to wane, there became more emphasis on relying on employees. There was more pressure to go union from the Eastern people who came in. A lot of concern to get communication strengthened so we wouldn't blow our cost structure. There was a lot of advantage from making employees feel they were getting a fair shake.

EIGs and MIGs were active in Boston, and their representatives also participated in regional and companywide forums. Employees at the Boston station expressed high expectations for inclusion in issues of companywide importance, such as the formulation of the Continental Lite strategy and the rewriting of Company Policies and Procedures.

Aside from customer service and the ramp, however, Continental employees were not satisfied with this form of representation and either had found or were seeking to find their own forms of representation through more traditional unions. In 1993, the pilots voted in a new, independent union. Soon after, the flight attendants' union, which had never been destroyed, became active again after 10 years of dormancy. And the mechanics became involved in a union drive that ultimately proved successful. Interestingly, in a company that was associated with the aggressive union-busting efforts of Frank Lorenzo, there was little evidence of local or top-level management opposing these efforts to re-unionize in the mid-1990s. A flight attendant base manager expressed what appeared to be the new attitude toward unions:

> When you have a union on board . . . in today's environment it's different from even seven years ago. It used to be combative. Now in the United

States we work together more. We are not trying to get as much as possible for the least work. These days everybody knows we have got to be lean.

In other words, Continental was no longer actively opposing unions, in part because the unions were now trusted to be more restrained with respect to their demands, in recognition of the competitive environment in which Continental was operating.

This new acceptance of unions also reflected the values of Continental's new leadership team, headed by CEO Gordon Bethune, and Vice President of Employee Relations Mike Campbell. Indeed, in Bethune's "Go Forward" plan for turning around Continental Airlines, unveiled in January 1995, one of the four components was "Working Together (to improve labor relations)." Bethune appeared to be striving for partnership with Continental's employee unions. However, this partnership was threatened by Continental's plan to create a code-sharing alliance with Northwest Airlines in 1998. Continental's pilots began informational picketing at selected airports, concerned that their job security was at stake. Clearly, a communication gap had opened up. According to the president of Continental's pilot union:

> If they really want this pilot group, this employee group, to buy off onto this transaction, they need to provide us with the information we need to make decisions about our careers. And if they won't share that information with us, that raises doubts. That raises suspicions. And they have nobody to blame but themselves.[6]

That problem was averted through more open communication between the company and its unions, but the incident demonstrated that Continental's new leaders could not relax their efforts to build trusting relationships with Continental's employees and their unions.

Labor Relations at United Airlines

The United employee buyout of 1994, in which employees purchased 55 percent of United's stock through wage concessions in return for board representation, seemed to be an ideal way to align employees' interests with those of management, and to do so in a way that would foster cooperation between employee groups. Under the employee stock ownership plan (ESOP), United's unions were represented on the board of directors, as well as in cross-functional problem-solving teams. However, support for the ESOP was shaky from the start. United's pilots, represented by the Air Line Pilots Association, took the lead in the employee buyout, though internal dissent among the pilots continued to surface throughout the period of the ESOP. United's mechanics and ramp workers, represented by the International Association of Machinists (IAM), joined the buyout but supported it by a narrow margin.

Nonunion employees, who made up a substantial percentage of United's frontline employees, including customer contact positions such as ticket agents, gate agents, and reservations agent, were given representation on the board of directors in return for their participation in the employee buyout. After the buyout, these customer contact employees who had been traditionally opposed to unionization decided to join the International Association of Machinists, the same union that already represented United's mechanics and ramp employees.

United's flight attendants, represented by the Association of Flight Attendants, agreed to join the buyout only if United agreed to stop its efforts to hire foreign-domiciled flight attendants, a move that they felt threatened their job security and that took some of the best-paying jobs away from their members. This condition was not met, and more significantly, the other unions did not back the flight attendants' position. As a result, United flight attendants did not participate in the buyout and were not represented on the board of directors. As United's new CEO at the time of the ESOP, Gerald Greenwald said that he was "committed to forging a mutually beneficial agreement with [the flight attendants]." The flight attendants' union responded: "If someone would come up with a good solution, I think we would entertain it."[7]

Rather than becoming more unified around the buyout over time, however, as observers had hoped, employees became increasingly divided over the buyout. The mechanics voted to leave the IAM and their ramp and customer service colleagues to join a new union just for mechanics, in part to reopen the question of whether to participate in the ESOP. The vote failed by only a narrow margin. The flight attendants' union continued to oppose the company plan to move some flight attendant jobs to overseas bases—and continued to withhold their support for the ESOP. Meanwhile, pilots pressured company leadership to make changes in management, in part to demonstrate to themselves that the power they had achieved through board representation was a reality.

Some United leaders found that initially there were positive changes associated with the ESOP. A ramp supervisor described the initial impact of the ESOP:

> There's been a significant amount of buy-in by the groups involved. . . . United has had a rancorous labor history—lots of strikes, ill will, very much "us and them" philosophy. With the ESOP, we're not talking about a little shift here—we're talking about 180 degrees. From open hostility to "we're all in this together."
>
> I used to have to come in here with a whip and a chair. In almost all cases it's taken a noticeable turn for the better. It's not to say that everybody runs out the door ready to load the airplanes. But it's made my job considerably easier.

Over time, other United leaders began to question the value of the ESOP. A Boston manager explained his disappointment with the ESOP:

> After the ESOP things got better. We would have hoped there would be a real change in attitude. But the IAM has a real difficult attitude. Their basic philosophy is different from managers. They think about what they can get out rather than what they can put in. You'd think the ESOP would bring a different attitude, but so far not. Instead it's "how can I get an easy hour? How can I get a paid lunch?"
>
> The IAM called in sick one day after Thanksgiving, then called a work slowdown, work by the rule book. Flights were delayed just long enough that you had to explain it. . . . It was happening all over sporadically, places with the strong union-type ties. This caused a lot of resentment between the employee groups. Customer services would have to deal with customers, bags would be piled up, it was difficult and hazardous. Relations were at an all time low. We are trying to get it back to where it was.

In addition to continuing problems in day-to-day workplace relations, the influence that employees had hoped to gain through board representation was not achieved, in the view of many. Rick Dubinsky, head of the pilots union for United and representative to the United board of directors, expressed disappointment in his farewell speech to members in October 2001:

I view the Board of Directors seat as "golden" but only as it relates to providing [us] with unparalleled access to information and the most secret inner workings of the company for which we fly. However, for the 25 percent-plus of the stock of this corporation that is held by the pilots, to be limited to only one board seat with minimal influence is a travesty.

In the last year and a half that I have been attending their meetings, the United board hasn't spent even 30 minutes discussing any issues germane to its employee owners, with the exception of complaining just how unreasonable and greedy are the pilots. This airline is being run and managed purely as a public company. Management has deep-sixed any vestiges of employee ownership and is patiently biding its time until the ESOP and its corporate governance structure "sunsets" about 15 years from now.

Partly as a result of disenchantment with the limited influence gained by employees through the ESOP and its failure to include the flight attendants, labor relations at United Airlines deteriorated significantly in the late 1990s.[8] United flight attendants began using a new form of striking developed by their colleagues at Alaska Airlines, called CHAOS (Create Havoc Around Our System), in which members publicly declared their intent to stage strikes selectively throughout the company, but without announcing beforehand when or where the strikes would occur. United flight attendants used this strategy during negotiations in 1997, 2000, and 2001, protesting outside airports and passing out CHAOS information to passengers. In addition to the uncertainty this strategy created for the company, it also created, by intent, a high level of uncertainty and anxiety on the part of customers.

Under these pressures, United's CEO Gerald Greenwald and President John Edwardson began to lose the support of United's board, particularly its employee representatives. In 1998, John Edwardson resigned as a result of lack of support from the board, and in 1999 the board elected James Goodwin to succeed Greenwald as chairman and CEO. Goodwin, a 32-year veteran of United Airlines, enjoyed the strong support of the Air Line Pilots Association and the International Association of Machinists. He brought in a new management team, including Rono Dutta as president, and Bill Hobgood as the senior vice president of people.

Under Goodwin's leadership in 1999 and 2000, however, the proposed merger with US Airways became a source of heightened conflict for all workgroups:

Pilots, fearful of pay and seniority changes as well as layoffs that could result from such a merger, created a slowdown that was quickly followed with similar actions by the mechanics. The summer of 2000 left United management with a sorry figure to cut in front of the flying public, who were outraged by delays and cancelled flights, not to mention unhappy United employees.[9]

Labor relations appeared to become even more adversarial in the wake of September 11, when proposals by labor representatives to cushion the impact of the layoffs were rejected by management. In addition, United's unions continued to question management's commitment to the concept of employee ownership. Goodwin abruptly resigned October 28, apparently in response to pressure from the board of directors and particularly its employee representatives. In his place, the board appointed John Creighton, a board member with the reputation of having worked successfully with Weyerhauser's unions in the 1990s to turn that company around. Upon his appointment, Creighton announced his intention "to work hand-in-hand with our employees and unions to accomplish this task by developing innovative solutions to the issues we collectively face."[10] However, the obstacles he faced in repairing United's broken labor relations were clearly considerable.

Labor Relations at American Airlines

At American Airlines, pilots, flight attendants, ramp workers, and mechanics were unionized, but a substantial number of its workgroups—gate, ticket, reservations, and operations agents—were not. Under the leadership of former CEO Robert Crandall, labor–management relations at American fluctuated between tentative and adversarial. American had fairly adversarial relations with the unions that represented its pilots (the Allied Pilots Association) and its flight attendants (the Association of Professional Flight Attendants). A leader of the pilots' union explained:

> Crandall always gets people mad. One example was when Crandall put that ad in the paper during the Christmas time conflict with the pilots in 1989. The ad was called AApology and basically blamed the pilots for everything, tried to make us look bad to the public.
>
> Bob Baker [executive vice president of operations], on the other hand, is really respectful of employees. I can call him anytime I need to talk. The new

VP of flight operations [who reports to Bob Baker] and the new chief pilot are also very good. The new VP is spending a lot of money and time trying to smooth relations with the pilots.

Sometimes it appears Crandall is acting unilaterally, without consulting with other members of management. Like when Crandall announced in Chicago recently, at a President's Conference, that 500 pilots would be furloughed. According to others who were there, Baker about fell out of his seat when Crandall announced that.

The union that represented American's ramp employees and mechanics (the Transport Workers Union) had more of a mixed relationship with the company, at times fairly cooperative and at other times conflict-ridden.

Under Crandall's leadership, American had been the first airline in the industry, in the early 1980s, to initiate two-tier wage contracts. Two-tier wage contracts were an attempt to reduce wage costs by negotiating separate lower rates for new employees, while protecting the wage levels of current employees. Although American was successful, the two-tier wage structure bred resentment among new employees. A representative for the ramp workers explained later:

> Until the 1983 contract, we had good contracts. Our contracts were democratic and fair. We wouldn't sell out one group to help another group. But starting in 1983, this principle was abandoned. The contract called for lower starting rates for new people and a slower progression once they got there. The new ramp workers would come in at $4.50 and never get beyond $5.50. They also did not get benefits for the first year.
>
> You should understand, being a woman. It's an ERA issue, equal pay for equal work. The guy beside me is doing the same work as I am, and he's making less. It's divisive.

By the time those new employees became the majority, they were ripe for dissent, and American suffered several labor-management conflicts in the late 1980s and early 1990s.

In addition to these controversial and only somewhat successful initiatives to reduce costs and increase productivity, Crandall's approach toward communicating with frontline employees was different from that of his predecessors. He began to communicate directly with frontline employees rather than solely through their union representatives. This approach in and of itself did not necessarily signal a lack of respect for employee representation—Southwest has always taken the approach of communicating directly with frontline employees as well as with their union representatives, and Continental Airlines under Gordon Bethune is well known for doing the same.

Crandall, however, had a tendency to question publicly whether American's unions were in fact representing the views of their members, thereby questioning the legitimacy of his employees' unions. When the unions expressed opposition to company initiatives, Crandall tended to express the view that the unions' opposition was not reflective of its members' views, then was taken by surprise by the strength of frontline opposition to management policies, as, for example, in the 1993 flight attendants' strike. Rather than working with the unions, Crandall appeared to be competing with them for the trust and loyalty of American's frontline employees. The strategy of going around the unions, and suggesting that they did not truly represent their members, was a risky one to pursue, particularly as a strategy for winning the trust of frontline employees.

By questioning the legitimacy of union representatives, Crandall helped to build an atmosphere of disrespect that infected relationships between employee groups, including those whose cooperation with each other was critical for American's operating performance. Crandall's questioning of union legitimacy threatened to undermine the teamwork that the company had worked so hard to build through training. According to an American gate agent in the Boston station:

> After the flight attendant strike, they tried to pit us union against nonunion. They made it look like the flight attendants were out to screw the company. They pitted us against another work group. They preach team but they don't practice it.

Other employees spoke with disrespect of their colleagues in other functions, and of the unions that represented those colleagues. An American pilot suggested to me:

> You know, if American really wanted cost savings, they should bust the TWU [the union that represented mechanics, ramp agents, baggage transfer

agents, cabin cleaners, and so forth]. They should get the mechanics out since they're the only skilled workers in the group. And bust the rest.

This comment was from a pilot who believed strongly in the right to organize, and who was a long-standing leader of the pilots' union. Pilots expressed similar attitudes toward the flight attendants' union. These patterns of disrespect for colleagues and their union representatives mirrored top-management attitudes at American under Crandall, and boded ill for coordination of the flight departure process.

American has experienced more harmonious labor relations overall since Crandall was replaced by Don Carty. A leader of the pilots' union looked back on the Crandall era and reflected on the changes brought by American's new leadership:

> Crandall once said at a critical point in negotiations that pilots were nothing but high-paid bus drivers. He paid for that comment. The company is more under the control of the operations people now, like Bob Baker, and they recognize the value employees can bring to operations. The lines of communication are opening up.

Summing Up

We have seen in this chapter that the quality of the labor/management relationship can influence relationships throughout the organization, with likely effects on organizational performance. Consistent with the argument made by Kochan, Katz, and McKersie in their classic book, *The Transformation of American Industrial Relations*,[11] a recent study shows that it is not the level of union representation, but rather the quality of the relationship, that determines organizational performance. Conflict reduces quality, efficiency, and financial performance, while a positive workplace culture improves these outcomes. Unionization by itself has little impact on these outcomes, either positive or negative.[12]

But surely there is some basis for the deeply held American belief that unions are bad for business. In *What Do Unions Do?* Richard Freeman and James Medoff report that union membership can produce loyalty to union goals at the expense of loyalty to company goals.[13] However, they found that union representation can also provide an avenue for employee voice in the organization, potentially creating a greater sense of shared goals with their employer, *so long as employees are not forced to choose between loyalty to their union and loyalty to their employer.* That is, union representation can reinforce shared goals between employees and employers so long as the employer recognizes and respects the role of the union, and seeks its partnership.[14]

Similarly, union membership can foster strong ties *among* employees.[15] When multiple unions are present, it may be even more critical for management to show the utmost respect for each one. Any disrespect shown by management toward one union tends to result in disrespect shown by employees toward their fellow employees, undermining critical relationships throughout the organization. Union representation can support cross-functional coordination and performance so long as employers show respect for employee interests as articulated through their collective voice.

At Southwest Airlines, respectful relationships between company management and the unions chosen by frontline employees appear to set the tone for respectful relationships throughout the company. As Southwest's leaders pointed out on several occasions, however, positive labor/management relations are not achieved once and for all. Rather they have to be reproduced every day. The relationship is never complete. As Beverly Carmichael, Southwest's newly appointed vice president of people, pointed out recently: "It's like any other relationship. You have to live it every day."

Build Relationships with Your Suppliers

[Southwest] makes the airport part of their team. We make a presentation to them, and then they turn around and make one to us, saying "here's how we see us working together." That's unheard of. It gives you the impression that, this is a group I really want to work with, as opposed to [other airlines] where you wonder if you can get them to call you back. With Southwest you want to see what you can do for them. I think it pays huge dividends. My reaction to how I'm handled by Southwest is that it makes me want to bend over backwards.

—Kevin Dillon, Director of Manchester (NH) Airport

SOUTHWEST HAS THE reputation of being an independent company that prefers to do things by itself. It doesn't pay travel agent commissions or participate in industrywide online reservation systems. Southwest has not joined any strategic alliances with other airlines, despite the increasing popularity of these alliances in the industry, and despite the preliminary evidence that alliances enable airlines to increase both market share and revenues.[1] Southwest outsources none of its services other than fueling and off-line heavy maintenance checks, while other airlines outsource fueling and catering, and in their smaller stations often outsource ramp and maintenance functions and occasionally even customer service functions. When asked why, President and Chief Operating Officer Colleen Barrett answered:

> We would prefer to just rely on ourselves and take that growth internally. There are advantages to alliances, but there's not another airline out there that could communicate with us. There are no airlines that have systems similar to ours. We do not want to hold for other airlines or slow our operations.

At the same time, however, Southwest relies on outside parties to do what it cannot do—manage the airports, run the air traffic control system, and produce the airplanes that they fly. With these outside parties on whom they must rely, Southwest has taken a proactive, partnership-oriented approach that appears to generate significant payoffs to both Southwest and the other parties in the relationship. As we will see in this chapter, these external parties are treated to the same kind of relationship-building efforts that we have seen throughout Southwest Airlines.

Partnering with Airports

Southwest stands apart from the rest of the airline industry in the emphasis it places on building partnerships with the airports it serves. Kevin Dillon, the manager of a small airport in Manchester, New Hampshire, relates his own experience in working with Southwest. Southwest first began flying to Manchester in 1998. As in most other cases, the "Southwest effect" on Manchester Airport was immediate and dramatic. Traffic grew by 75 percent in the first year, and the average one-way fare dropped from $350 to $129. Before coming to Manchester Airport, Dillon had spent 21 years managing operations at larger airports, including Kennedy, LaGuardia, and Logan Airports. Dillon contrasted his experience with Southwest to his usual experience with airlines:

> I wasn't used to this. I went to Dallas for my first meeting with their corporate people. There were 12 people around the table, including LaPorte [Southwest's station manager for Manchester], their regional marketing person, their facilities people, and their senior route planning people. They had Pete McGlade and John Jamotta there—the guys that go around in disguise to figure out where to put Southwest's next flights! If I could sit down with a

route-planning analyst at American Airlines, the most junior person who crunches the numbers, I would be lucky.

One benefit of this partnership approach has been joint problem solving, resulting in new solutions to problems that would otherwise have constrained Southwest's ability to grow.

> Southwest seems to have a knack for pulling pearls of wisdom from people where you wouldn't even know to look for them. They wanted to know about route access to this airport and as we talked about it we came up with some new solutions that we've implemented.

Southwest's internal relationships, particularly its high levels of shared goals, shared knowledge, and mutual respect, bolstered its ability to partner effectively with external suppliers.

> At Southwest, they just don't have any egos. I'll go to make a pitch to them and they'll have everyone there from all the functions. The business guy will say X, the facilities guy will say Y, and the maintenance guy will say Z, and they'll all be on the same page. They jointly come to a decision, usually right there in the meeting. There's no ego.

Dillon noted that he has been involved in well-functioning relationships with other airlines as well. The Southwest difference, however, is unmistakable.

> Even at Continental it's not like Southwest. Their manager of route planning is a good guy, but you're dealing with a bureaucracy. He might like the idea but he's got to take it to his manager who takes it to his director, who has to put it in his strategic plan.

Airport managers can become part of the Southwest family by being included in the ritual of after-work parties. According to Dillon:

> I hear that you've really arrived when they invite you to one of their Friday afternoon deck parties down in Dallas.

Partnering for Security after September 11, 2001

Partnerships between airlines and airports are more than fun and good business, Dillon argues. When the goal is to provide security without unnecessarily inconveniencing the passenger, the airline/airport partnership can play an essential role.

> One of the problems you always find in security is fragmentation. As the airport manager, I am responsible for all security here except passenger and baggage screening. That's the airlines' job. So everybody can point fingers—the FAA, the airlines, and the airports. There are lots of loopholes if you want to take advantage. If you want to, you can be very lax.
>
> According to the mandate that was just handed down [after September 11], it's not clear who has the responsibility for screening bags—it's just clear that 100 percent have to be screened starting in 60 days. So nobody is moving yet. The airlines are waiting for the feds or airports to do it.

However, while other airports have suffered from long lines and passenger inconvenience, Manchester Airport has been able to make progress, thanks in part to its partnership with Southwest Airlines.

> I see security as a strategic customer service issue. . . . Wait times are a huge issue for us. We've doubled the amount of staffing, never letting wait times exceed 20 minutes. Logan couldn't tell you how long their wait times are. Neither could O'Hare. And that's not because security is an airport responsibility at Manchester. [The responsibility for security] belongs to the airlines here, just like at other airports. But the largest carrier at an airport or in a terminal is usually the primary contractor for security. And here it's Southwest.
>
> So I proposed to Southwest—if you double staffing at the checkpoints, we can market this. We'll help pay for the additional staffing. It was easy to get it done here, given Southwest. Other airlines would tell you—"we run security." But not Southwest. And they haven't sent us a bill yet.

Helped by its partnership with Southwest, and the relatively short wait times that have resulted from this partnership, Manchester Airport has performed well relative to its major competitor, nearby Logan International Airport.

Manchester only has 3 million passengers per year compared to Logan's 27 million. But we are gaining market share. Since September 11, . . . people are thinking differently about flying. . . . It's helped us. Our traffic is actually up from a year ago, even though the industry cut flights by 20 percent. Some of our airlines have been using the cuts in flights to redeploy aircraft from other airports to here, to increase their flights from Manchester, because they see the passenger demand.

The partnership between Manchester Airport and Southwest Airlines has benefited not only these two parties, but also the other airlines that fly to Manchester. The efficient security system made possible by the partnership has increased the attractiveness of Manchester Airport for the passengers of American, United, Continental, and all the other airlines that fly to Manchester. In this respect, there have been positive spillover effects for the industry resulting from Southwest Airlines' practice of building partnerships with the airports where it is the dominant carrier.

Partnership Challenges

At other airports, Southwest has faced more substantial challenges in forging a partnership. Baltimore-Washington International Airport (BWI) is one case in point. In 1993, Southwest selected BWI in Maryland, 30 miles from Washington, D.C., as its gateway to the East Coast. Service to Cleveland and Chicago began on September 15. One year later, the airport broke ground on a $27.6 million expansion project to extend the terminal and create six more domestic gates. Southwest signed up for all of them. Through the 1990s Southwest added more cities to its nonstop service from Baltimore. After just 7 years, Southwest's share of Baltimore passengers in 2000 reached 34 percent, displacing US Airways, the long-time leader. Baltimore had become one of Southwest's eight "mega-stations"—so called because it offered more than 100 flight departures per day. Given the continued growth in number of flights projected by management, Southwest's Baltimore gates would reach capacity limits later in 2001. Southwest's bag sorting area had already reached its capacity. In mid-2001, Baltimore directors began planning the renovation of Concourses A and B to provide more gates for the company.

Even once Southwest became the dominant carrier at Baltimore, the airport leadership responded somewhat reluctantly to Southwest's needs and its desire to play a partnership role in airport operations. According to a frontline operations agent at Southwest's Baltimore station:

> This was US Airways' territory. It's been kind of hard to get things done here. They had friends, and as we grew, we started bumping them. Considering everything, we have a pretty good relationship with this airport.
>
> We added more x-ray machines to improve the flow, shorten the lines. We went from four to seven machines after September 11. It was our initiative to get the lines down. It's in our best interests and in the airport's best interest too, to get the lines down.

Matt Hafner, regional director for Southwest, concurred:

> It's been tough working with this airport. We like to partner, but this one has been very political. It's getting better now, maybe because US Airways is looking weak. But we've also just had our leadership [top management team of Southwest Airlines] here meeting with the head of the state DOT. I think that has helped. We are finally getting action on some things we needed last year. They weren't used to the way we operate, coming in, needing to change things. We changed their jobs.

Jim Wimberly, executive vice president of operations for Southwest, had a broader perspective on the challenge that Southwest poses for airports:

> We challenge the infrastructure and the airport leadership in many airports where we fly. Our presence brings demand for extra parking space. . . . That "Southwest effect" creates a real challenge for airport directors. [In the case of Baltimore-Washington International] our growth has put many more issues in front of the Maryland Aviation Authority than they traditionally have had to deal with. New road capacity, provisioning facilities, ticket counter positions, conveyer belts for baggage, new parking garages, rerouting roadways, updating the master plan, getting noise studies done—you name it. When we go into a city, we create orders-of-magnitude growth, not incremental, so we have to work closely with the airport or it won't work.

Partnering with airports has been essential for Southwest's success, Wimberly explained:

It is difficult to run an airline if you don't have cooperation of the airports. Our airplanes don't work too well without those strips of concrete on either end.

Southwest has benefited from trying to understand the perspective of the other party, Wimberly explained:

You have to understand the political realities of airport administration. While they might be doing all they can to promote Southwest's growth, they are having to explain to city council why they leased ten gates to one airline and only two to another. We can help politically and educationally. Our Government Affairs department gives information to the local chamber of commerce about the economic growth that is brought by low-fare airlines. And the grassroots activities of our passengers who want that low-fare service definitely help.

It also helps that Wimberly, who plays a major role in Southwest's airport relations, served as the airport director at Houston's Hobby Airport during its high-growth period before joining Southwest's management team. As a result of his previous job experience, Wimberly has observed the relationship from the airport's perspective:

Hopefully I've brought a little understanding of the political realities that airports have to deal with. If you want to succeed in a city [as an airline], and you don't have the backing of the airport, you could be fine on the surface but have some bruising realities behind the scenes on a daily basis.

Partnering with Air Traffic Control

In addition to partnering with airports, Southwest also prides itself on its partnership with another critical player in the industry—air traffic control. While most airline employees take for granted the governmentally mandated role of air traffic control, and complain bitterly when the job is performed in a way that seems to cause unnecessary negative consequences, Southwest seeks to build a positive working relationship with air traffic controllers. Wimberly explained Southwest's approach:

We have good relations with air traffic control. We make routine visits to air traffic control towers in all the airports we serve. We take them hamburgers. They appreciate our flexibility and our willingness to work with them.

According to Colleen Barrett, president and chief operating officer of Southwest, a key ingredient of the partnership with air traffic control has been the Southwest pilots:

> Most pilots have strong egos. We turn pilots and air traffic control people into partners. Herb is always told about the civility of Southwest pilots when he makes tower visits, and it pays handsome dividends. The people in the tower are amazed at the civility of our pilots. We practice the golden rule with them just as we do with everyone else.

Wimberly agreed:

> Our pilots . . . are comfortable with making changes in speed and altitude to accommodate air traffic control. They are willing to be flexible.

Partnering with Aircraft Manufacturers

A third critical supplier for Southwest, or any airline, is the aircraft manufacturer. Southwest is one of the few airlines in the world to fly only one type of aircraft—the Boeing 737. Southwest has reaped various benefits from this decision, including the benefit of being able to build its flight operations around a single operating platform. Most airlines hesitate to purchase their aircraft from only one manufacturer, despite the benefits of operational consistency, because they want to maintain leverage as a purchaser of aircraft. They fear being taken advantage of if they become reliant on a single supplier. The risk of hold-up is common in supplier relations,[2] and one that most theorists recommend be minimized by diversifying suppliers, and avoiding at all costs becoming reliant on a single supplier, particularly for a high-cost item that is essential to one's operations.

However, Southwest has addressed the perennial concern of supplier hold-up in its own characteristic way—by building a mutually beneficial partnership with Boeing. Colleen Barrett explained Southwest's approach:

> With Boeing, it's like with everyone else. We try to make them understand that what's good for us is good for them. When you are the launch customer for an aircraft, there are lots of advantages. When you're as good a customer as we are, they listen. We don't go along with the crowd. Boeing likes us because of our history. They know our philosophy now, so they know we do not want "one little change" that will drive up the cost. Our way is actually less costly.

John Denison, Southwest's former executive vice president of corporate services, emphasized the long-term nature of the relationship:

> We would probably not change companies unless a partner company ceased to be a good partner. It is relationship-driven. If we think a product is good for us and good for our customers, it is good for Boeing.

One of Southwest's chief pilots described Southwest's relationship with Boeing from his perspective:

> We are the largest customer of the Boeing 737-300 and 500. We developed the 737-700 with the FAA and Boeing. We keep the procedures as much the same as possible between aircraft types. There are benefits with spare parts, not so expensive.

How are decisions made about aircraft configurations? he was asked. He laughed, then replied:

> It's very unstructured. I don't mean it to sound bad. It's a good thing. There's a lot of free flow of information. The four chief pilots in the four bases are involved. Directors of training and standardization are involved, and the vice president of flight operations. There's a group of six or ten to discuss issues, but there's also an open exchange between the executive vice president of operations, the head of maintenance, the head of the aircraft reliability program, and the reps from Boeing. There is a synergistic effect of everyone passing information around. Ideas go out, people take positions then try to persuade each other. We are quite direct. People are not afraid to speak. You don't see a lot of territorialism.

The relationship between Southwest and Boeing appeared similar to the relationships observed between Southwest and its airport directors, characterized by a free flow of information with the potential to offer benefits for both parties beyond what is achieved in more traditional supplier relations.

Benefits of Partnering with Your Suppliers

We see that Southwest has invested substantial time in developing effective partnerships with the three outside parties on which it is most dependent—airports, air traffic control, and aircraft manufacturers. Each of these parties provides a critical resource to Southwest that Southwest cannot produce on its own. Organizational scholars Russell Johnston and Paul Lawrence call these partnerships "value-adding partnerships," arguing that such partnerships have advantages over independent companies trying to negotiate with each other in the absence of a partnership, and advantages over vertically integrated companies that bring all activities in house.[3] Value-adding partnerships are "a set of independent companies that work closely together to manage the flow of goods and services along the entire value-added chain." Value-adding partnerships allow each party to focus on what they do best—in the case of Southwest Airlines, Southwest can fly the airplanes, while the airports manage the ground facilities, the U.S. government monitors air traffic control, and Boeing makes the airplanes. And yet the partnership between Southwest and each of these parties generates better outcomes for each party than any could achieve in a more traditional supplier relationship.

Value-adding partnerships can be observed in other industries as well, where some of the most successful organizations are those that have built close partnerships with their suppliers. In the auto industry, for example, supplier integration has been on the increase since auto manufacturers learned from the Japanese model about the benefits of close collaborative relationships. A recent study of auto industry supplier relationships found

> . . . an extraordinary increase in communications between customers and suppliers, independent of formal status as independent or vertically integrated. The volume of face to face, fax, phone, and e-mail exchanges was huge and increasing. All types of interaction occurred, on average, between a daily and weekly basis.[4]

In the apparel industry, a similar trend has occurred:

> Until recently, most channels in the textile and apparel industries have been characterized by arm's-length relationships among relatively autonomous firms.[5]

But now the successful apparel manufacturers and retailers are those who have developed well-integrated supply chains, in which information and know-how are readily shared across organizational boundaries. Similar partnerships have emerged in the distribution of drugs and health-care products.[6] In the delivery of health services, value-adding partnerships are beginning to emerge among hospitals as managed care dictates shorter lengths of stay in acute-care hospitals, requiring that most care be provided by external parties. Some hospitals have found that the same capabilities that improve the coordination of care internally can be leveraged to improve the coordination of care with external parties.[7]

Summing Up

Southwest's partnership approach is radically different from the traditional approach to supplier relations. In the old model, organizations were independent parties who transacted with each other at arm's-length through formal contracts, keeping information close to the chest. Cooperation occurred only within organizations, while careful arm's-length negotiation with minimal information sharing was the normal mode for dealing with parties external to the organization.[8] But when there is more uncertainty in the environment, there is much more that organizations can learn from one another. Because of the benefits of learning, both parties have more to gain than to lose from the sharing of information. Although there may be doubt and mistrust at the outset, "once the cooperative exploration of ambiguity begins, the returns to the partners from further joint discoveries are so great that it pays to keep cooperating."[9] Ultimately, this ability to partner is an acquired skill like any other, and one with potentially significant effects on organizational success.[10]

What additional insights do we gain from the example of Southwest Airlines? We learn that relationships are critical for coordinating across organizational boundaries, just as they are critical for coordinating across functional boundaries. In order to partner effectively with the outside parties whose cooperation Southwest has deemed critical for its own success, Southwest seeks to build relationships of shared goals, shared knowledge, and mutual respect with them. Indeed, the same relational competence that Southwest employees have developed in their internal relationships has been leveraged and extended to their relationships with outside parties. By treating these suppliers as partners, Southwest effectively extends its sphere of influence beyond its employees to encompass its entire value chain.

Building High Performance Relationships— And Keeping Them

How the Ten Southwest Practices Reinforce (or Undermine) Each Other

T HROUGHOUT THIS BOOK we have seen that Southwest Airlines' extraordinary performance is not due simply to its outstanding leadership, its funky culture, or its unique operating strategy, although it has all three. Rather Southwest's extraordinary performance can be traced to a set of organizational practices that deliberately overcomes the divisive effects of functional boundaries by transforming relationships between management and frontline employees, among frontline employees, and with key external parties. Coordination is supported by a coherent set of organizational practices that encourages people to think of their jobs not as a set of discrete tasks, but instead as linked to broader processes involving people in other functional areas. In many work settings, including the airline industry, the functions involved in delivering a particular product or service are divided by status, expertise, and geography. It is Southwest's attention to relationships—"designed in" through a consistent set of organizational practices—that accounts for much of Southwest's performance advantage. See Exhibit 15–1 for a summary of these practices.

This is good news because it means that other organization can adopt Southwest's powerful organizational practices without attempting to re-create its culture. Adopting a set of organizational practices may involve

Exhibit 15–1 Ten Southwest Practices for Building High Performance Relationships

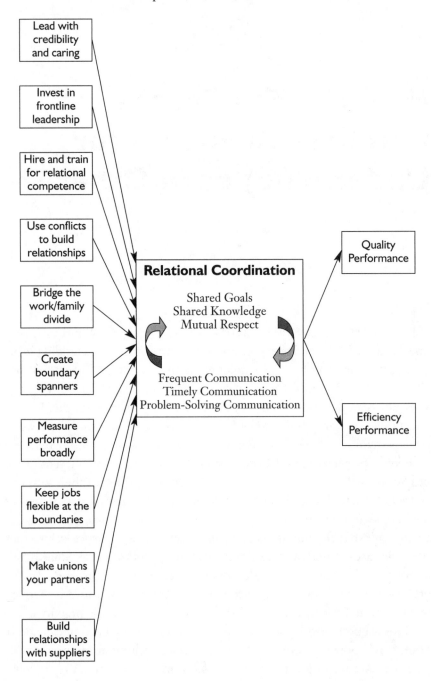

a significant investment of time and energy, but it is more feasible than trying to adopt the culture of another organization. And as we have seen, these organizational practices ultimately do support the culture for which Southwest is so well known.

However, these organizational practices are not stand-alone elements. Rather they are mutually supporting, so that their total effect is likely to be more than the sum of their individual effects. The organizational practices identified here are expected to be more effective if they are adopted in conjunction with the others, rather than being adopted in isolation. Consistency among practices is beneficial in the sense that each one increases the effectiveness and sustainability of the others. Indeed, if some of your organizational practices work to undermine relationships, the careful investments you have made in other organizational practices may be effectively wasted, or at least seriously diluted.

The following sections consider the potential consequences of only partially adopting the 10 practices that were described in Part 2.

Lead with Credibility and Caring

Perhaps you have put into place all the other organizational practices, but you have a top-management team that does not have a credible, caring relationship with frontline employees. Like American, Continental, and United Airlines at various points in their history, as we saw in Chap. 5, many organizations have suffered years of mistrust between management and frontline employees. For these organizations, it is no small task to reverse this mistrust and restart the relationship from scratch. However, without credible, caring top leadership, the other organizational practices are in jeopardy. The behavior of top leadership serves as a model for the rest of the organization, helping to illustrate and animate the principles that underlie the other organizational practices that you have put into place.

The credible leadership of Herb Kelleher and Colleen Barrett has created credibility throughout the organization, and serves as a foundation for other leaders throughout the company, including the frontline supervisors. "It makes our jobs so much easier," said a mid-level manager at Southwest Airlines. "When Herb or Colleen says something is bad, you know it's bad." Without credibility on the part of top leadership, there would be no chance of a long-lasting partnership with employee unions, or with external suppliers. In addition, the caring leadership of Herb Kelleher and Colleen Barrett has helped to create the basis for strong familylike ties within Southwest, and a concern for supporting the family relationships of employees at home. It is clear that top leadership is not the be-all and end-all to strong organizational performance, but that top leadership plays a critical role in either supporting or undermining the effects of the other organizational practices.

Invest in Frontline Leadership

You might adopt the overall system of practices, but decide to employ a relatively small number of supervisors per frontline employees, perhaps to save on staffing expense. As we saw in Chap. 6, frontline employees would likely receive less coaching and feedback on their work, and would look instead to quantitative performance measures to figure out how they were doing. These measures tend to be less effective at capturing things like helping across functional boundaries, and more effective at capturing performance of a specific job. The second outcome of reduced supervision, we also saw in Chap. 6, is that frontline employees tend to have a less personal relationship with management. There are fewer opportunities to hear a management perspective, and thus more opportunities for the gulf to widen between management and nonmanagement employees. As a result, it is a much bigger job for the organization's top leadership to reach the frontline employee, with less help from frontline leadership. Similarly, a reduced supervisory staff may undermine your efforts to make unions into partners rather than adversaries. With reduced supervisory staff, there is less opportunity for day-to-day conversations through which to work out a set of shared objectives between management and nonmanagement employees. As a result, the negotiating table becomes less a place to formalize an ongoing conversation and more a place for strangers with competing objectives to meet warily.

Hire and Train for Relational Competence

Consider, for example, what happens if you adopt all of the organizational practices outlined in Part 2 except that, contrary to Southwest's approach as shown in Chap. 7, you continue to hire and train employees without regard for their relational competence. Say you continue to hire and train your pilots (or engineers or physicians) to exhibit a command personality with their fellow employees. Your new performance measurement system that holds all employees involved in a particular work process jointly accountable for outcomes will be seriously undermined. Other employees participating in the work process will not feel it is fair to be held responsible for outcomes over which they had little say. This is exactly what happened when the pilots at American Airlines became members of "departure teams" in which they were held jointly accountable with the gate agents for decisions about whether and how long to hold a flight. Because American's pilots were still hired and trained to exhibit a command personality, they had no concept that the gate agents might have a valuable perspective to contribute to the decision. Cecil Ewell, former chief pilot and vice president of flight operations at American Airlines, pointed out just before the program was terminated:

> There are real problems with the way that program is working right now. The pilot thinks he is in total control and that the ground workers don't know as much. The gate agents are getting around the pilots by cheating, saying they already got approval from the pilots when they didn't.

Similarly, if employees continue to be hired and trained without regard for relational competence, any efforts to use conflicts as an opportunity for learning, bringing them out into the open rather than submerging them, are likely to backfire. New procedures for conflict resolution are not likely to succeed if relational competence is not fostered in the hiring and training processes. Finally, what happens if you develop flexible job descriptions asking employees to do whatever needs to be done to make the operation a success, and yet those employees continue to be hired and trained without regard to relational competence? Those flexible job descriptions may backfire because employees will not be equipped to deal with the fuzzy boundaries between their own job and the jobs of their colleagues. At the very least, the flexible job descriptions will be rendered relatively useless as employees choose to remain within the safe territory of their own jobs.

Use Conflicts to Build Relationships

Let us consider another scenario. Say you adopt all of the organizational practices outlined in Part 2, except you downplay the importance of conflicts among employees. Rather than using conflicts as an opportunity for learning, as we saw Southwest do in Chap. 8, you take the more common approach of brushing them under the table, hoping the parties will forget their problems or work them out on their own. This would be a serious mistake. Several of your other practices create the potential for conflict, and you need to be ready to address those conflicts proactively when they arise. For example, flexible job descriptions are great in terms of expanding the scope of responsibility, but they do create the potential for conflicts that would not otherwise arise. The expectation that you will do your own job, plus *anything else* that might be necessary to help the operation succeed, blurs the boundaries between jobs and creates more areas that are open to interpretation and thus conflict.

Likewise, broad performance measures that hold people jointly responsible for outcomes can create conflict. If you are responsible only for your own task, there is less opportunity for conflict. If instead you are responsible for the outcome of the overall work process, along with the others who are engaged in that work process, there is less clarity about whose fault it is when something does go wrong. Proactive conflict resolution can make the difference between letting these conflicts fester or using them as an opportunity for learning about the overall process and the role that each party plays in it.

Bridge the Work/Family Divide

This organizational practice in particular looks like one that is "nice to have" but not essential to the overall effectiveness of the other practices. And yet it is. All of the practices outlined in Part 2 are designed to build strong working relationships that support high performance. To be truly engaged in strong working relationships, it was argued in Chap. 9, a person must be able to bring his or her real self to the workplace. Southwest's efforts to make the workplace feel like a family helps to cement those working relationships at a deep level of commitment, by creating a strong sense of collective identity at work.

The hazard of these familylike relationships at work, as Southwest's managers are well-aware, is that employees will neglect their own family relationships, creating dysfunctional home lives that will eventually undermine employee well-being and performance. Accordingly, Southwest seeks to support and strengthen the family ties of their employees, through flextime policies and emergency funds to help employees in need. One young employee told me about confiding a family problem to his supervisor and being immediately excused to deal with it, along with some cash to address the emergency. By supporting the family and non-work commitments of its employees, and by making the workplace itself feel like a family where one can be one's true self, Southwest gains the loyalty and commitment of its employee at a deep level, thus providing a foundation for all its other practices.

Create Boundary Spanners

Say you put into place the other relationship-intensive practices of Southwest Airlines, but then decide to rely on a technology interface rather than a human interface for coordinating your work processes. As we saw in Chap. 10, some work processes have very distinct functional boundaries and therefore benefit greatly from using a human boundary spanner to coordinate them. A boundary spanner like the operations agent at Southwest plays an informational role, helping to collect and transmit information from one function to the other, including subtle contextual information that is not easily codified and transmitted through a technology interface. But Southwest's boundary spanner also plays a social role, helping to build shared goals and a shared understanding of the work process so that each party is more likely to take the right actions when there is a need to adapt quickly to changing circumstances.

When information technology is used to *replace* the role of the boundary spanner, some of these shared understandings will start to break down over time. Supervisors are likely to fill in the breech, spending their time coordinating across functional boundaries, thereby detracting from their role in providing coaching and feedback to frontline employees. With less active coaching and feedback from frontline supervisors, there is additional pressure on the performance measurement system to provide feedback to employees. As a result there may be an increased emphasis on doing what can be readily measured, typically activities within the bounds of a given functional area, neglecting the critical activities at the boundaries.

Measure Performance Broadly

Instead of using Southwest's approach toward measuring performance, as described in Chap. 11, you could decide to take the traditional approach to performance measurement, measuring performance "by the numbers" and assigning outcomes to individual departments. However, cross-functional performance measurement is central to Southwest's system of organizational practices. Without it, there is no need for flexible work rules, and far less need to hire and train people for relational competence. These other organizational practices would become unnecessary, wasted investments.

In addition, when performance measures are functionally specific, the coaching and feedback role of frontline supervisors becomes far less critical. The coaching and feedback role of supervisors is particularly useful for helping employees understand how their own actions affect overall process outcomes. When one's performance is measured only in terms of one's own functionally specific tasks, feedback is more straightforward and supervisors have less value to add to the process. This approach was exemplified by American Airlines, where control of the operation was achieved through functionally specific performance measures, rather than through supervisory coaching and feedback.

Keep Jobs Flexible at the Boundaries

If you put into place all the other relationship-intensive practices, but do not have flexible work rules, what harm could that possibly do? Quite a bit, potentially. If all other practices in the organization are geared toward minimizing functional divisions, and yet there are rules in place to discourage or actively prevent employees from performing the work of others, the message to employees is confusing and frustrating. Why hire and train for relational competence if one's ability to help others in a pinch is highly restricted? This was the reasoning at American Airlines, where a supervisor said, "the workgroups are so well-defined that they are not allowed to help out, so we don't look for that [when we hire]. It would cause problems." Similarly, why create a performance measurement system designed to encourage helping out across functional boundaries when job descriptions prevent it?

As we saw in Chap. 12, rigid job descriptions tend to reinforce beliefs that certain work is the territory of certain people, and that others are not entitled to do it, even in circumstances where it would clearly make sense for the sake of operational performance. This territoriality undermines the principle that is communicated by your other organizational practices, making them a wasted investment at best, or worse, creating cynicism as to the organization's true principles.

Make Unions Your Partners, Not Adversaries

What if you have invested carefully in building the other organizational practices, and yet have developed an adversarial relationship with one or more of your employee unions? What harm could this do? As shown in Chap. 13, positive labor/management relations have the potential to further cement the loyalty of employees to the company. The loyalty that employees feel toward their company is magnified when the union they belong to is engaged in a mutually supportive partnership with the company. An adversarial relationship, by contrast, forces employees to choose between loyalty to their union and loyalty to their company, resulting in divided loyalties within and among employees.

Second, the importance of labor/management partnership for achieving flexible job descriptions cannot be underestimated. In any unionized setting, job descriptions are subject to contractual negotiations. One of the surest outcomes of adversarial labor/management relations is an attempt to negotiate rigid job descriptions to protect union members from being taken advantage of by unscrupulous managers. In addition, an adversarial relationship can result in job actions taken by one work group against the company, putting stress on the other work groups and thus undermining the quality of relationships among frontline employees.

Build Relationships with Your Suppliers

Finally, what result can you expect if you have developed all of the practices to support strong relationships within your organization, but you still have arm's-length relationships with some of your most important suppliers? At the very least, there is a missed opportunity—you are missing the chance to leverage your internal relational capabilities to create strong relationships with external parties, and thereby missing out on the operational benefits that can result from external partnerships. At worst, there is the same problem that can occur with any inconsistent organizational practice—the message that employees receive is not clear, which can lead to confusion or cynicism about the organization's true principles, and thus to an erosion of those principles. Simply put, if we treat the airports, air traffic control, and the aircraft manufacturers with disrespect, jockeying for the most favorable position for ourselves without regard for their interests, then that same us/them approach may come to infect our internal relationships as well.

Summing Up

Southwest's success is not due to one particular organizational practice or another, but rather to the overwhelming consistency among them. As we have seen, each organizational practice tends to reinforce the others or, if designed in a way that is inconsistent with relational principles, tends to undermine the others. The idea that high performance depends on *bundles* of organizational practices—rather than individual practices—is a powerful one that extends to other industry settings. Evidence from the auto industry,[1] the apparel industry,[2] the steel industry,[3] and the telecommunications industry[4] shows that bundles of practices can have powerful, positive effects on performance. This book is part of a series of studies that shows how bundles of mutually reinforcing organizational practices can launch organizations onto a high performance trajectory.[5]

In their seminal work on organization design, Paul Lawrence and Jay Lorsch made perhaps the earliest case for the benefits of consistency:

> A new form of consistency can be achieved. Each of the discrete practices . . . can be consistent with the other practices, . . . so that all will reinforce the desired task performance.[6]

Since then, from the work of Jay Galbraith to the work of David Nadler and Mike Tushman, alignment among organizational practices has been considered to be integral to high performance.[7] Economists have shown that the performance advantage from consistent organizational practices is due to "complementarities" among them.[8] Practices are complementary if adopting one increases the benefits of having the other, or if *not* adopting one *decreases* the benefits of having the other. Because of the psychological dynamics of reinforcement, consistency is likely to be particularly important for organizational practices that are designed to influence employee attitudes and behaviors. When an organization sends mixed signals—on one hand we select and train employees for relational competence, but on the other hand performance measurement is functionally based—the result is confusion and cynicism about the organization's true principles, undermining investments in both practices.

Most U.S. firms have implemented some form of innovative work system or human resource practices over the past decade,[9] and many of them are designed to strengthen relationships between management and frontline employees, or among frontline employees themselves. However, the question is whether these innovations are sufficiently coherent and consistent to transform relationships, or whether they are sporadic, separate efforts that leave key relationships fundamentally untransformed. As we have seen here with Southwest, effective organizations typically have a configuration of mutually consistent practices rather than a single key practice that makes them effective,[10] while imitating organizations tend to adopt only some of these practices.[11] Organizational experts have recognized the difficulties of transferring best practice from one organization to another, but have concluded that successful learning from another organization requires managers to adopt the whole system of mutually consistent practices in order to achieve desired performance outcomes.

To learn successfully from Southwest, I have argued, the key is to adopt organizational practices that support relationships over the long term, between managers and frontline employees, among frontline employees, and with external parties, and to be rigorous about seeking consistency among these practices. One bad apple—or inconsistent practice—really can spoil the whole bunch.

CHAPTER

16

Learning from Southwest

Efforts by American, Continental, United, and JetBlue

[Continental] wanted to buy Southwest—it was a serious plan. But Southwest wasn't interested. So why not just emulate them? . . . Our industrial engineers went there to visit. Southwest invited our people into their little world. Mr. Kelleher said, "Come on in, ask anything you want." I don't understand why.

—Customer Service Manager, Continental Airlines

We took what we thought worked best for Southwest and best for United, and made the United Shuttle. People from across the system were involved. . . . It was amazing to me that [Southwest] was so open.

—Operations Coordinator, United Airlines

NOT SURPRISINGLY GIVEN its phenomenal record of success over three decades, other organizations have begun trying to learn from the Southwest model. As noted at the beginning of this book, these efforts to learn from Southwest have become widespread only recently, as observers have come to realize that Southwest is more than a funky niche airline. But everyone focuses on and seeks to imitate different aspects of the Southwest model. The result is something like the story of the three blind men and the elephant, in which each man observes a different part of the elephant and draws his own conclusions about the whole elephant based on the one part he has observed.

The Southwest model has three primary components. First, there is a *relationship* component. As shown throughout Part 2, this relationship component is strengthened by 10 distinct organizational practices that have evolved over time at Southwest, from credible, caring leadership to long-term supplier relationships. Second, there is a *product* component in which simplicity is the central feature—snacks rather than meals, a single class of seating, no reserved seats, and so on. Third, there is a *structure* component in which the point-to-point route structure and single air-craft type are the central features. Part 1 demonstrated that the relation-ship component of the Southwest model yields substantial gains in quality and efficiency independent of the product or structure compo-nents of the model.

It is important for the reader to keep in mind throughout this chapter that these three components—product, structure, and relationship—are present and can serve as the basis for competition in any industry. In the retailing industry the *product* component has played a key role, as in the case of Kmart and Wal-Mart identifying an unmet demand for a low-lux-ury, high-convenience shopping experience with an emphasis on selec-tion and availability. The *structure* component has also played a key role in the transformation of retailing, in the form of large store spaces and supply networks to achieve rapid product replenishment. Finally, the *relationship* component has also played a key role in this transformation, particularly the relationships with external parties such as manufacturers and distributors that enable rapid replenishment.[1]

This chapter makes a point that is relevant far beyond the airline industry—that strong relationships can play a critical role in the compet-itive arena, but they are difficult to achieve. We will see some attempts to adopt the relationship component of the Southwest model, and some common pitfalls.

Efforts by Other Airlines to Learn from Southwest

The *product* component of the Southwest model is the component that has been most frequently imitated by others in the airline industry. It is easy to see why. The nature of consumer demand has changed over the past several decades, with a growing demand for low fares. This change began with deregulation of the industry in 1978 and the subsequent rise of fare competition. Traditional airlines have continued to rely on business travelers to pay high fares to subsidize the cheap fares they offer to fill the rest of the seats. As of the late 1990s and early 2000s, however, it was no longer clear that business travelers would continue to pay those high fares. A multitude of airlines have sought to imitate Southwest's simple product in an attempt to offer the low fares that consumers are increasingly looking for. Early on, People Express and Texas International tried to serve this market. More recently, we have seen efforts by ValuJet, Mesaba Air, Midwest Express, Continental Lite, the United Shuttle, US Airways' MetroJet, AirTran, the Delta Connection, and JetBlue Airways.

Some of these imitators have also sought to imitate the structure component of Southwest—particularly its point-to-point route structure. A point-to-point route structure provides little in the way of pricing power, relative to a hub-and-spoke route structure. Airlines have pricing power in their hubs due to their market share and due to their ability to limit other airlines' access to their hubs.[2] According to American Airline's senior vice president of planning, a hub generates up to 20 percent more revenue per plane for American than a comparable point-to-point flight.[3] Northwest Airlines similarly relies on its hubs to raise prices beyond what is possible on more competitive point-to-point routes, thus the term "fortress hubs." According to Northwest's leadership:

> Northwest got to be profitable by focusing on a very pure version of the network [hub-and-spoke] strategy. We focused on our sources of competitive advantage and built a network around them. . . . We eliminated our routes up and down the West Coast. We eliminated some flying from Boston. We eliminated hubs at Washington, D.C., and elsewhere that couldn't reach critical mass.[4]

As a point-to-point carrier, by contrast, Southwest has relatively little pricing power. But as the examples of JetBlue Airways and AirTran show, one can use a hub-and-spoke route structure to deliver a low-fare, simple product. JetBlue flies nearly all of its flights into and out of its JFK hub and is now starting to develop a second hub in Long Beach, California. AirTran does the same with its Atlanta hub and is starting to develop a second hub in Baltimore. The difference from the traditional hub-and-spoke airlines is that JetBlue and AirTran do not appear to use their hubs as a source of pricing power. The low-fare, simple-product component of the Southwest model therefore appears to be compatible with a hub-and-spoke route structure.

Attempts to learn from Southwest and adapt to the changes in consumer demand have taken two different forms. Several of the major airlines—American, Delta, Northwest, and US Airways—attempted to maintain a traditional product mix and the traditional hub-and-spoke route structure, while at the same time attempting to improve quality and efficiency performance through improved coordination of the flight departure process. To do this, they sought to understand the relationship component of the Southwest model, and in particular how frontline employees could work more effectively together across functional boundaries. American Airlines will be used to illustrate this first group of airlines. A second group of airlines adopted some version of Southwest's relationship focus and its low-fare product, and sometimes but not always adopted its point-to-point route structure. Continental Lite, the United Shuttle, and JetBlue Airways will be used to illustrate this second group of airlines.

American Airlines

The leadership of American Airlines made several efforts in the 1990s to improve cross-functional coordination of the flight departure process. An IBM study conducted for American in 1991 found that at American, "the departure process was a set of parallel lines that didn't intersect," according to a human resource manager at American. Following that study, station-level experimentation, high-level task forces, and process advisory teams all focused on fixing the awkward handoffs between functional areas and streamlining the flight departure process. At one station, the functional groups involved in departures were placed under common management in an attempt to reduce the departmental boundaries that were believed to restrict coordination. Managers used training sessions and job trading to increase understanding across employee groups. Flight attendants agreed to "tidy" the aircraft on through flights.

These efforts were geared toward improving on-time performance and customer service as well as trying to shorten turnaround times, but not toward imitating the Southwest product. Ever since discussions at

American in the early 1990s about launching a Southwest-like product, which faltered on a disagreement between management and the pilots union about work rules, American management was relatively united in the decision not to imitate the Southwest product. But Southwest's practices were still seen as relevant in certain respects. The vice president of field services explained:

> We view Southwest as a different product. I'm not sure how relevant it is to us. But teamwork is essential in either area. Teamwork is just as essential to us.

Like the other major airlines, American faced the most competition from Southwest in short-haul markets. As shown in Chap. 2, Southwest's ability to turn planes quickly at the gate was a source of competitive advantage in all markets, but particularly in short-haul markets where time on the ground was a larger component of overall costs, relative to time in the air. American chose to withdraw from these routes rather than compete with Southwest, citing high labor costs as the primary reason for its inability to compete. According to a member of American Airlines' top management team:

> American is not competing with Southwest. . . . We are getting out of short haul. Crandall is saying to the unions, reduce my costs and we'll grow again. We'll go back into short haul. The labor contracts are key to getting back those markets. But we are pretty set on that strategy now anyway, even if the contracts did change.

However, American abandoned some of its short-haul markets in a way that allowed the airline to maintain control over them. When American withdrew from its San Jose hub in the face of low-cost competition from Southwest, the company leased its gates to low-cost, new entrant Reno Air and set up a frequent flier partnership with that airline.[5] Reno became a direct competitor of Southwest, in effect acting as a proxy for American Airlines. Midway Airlines, based in Chicago, was another new entrant that formed a partnership with American Airlines. It came back into business 2 years after shutting down, initially flying only between Chicago and LaGuardia. In March 1995 Midway formed a partnership with American as American withdrew from its Raleigh/Durham hub, and began flying routes that American abandoned. In return, Midway was able to reward its passengers with American frequent flier miles. Southwest also began flying those routes. Again, American appeared to be using a low-cost, new entrant to compete as a proxy in short-haul markets. According to a former American Airlines employee:

> Midway was started by a former American manager. . . . American helped put him into business. The pilots are upset about this. But we'll keep having these partnerships unless we get lower costs from the unions.

Exiting short-haul markets was not a sufficient solution, however. Even in its long-haul markets, American needed to improve efficiency. By 1994 Crandall estimated that American Airlines faced low-fare competition in nearly 40 percent of its domestic markets.[6] American's hubs enabled the company to generate up to 20 percent more revenue per plane than a comparable point-to-point flight.[7] This revenue advantage, however, was lost through high labor costs and low productivity, said a company spokesperson. American tried to address these costs by seeking to reduce wages through negotiations with its unions and through outsourcing airport functions to lower-paid employees. In early 1995, American contracted out noncore customer service functions in the 30 largest stations, and all customer service functions in the other stations. The noncore functions included "baggage service, parcel service, and the customer service reps out in front of the counter," said the Los Angeles customer service manager. "We will outsource this work, and we won't hire new ones. The company doesn't want to hire full-time permanent employees."

Improvements to the flight departure process offered an alternative way to compete—by raising productivity rather than by cutting wages or outsourcing work. Yet the multitude of experiments and efforts to improve the departure process at American did not lead to the implementation of lasting solutions. According to a human resources manager at American:

> Many efforts have been made, but parallel rather than building on each other. . . . Studies are done, with findings and recommendations, but nothing happens. Operational issues don't become strategic issues, unlike at Southwest. Everybody has concerns about the departure process, but it never gets anywhere.

For example, there was an attempt to form flight departure teams, in which the pilot and the gate agent would decide together when it was time to depart, with the joint discretion to hold the flight for additional passengers, baggage, or cargo (see Chap. 11). However, pilots were limited in their ability to work as part of a team with other employee groups. Rather than deciding in conjunction with the other employee groups, pilots reportedly insisted on being the first among equals. According to the chief pilot and vice president of flight operations:

> There are real problems with the way that program is working right now. The pilot thinks he is in total control and that the ground workers don't know as much. The gate agents are getting around the pilots by cheating, saying they already got approval from the pilots when they didn't.

The executive vice president of operations suggested that:

> The performance is dismal. Dismal. We are doing the customers a disservice. The lesson is that captains without the right knowledge base cannot make decisions properly.

Pilots were limited in the decisions they could make, according to these managers, because they did not understand the perspectives of the other groups well enough to make the relevant trade-offs. The initiative was considered a failure and dropped.

In 1995 it appeared that a new approach would be adopted at American Airlines. After Don Carty replaced Robert Crandall as the CEO of American Airlines, a new set of leaders appeared to have a clear strategy for operational improvements in the flight departure process. An executive vice president explained American's new objectives:

> We want an environment that would foster improved communication and more productivity. Maybe cross-functional coordination is the way to get that productivity. We're not thinking so much about reducing turnaround time, but we do want to know how to use fewer people and still get good results. We are interested in process-related productivity benefits. . . . Speeding turnaround time isn't one of our main objectives. Until we change the scheduling philosophy, we are constrained in reducing ground time. With our long-haul route system, we need the hub-and-spoke so there are limits to how much we can reduce turnaround time. . . .

But don't get me wrong, speed is important. Say our average time is 40 minutes. If we could work on getting all turns down to our shortest—say 30 to 35 minutes—just taking off that 5 minutes could tighten up the entire complex, and give expedited service for the customer. And it would improve aircraft utilization.

To achieve better coordination of flight departures and the efficiency gains associated with it, however, American would have to reconsider its organizational practices and how they could better support relationships among frontline employees.

In sum, American's strategy for responding to changed consumer demand was threefold—cut labor costs through outsourcing and contract renegotiation, withdraw from short-haul markets and compete instead through partnerships with smaller, low-cost carriers, and improve the efficiency of the flight departure process through improved cross-functional coordination. In this strategy, however, relationships were left fundamentally untransformed, due to the sporadic, disconnected nature of the efforts to improve flight departure performance and due to the lack of support from American's organizational practices. For example, trying to get pilots to engage in teamwork with the ground crews around flight departures was virtually impossible, given that American was still hiring and training its pilots to exhibit a "command personality" (see Chap. 7). In addition, American was simultaneously attempting to reduce costs through outsourcing jobs and farming out its short-haul flights, undermining relationships with its employee unions. Worst of all, as we saw in Chap. 5, Crandall's leadership and attempts to influence employees through fear of his "Transition Plan" left a legacy of distrust that new leaders had to invest considerable time and effort to overcome.

Continental Lite

Continental Airlines was also concerned about its inability to compete in short-haul markets. Led by then-CEO Bob Ferguson, Continental explored the Southwest model. According to a Continental customer service manager, these plans went so far as to consider purchasing Southwest. With the help of two Southwest Airlines marketing veterans, Don Valentine and Sam Coates, and the flexible work rules achieved in the 1980s when Frank Lorenzo abrogated Continental's union contracts, Continental was expected to have the best chance of any of the major carriers to emulate the Southwest model. Herb Kelleher, Southwest Airlines' CEO, said that relative to other major carriers, "Continental has a lot more latitude to attempt it."[8]

Continental's "airline within an airline"—Continental Lite—began to fly in October 1993, offering no-frills, high frequency point-to-point service at low fares. In March 1994, Continental Lite expanded to include 62 percent of Continental's flights. Continental Lite offered low fares, made possible by turnaround times of 20 minutes, down from Continental's usual 50-minute turnaround. The faster turnarounds were achieved in part through improved coordination. The stated goal was to use new work practices to speed turnarounds throughout Continental's operations. "It's supposed to infect the whole bloody company," said one of Continental Lite's leaders.[9]

By fall 1994, Continental Lite got its employee productivity and aircraft utilization to target levels in most cities. The implementation appeared to be successful in some sites based on the levels of communication and relationships measured in an employee survey, and based on Continental's success in getting the planes turned in less than 20 minutes. But quality suffered seriously. "On-time performance dropped precipitously and customer complaints—the old and persistent Continental bugaboo—rose."[10] These performance problems, along with an inability to raise revenues to a sustainable level, inspired doubt by some industry observers that the experiment could work.

The problems identified under the new leadership of CEO Gordon Bethune in the fall of 1994 included both the lack of a suitable fleet and a lack of the critical relationships needed to make the schedule work. Bethune explained:

> One of our other problems is to get buy-in across departments. If you're late, is it the guy who carries out the schedule or the guy who writes the schedule? [We have to stop writing schedules] that we can't meet. It's called buy-in. You can't operate without it.

In addition, the company's maintenance assets were still fundamentally configured for a hub-and-spoke operation, in which aircraft depart from and return to hubs, allowing maintenance to be centralized in the hubs. In Lite's point-to-point operation, aircraft were scheduled to go from small city to small city in a linear fashion, creating severe logistical problems when breakdowns occurred. This was construed alternatively as a failure of the maintenance department, and as a failure at the strategic level to put resources where they were needed to operate a non-hubbed route structure.

A fourth problem was the choice of markets. Many of the point-to-point routes that were not linked to Continental's hubs on either end were doing poorly. The route selections had been made without adequate attention to customer demand. A Continental station manager explained:

> The difficulty on the marketing side is that we took 10 years of Southwest data and did regressions. We said if we do x we'll get y. We figured if we drop fares this much, we'd get this much traffic. But we didn't factor in the traffic potential of the individual city pairs.

On top of this, Continental encountered resistance to Lite by its business customers, members of the Elite and OnePass programs, because of the loss of the amenities they had come to expect. Station employees noticed this problem early on in the experiment. Boston's customer service manager explained:

> If you take something away, it takes a little getting used to. Our marketing department monitors this very carefully. We board first class last in Lite, not first. There is no preboarding drink. There is not the wonderful little amenity of watching everyone board while you have a drink. We have a brochure to explain these policies. We put it in a positive light, saying that you will have more time in the station to make those last-minute calls. We say you won't have to sit there and have everyone crowd past you. There will be no first-class meal, but there is a complimentary drink.

To accommodate customer expectations, station personnel bent the rules of Lite. The quick turns were "very unrealistic," according to a Boston customer service supervisor:

> You can't throw a person into a seat. You can cajole, announce, suggest. We are not supposed to, but we do a courtesy boarding for our OnePass members any time they want. We can't stop that. It's part of our culture. One thing I couldn't understand, couldn't express. With short-haul strategy, you need a

short-haul culture. There should be no courtesy boarding. But we still did it. We wouldn't hurry. BusinessFirst people loved it. But it didn't jive with Lite.

For the most part, employees did follow Lite procedures, and as a result, they believed, business travel on Continental declined.[11] The OnePass frequent flier program fell from number one in the industry to number five.

Throughout the fall of 1994, Bethune and his new leadership worked to solve these problems. According to Bethune:

> We have recovered significantly operationally. We're learning how to run a different kind of system. We've put pilots where they need to be. We've put mechanics and parts where the airplanes are. We have recovered from the lack of organization in the implementation of the strategic plan.[12]

Bethune estimated that 20 percent of Continental Lite's routes did not work, primarily the routes that were designed to avoid the hubs, and began to cut service on them. Bethune set up a cross-functional scheduling team to achieve improved integration between scheduling and operations.[13] And to adjust to declining numbers of business passengers, a plan was announced to reduce the number of BusinessFirst seats from 19 to 10 percent by May 1995 and increase the number of coach seats.[14]

In January 1995, the changes accelerated as Continental began to reposition itself once again as a hub-and-spoke carrier. Bethune estimated that it was 32 percent of Lite's routes that didn't work, rather than just 20 percent, and started to cut all nonhub routes. The role of Continental Lite was reconceived as "the short-haul anchor to Continental's hub operations, providing substantial feed to long-haul operations,"[15] rather than an innovative new stand-alone product. Fares were increased $20 to $40 on most Lite routes, setting off a round of fare increases throughout the industry. Bethune reversed the strategy on Elite and OnePass travelers by restoring many of their privileges and meeting personally with them at his home to make amends. Don Valentine left the company at the end of the month still calling the Lite strategy a success. In the March 1995 schedule, however, the route structure reverted completely back to hub-and-spoke. The Cleveland station manager explained:

> We went back to the old way March 1. The load factor changed six percentage points right away. Better connects. Reliability is way up. It's very simple

to explain—it's the linear [point-to-point] flying pattern we implemented with Continental Lite [that didn't work]. Very simple.

Continental had learned that the Southwest model in its entirety "is a completely different way of running an airline,"[16] and that neither the low-fare product nor the point-to-point route structure made sense for Continental to adopt at that time. But the relationship component of the Southwest model was still relevant to Continental, Bethune decided, and he continued to build this component through the remainder of the 1990s and into the early 2000s. In particular, improved cross-functional coordination of the flight departure process that was learned during the Continental Lite experiment continued to be relevant, even while selling the traditional high-fare product and while using the hub-and-spoke route structure. Bethune also worked hard during this period to build strong relationships between management and frontline workers, taking a nonadversarial approach to union organizing efforts and appearing to overcome a history of adversarial union/management relationships, as described in Chap. 13.

In some respects, Continental learned the most important lessons from the Southwest model. Still, Continental's organizational practices were not consistently supportive of relationships among frontline employees. In addition, with the growing demand for low-fare air travel in the late 1990s and early 2000s, Continental's return to the high-fare approach put it in a tight position, along with the other high-fare airlines.

The United Shuttle

The United Shuttle was designed to imitate the Southwest model on United Airline's short-haul routes, focusing on quick turnarounds for high aircraft utilization, and trying to build the cross-functional teamwork to make these quick turnarounds possible. The Shuttle was United's response to a worrisome Southwest incursion into United's California markets. In October 1994, United began Shuttle operations in California markets where it had steadily been losing market share to Southwest.[17] *Air Transport World* reported:

> United Airlines has launched its low-cost, high-frequency Shuttle by United service with initial flights to eight city pairs in a move aimed at regaining critical West Coast market share during a head-to-head competition from South-

west Airlines. Aggressive competition from carriers such as Southwest has cut sharply into United's regional profits in recent years and forced the carrier to cut back on routes where it could not directly compete with low-cost airlines.[18]

The establishment of this quick-turnaround operation was a key part of United's July 1994 employee buyout agreement. After having proposed to abandon unprofitable short routes, much as American did in Spring 1993:

> [CEO Steven] Wolf made clear that unless the unions come around, United would farm out the short haul routes. "It's not a management decision," he said. "It's a marketplace decision."[19]

United would contract out its short-haul routes to a lower-cost airline, said Wolf, much as American had done, and that airline would feed United's long-haul routes, unless the three major unions were willing and able to deliver productivity increases of about 10 percent.

> United's pilots asserted that their contract barred the airline from [spinning off a smaller airline to compete with Southwest on short flights], and suggested that they might stage a strike if it pursued such a venture. Subsequently, United's largest unions decided to try to gain control of the company.[20]

In the final agreement there was a provision for up to 125 of United's aircraft to be dedicated to the Shuttle by 1998.[21] Although this near-conflict with the pilots seemed an inauspicious way to start a new competitive venture, some United managers, including the manager of the Los Angeles station where the Shuttle was first launched, took a more hopeful perspective:

> The timing was terrific. With the industry changing, employees wanted a voice. The ESOP gave us an opportunity.

Like Continental Lite, United's "airline within an airline" was modeled after Southwest in some important respects. Practices were implemented to support cross-functional coordination and were intended over time to influence operations throughout the whole company. Soon after the Shuttle began operation, CEO Gerald Greenwald said in a speech:

Shuttle by United will be a catalyst for change. . . . We'll take the best of United and put it to work with our Shuttle—and what we learn from the Shuttle, we'll channel back, to change the way the rest of the company does business.[22]

Operationally, the challenge was to figure out how to reduce turn times to 20 minutes while still retaining some of United's traditional amenities. The Los Angeles station manager described the thought process:

If we could get to the goal and still have seat assignments [for passengers], it would be win/win. Five or six of us worked on this. We went through count-less variations of how to board quickly. The solution was to board window seats, then middle, then the aisle. The solution for assigned seats was to give assigned seats at the gate, after checking in.

From here, the innovations were made by "max mix" teams—teams made of up employees and managers from diverse functional groups. "This is the cornerstone of the Shuttle," said Jim Hardigan, regional vice president of ground handling for the West Coast and leader of Shuttle development in the early stages:

From that point, I acted as the facilitator. We got 150 people together and said, write the playbook. We wanted it done by people who do the job level of detail. We really let them get into it. Because they were cross-functional, they came up with a playbook that was working right from the get go.

The designers of the United Shuttle attempted to learn from South-west, but selectively. The Los Angeles station manager explained:

We like a lot of what Southwest does. But our goal is not to be Southwest. We started by asking, what is our customer base? What would they like?

Even beyond the design phase, there was active learning from South-west, especially where the Shuttle and Southwest operated in the same airports. According to a Shuttle supervisor:

We're curious. We've been mostly evaluating their boarding process and uniforms. Timing their turns.

At the beginning, the United Shuttle achieved high levels of coordination among frontline employee groups, levels that were nearly as high as those found at Southwest Airlines. In a study conducted soon after the Shuttle was launched, turnaround time and staffing productivity were near those of Southwest Airlines, and service quality numbers were significantly above the rest of United (results reported in Chap. 3). However, much of that success was due to the initial enthusiasm and goodwill around the design of the Shuttle and the employee buyout of the airline. That enthusiasm at the United Shuttle was not sustained by organizational practices designed to support relationships among frontline employees and between management and frontline employees.

Aside from its Shuttle operation, United maintained the traditional hub-and-spoke strategy of gaining a revenue advantage through its domination of key hubs, and contracting out the uneconomical short-haul routes to regional partners. Like American Airlines, however, United also tried to reduce costs in its hub operations by reducing turnaround times and staffing levels where possible. Like Continental, United did this by attempting to leverage the lessons learned from its quick-turn operation into the rest of the organization.

At its peak, the Shuttle served 22 cities and offered 469 flights per day. However, the United Shuttle never expanded beyond the western United States. Finally, 7 years after its founding, when the September 2001 terrorist attacks depressed consumer demand, United announced that it would discontinue Shuttle flights altogether on October 31, 2001.[23] Still, there are ongoing attempts at United Airlines, particularly in the form of cross-functional problem-solving teams (see Chap. 7), to leverage the best lessons of the Shuttle throughout the United system. These efforts are being overshadowed, however, by difficult labor relations at United, and by the unmet expectations associated with the employee buyout.

JetBlue Airways[24]

New entrants—such as Morris, ValuJet, Reno, the new Midway, and JetBlue—imitated various aspects of the Southwest model in an effort to take short-haul routes from the major airlines. Since JetBlue was expected to have the best chance relative to other new entrants of capturing the best of the Southwest model, we focus on JetBlue in this chapter. Like Southwest, JetBlue offers a relatively simple product, with little meal service, at relatively low fares. However, JetBlue also distinguishes itself from Southwest by offering reserved seating, leather seats, and television at every seat, and it has a more traditional hub-and-spoke route structure and a more traditional mix of long- and short-haul flights.

JetBlue Airways entered the industry later than the other new entrants and was the best-funded start-up in U.S. aviation history, founded in early 1999 with an initial capitalization of $130 million and with several former members of Southwest's top management team. JetBlue founder David Neeleman had gotten his start in the airline business in 1984 when he partnered with June and Mitch Morris to run Morris Air. After joining Morris Air's management team, Neeleman raised $20 million in venture capital, and in just over one year increased the value of Morris Air from approximately $59 million to $130 million. Herb Kelleher, former CEO of Southwest Airlines, watched the growth of Morris Air and its route network centered in Salt Lake City, Utah, and decided to make an acquisition. Southwest had always prided itself on growing from within at a steady rate of 10 to 15 percent per year. But Morris Air was so similar to Southwest, by design, that Kelleher believed the merger would be a success.

Neeleman and the Morris family sold Morris Air to Southwest Airlines in 1993, and Neeleman joined Southwest's top management team as an executive vice president. Rumors abounded within the company that Neeleman was slated to be Kelleher's successor. That, along with Neeleman's aggressive, restless personality, always seeking to innovate, reportedly created tension in Southwest's top management team. Ann Rhoades, as the executive vice president of people for Southwest Airlines at the time, was given the task of letting Neeleman go in 1994. According to Rhoades:

> David . . . was ahead of Southwest in technology. He initiated the e-ticket at Southwest. But he didn't fit the culture.

Though disappointed, Neeleman did not drop out of the industry. Having signed a 5-year noncompete agreement with Southwest as part of the Morris Air sale, he turned to developing a new reservations system called Open Skies (sold to Hewlett-Packard in October 1998). Neeleman then went on to work as a consultant to a Canadian low-fare start-up carrier, WestJet.

In 1998, when the noncompete agreement with Southwest Airlines ran out, Neeleman decided to capitalize on his Morris Air, Open Skies, and WestJet successes to develop a new start-up airline. He wanted to follow the successful example of Southwest, stimulating demand in underserved markets with low fares, enabled by the highly productive use of employees and aircraft. To help emulate the Southwest model, Neeleman hired two former Southwest Airlines executives, John Owens, the treasurer of Southwest Airlines for 14 years, as his chief financial officer, and Ann Rhoades, the head of Southwest's People Department for 6 years, as his executive vice president of human resources.

Neeleman wanted to learn from the Southwest model, but he also felt he could improve it. His new airline would improve the passenger experience with technology, and would use technology to increase employee and aircraft productivity even beyond the record levels achieved by Southwest. Neeleman illustrated his idea for a new type of airline by describing his experience with his local dry cleaners. "I hate long lines," he said. "When you go to the dry cleaners, why can't they already have your credit card number so all you do is pick up your clothes without having to stand in line?" While at Southwest, he noticed that in spite of the emphasis on efficiency, passengers would have to stand in as many as three lines; one to check bags, another to get a boarding pass, and again to get in the boarding queue to avoid being stuck in a middle seat.

Based on his earlier industry experience, Neeleman had several ideas about how to start a new airline that would capitalize on technology and make the customer experience better than existing offerings. First, he believed that a start-up needed to be well capitalized:

> A number of airline start-ups did many things correctly but were not adequately capitalized. There's nothing worse than running a business and scraping for capital. I decided that I wouldn't do another start-up without enough funding. With an airline, there are so many moving parts that it's important to have enough capital.

Neeleman wanted to set up an airline that would leverage technology for safety and efficiency and with a commitment to people. In describing his approach, Neeleman said:

> We're a new kind of low-fare airline, with deep pockets, new planes, leather seats with more legroom, great people, and innovative thinking. With our

friendly service and hassle-free technology, we're going to bring humanity back to air travel.

The strategy was to use new airplanes, offer great personal service, and create a state-of-the-art revenue management system and a single class of service with fares averaging 65 percent less than the competition. In doing this, all seats would be assigned, all travel would be ticketless, there would be no discount seats, and all fares would be one-way with a Saturday night stay over never required. JetBlue would strive to be truly customer-friendly, with computer terminals that could be rotated to show the customer what the agent was looking at, giving a $159 voucher whenever a flight was delayed for more than 4 hours for reasons other than weather or air traffic, and giving a $25 voucher for misplaced bags. Like Southwest, JetBlue's target market was "people who aren't going to travel, people who are disgusted with their current choices, people who would drive, or people who wouldn't go at all."

Consistent with the Southwest model, Neeleman planned to use a single aircraft type. Given his experience with Morris Air and Southwest, he felt that the obvious choice was the Boeing 737, made famous as the only aircraft Southwest Airlines would fly. In the end, however, JetBlue entered into a contract to purchase Airbus A320s instead of Boeing 737s, giving them a seat capacity of 165 seats per plane rather than the 137 seats offered by the Boeing 737.

JetBlue's head of flight operations, Al Spain, focused some of his early efforts on streamlining the flight departure process, with the goal of achieving "the perfect 30-minute turnaround." One of his major innovations was the use of the pilot as the boundary spanner in the flight departure process. Instead of having one operations agent assigned to lead each flight departure, as we saw at Southwest (see Chap. 10), the pilot played that role at JetBlue. Armed with a laptop in the cockpit, JetBlue's pilots gathered the needed information from each function involved in the flight departure and made final decisions regarding weight and balance. It was a highly innovative solution to the coordination challenge. Like Southwest, JetBlue recognized the importance of having a boundary spanner role and staffing it well; that is, one boundary spanner exclusively dedicated to each flight departure. Unlike Southwest, however, JetBlue gave this central role to the pilot rather than the operations agent.

JetBlue also gave a great deal of attention to building relationships by focusing on shared values. For Ann Rhoades, executive vice president of human resources, organizing the airline around values was the highest priority:

> Values were central at Southwest Airlines, but they just happened. I think it's better to decide up front what they will be.

In an early top-management retreat, five values were chosen as central: Safety, Caring, Integrity, Fun, and Passion. New employees were carefully hired and trained with respect to these values, though there appeared to be less focus on hiring and training employees for relational competence than we saw at Southwest (see Chap. 7).

JetBlue deliberately departed from other organizational features of the Southwest model, most notably in its approach to unionization. According to Rhoades:

> We are not like Southwest Airlines in this respect. Herb [Kelleher] invited the unions in from day one. We prefer to operate without unions. If I have the opportunity to be a leader without work rules, I strongly prefer that. Not having a union creates a team environment. As long as we are working together well, we won't need unions.

Dave Barger, chief operating officer, took a similar position:

> We need to daily create the positive environment to keep this place union-free. We don't need unions. If our people think we need unions, boy have we failed.

Similar to Southwest, JetBlue's intent was to offer pay and benefit packages that met the industry standard. However, JetBlue designed the flight attendant position to encourage people to stay short-term rather than long-term in the job, offering no pay increases associated with seniority. According to Rhoades:

> We believe in taking care of people. But we do not believe in staying there forever. We believe firmly that some jobs are short term. We've designed the flight attendant job to be from 1 to 5 years in duration.

After just 6 months of operation, JetBlue turned in its first monthly operating and net profit. JetBlue's founders had built an airline with 48 flights per day to 9 of the 44 cities initially listed in JetBlue's FAA filing as target destinations. The company had carried over 500,000 passengers. In doing this JetBlue had compiled an on-time record of 80 percent, compared to 74 percent for the 10 largest U.S. airlines, and had received, according to Department of Transportation accounts, only 0.6 complaints per 100,000 passengers, compared to an average of 2.99 for their major competitors. Dave Barger commented:

> The operational performance figures would be very impressive for an established airline, but they are spectacular for an airline that began flying just over 7 months ago, especially considering the difficult weather conditions experienced this summer along the East Coast.

All in all, things were going well on the operational side, although in the spring of 2002 those numbers declined somewhat. JetBlue managers decided to give up the attempt to do a 30-minute turnaround, and instead adopted a turnaround time that ranged from 35 to 55 minutes, depending on the nature of the flight. JetBlue's turnaround times were therefore 35 to 55 minutes for a 165-seat aircraft, while Southwest's turnaround times were 20 to 30 minutes for a 137-seat aircraft. In effect, JetBlue's turnaround times were 75 to 83 percent longer than Southwest's, even though its aircraft seating capacity was only 20 percent greater.

In the wake of the September 11 terrorist attacks, JetBlue was one of the U.S. airlines that did not lay off any employees, despite the dramatic decline in passenger demand that followed. This move suggested that JetBlue shares Southwest's concern with maintaining strong relationships. JetBlue also has the same conservative financial practices as Southwest, enabling it to avoid layoffs and maintain relationships through good times and bad, as we will see in the next chapter. At the operational level, JetBlue like Southwest recognizes the need for a boundary spanner to play a central role in coordinating each flight departure, helping to foster communication and relationships across functional boundaries.

However, other organizational practices that we see at Southwest have not yet evolved at JetBlue. JetBlue's focus on relationships thus far has been primarily on relationships between management and frontline employees, neglecting somewhat the relationships among frontline employees that are central to achieving quality and efficiency performance at Southwest Airlines. In addition, JetBlue is seeking to build relationships while avoiding union representation, unlike Southwest. The belief that the absence of unions in and of itself can create a team environment is a risky one, and one that runs counter to the Southwest experience as outlined in Chap. 13. We have seen that unions who are actively engaged in a partnership with management can bolster teamwork. JetBlue runs the risk of having adversarial relationships with its future unions, should its employees decide at some point that they wish to be organized, simply because of its early position regarding union avoidance.

Summing Up

This book has argued throughout that relationships of shared goals, shared knowledge, and mutual respect are a source of competitive advantage that has enabled Southwest to change the terms of competition in the airline industry. We have now seen that other airlines have tried to learn from the relationship component of Southwest's model, whether as part of the traditional hub-and-spoke model (American), as part of an "airline within an airline" (Continental and the United Shuttle), or as a new entrant (JetBlue). The question, however, is whether these efforts have been sufficiently coherent and consistent to transform key working relationships, or whether they are sporadic, separate efforts that leave relationships fundamentally untransformed.

As noted above, relationships at American Airlines were left fundamentally untransformed, as a result of the sporadic, disconnected nature of the efforts to improve the flight departure process and the lack of support from American's organizational practices. For example, trying to get pilots to engage in teamwork with the ground crews about flight departures was virtually impossible, given that American was still hiring and training its pilots to exhibit a "command personality." In addition, American was attempting at the same time to reduce costs through outsourcing jobs and farming out its short-haul flights to lower-cost airlines, undermining relationships with its unions. Worst of all, Crandall's leadership and attempts to influence employees through fear of his "Transition Plan" left a legacy of distrust that American's current leaders are still working hard to overcome.

At the United Shuttle, the early evidence was that high levels of cross-functional coordination had been achieved, with outstanding operational results. However, much of that success was due to the initial enthusiasm and goodwill around the design of the Shuttle and the employee buyout of the airline. That enthusiasm at the United Shuttle was not sustained by the adoption of a set of organizational practices designed to support relationships among frontline employees and between management and frontline employees. Still, there are some ongoing attempts at United Airlines, particularly in the form of cross-functional problem-solving teams (see Chap. 5), to leverage the best lessons of the Shuttle throughout the United system. These efforts are being overshadowed, unfortunately, by difficult labor relations at United and by the unmet expectations associated with the 1994 employee buyout.

Continental Lite was also abandoned after a hopeful start. In abandoning Continental Lite, however, Continental did not throw out the baby with the bath water. Bethune recognized the value of building the relationship component of the Southwest model, even while reverting to a high-fare product and the hub-and-spoke route structure. Since his arrival at Continental, Bethune has worked hard to build trusting relationships with employees and their unions. However, Continental's efforts to build relationships among employees seem for the present time to rest largely on monetary incentives for on-time performance, whose long-term effects remain to be proven. Other supporting practices are not yet in place.

JetBlue appears promising in many respects. Not only has JetBlue been the most highly capitalized start-up in the history of the industry to date, it also began with the help of three former members of Southwest's top management team. It has developed a low-fare product with a few additional amenities that customers seem to appreciate. Some of Southwest's relationship focus is apparent at JetBlue, with the creation of a boundary spanner (in this case, the pilot) to coordinate flight departures and a concern with values in the hiring process. Yet several key ingredients of Southwest's model have been neglected—there has been no attempt to use union representation to foster strong relationships between management and frontline employees, and there is little evidence of Southwest's intense focus on building relationships *among* frontline employees. Indeed, the management team seems to hope that teamwork will thrive simply given the absence of unions. JetBlue therefore risks the sustainability of its early success. After the initial enthusiasm of a start-up organization is replaced by a daily routine, a consistent set of organizational practices is needed to support and sustain strong working relationships.

Thriving under Pressure— Southwest's Response to September 11 and Other Crises

We've always said we'll do whatever we can to take care of our people. So that's what we've tried to do.
>—Director, Office of Financial Analysis, Southwest Airlines

When it gets bad everywhere else, it's good here [at Southwest].
>—Local President, Transport Workers Union

If there ever was a stress test for a good business, this is it.
>—Kevin Murphy, Morgan Stanley Airline Industry Analyst

SOUTHWEST AIRLINES HAS enjoyed a tremendous 31 years of successful operation, marked by a record of consistent profitability in each year other than its first. Perhaps the most impressive characteristic of Southwest is the sheer sustainability of its success, year in and year out. However, the airline industry is changing around Southwest Airlines. Security measures imposed after September 11 have posed a tremendous challenge for Southwest's quick turnaround strategy.[1] Meanwhile, as we saw in

Chap. 16, Southwest's competitors are attempting to copy the Southwest model, trying to respond to the same market forces that have spurred Southwest's own phenomenal growth. Well-funded start-ups like JetBlue are trying to improve on Southwest's low-fare product by adding several amenities that customers seem to appreciate. Other changes are apparent as well. The labor market is being reshaped by a new generation of service workers who expect high rates of pay, but who appear to offer lower levels of commitment. New technologies are available to improve the scheduling of planes and to expedite the travel experience, and the Internet is becoming a central means of ticket sales and distribution. Airlines are expanding the reach of their networks through global alliances. The U.S. government is attempting to improve customer service through regulation. Southwest, as the only consistently profitable major airline in the United States, is in a prime position to fall into the competency trap[2] — the trap that follows from relying on past successes to the point of failing to respond appropriately to new challenges.

This book suggests that Southwest's sustainability in the face of new challenges thus far is due to strong relationships among its employees, managers, unions, and suppliers. Relationships are a primary source of resilience and, if carefully cultivated, can help an organization become stronger rather than weaker in the face of external pressures. We have seen that Southwest carefully nurtures these relationships through its 10 mutually reinforcing organizational practices. An equally important ingredient of Southwest's sustainability, we see in this chapter, is its refusal to take actions that would undermine organizational relationships over the long term, even when short-term pressures seem to demand such actions.

Resilience in the Face of Competition

Southwest is accustomed to competitive threats and has weathered them by relying on the relationships that give the organization its strength. The story of how Southwest responded to a price war from Braniff in its earliest days is legendary.[3] In an attempt to dislodge Southwest from the Dallas/Houston market, Braniff offered a fare that was below its own costs, and even below Southwest's costs. Southwest employees responded to the competitive threat in two ways—first, by lowering its fares to meet Braniff's and asking customers to pay the usual fare if they wanted to help Southwest continue to fly in the Dallas/Houston market.

And second, by figuring out how to turn airlines more quickly at the gate through improved coordination, thus getting higher utilization out of its most costly asset. Thanks to these initiatives, Braniff failed to dislodge Southwest and ultimately failed to remain as a viable presence in the industry. Southwest went on to succeed, continuing to rely on its internal and external relationships as a source of strength and resilience in the face of competitive threats.

Later, Southwest employees experienced considerable anguish as established airlines and new entrants sought to imitate the Southwest model in the mid-1990s. Fare competition from other airlines that were seeking to imitate Southwest took a toll on Southwest's profitability, which dropped 48 percent in the fourth quarter of 1994. The United Shuttle forced fare wars in several of Southwest's West Coast markets, while Continental Lite and US Airways forced fare wars on the East Coast, particularly on Baltimore, Cleveland, and Chicago routes. Lower profits and the fear that Southwest would lose its distinctive basis for continued profitability as others learned to imitate it led to a 54 percent decline in Southwest's stock price from February to December of 1994. According to the Los Angeles station manager:

> The United Shuttle is all that's on our minds right now. We just watched a feature on *48 Hours* about us and the Shuttle. They say the United system is far too rigid to provide good customer service. But our stock started at 30 this year and now it's down to 17.

Through videos sent to their homes and through his annual "Message to the Field," CEO Herb Kelleher emphasized to Southwest employees that they must take the challenge from the United Shuttle very seriously and strengthen their teamwork, because the Shuttle was a challenge to Southwest's existence. "There is so much competition out there that people are really pulling together," said a Southwest customer service supervisor. Because of this employee response, Southwest continued through this stressful time to deliver service in its reliable way, at low fares, and by the third quarter of 1995 was back to its usual level of profitability. After Southwest had held its own in California against competitive threats from the United Shuttle, the company turned its attention to the East Coast, where US Airways' MetroJet and Delta Express were posing similar competitive threats.

By 2002, Southwest faced a different set of competitors. Continental Lite had failed in the mid-1990s, while the United Shuttle and US Airways' MetroJet experiments were terminated in late 2001. Delta Express remained but had reduced its number of flights by 50 percent after September 11, 2001, and by mid-2002 had not yet resumed its growth. However, the emergence of JetBlue Airways as a very well funded start-up with a wealth of experience from Southwest-trained executives appeared to be a potentially daunting challenge for Southwest. Indeed, Herb Kelleher gave JetBlue a vote of confidence soon after it completed its first year of operation, saying "Keep an eye on JetBlue. That could prove to be a successful operation."[4] Other Southwest leaders spoke highly of JetBlue and of its CEO David Neeleman, who had worked for Southwest briefly after Southwest bought Morris Air from him in the mid-1990s. According to Southwest's East Coast Regional Director Matt Hafner:

> We respect JetBlue. And we respect David Neeleman. . . . JetBlue is a force to be reckoned with.

At Southwest's growing hub at Baltimore-Washington International, employees were well aware of the competition facing Southwest, including both JetBlue and low-fare carrier AirTran. However, frontline employees generally expressed a positive attitude with regard to their competition. According to a Baltimore operations supervisor, who had been with Southwest for 5 years:

> It's good for us to have competition. That's when we do our best. We've always had competition. We need it.

Resilience in the Face of Growth

Southwest has been challenged not only by competitive threats, but also by the tremendous growth opportunities that have resulted from its success. Even with Southwest's highly disciplined, self-limited growth rate of 10 to 15 percent per year, inevitably there were bumps in the road. As Southwest grew bigger and more geographically dispersed, things that had once seemed easy required more conscious effort. Colleen Barrett, president and chief operating officer of Southwest, said:

I have been here from day one, and it's almost cyclical. You have to go back in with long-timers, reinforce and remind people. We get a little complacent. We had a company culture here before I knew what it meant. The main goal is to maintain it. But it gets difficult as we grow.

One enormous growth-related challenge, given Southwest's highly selective hiring process, was the challenge of finding frontline staff, particularly at stations where Southwest's local rate of growth was extremely high. In a March 2000 interview, members of Southwest's top management team described these challenges. According to Libby Sartain, then–vice president of people:

We struggle with finding and keeping entry-level people in this labor market. The company has initiated different pay schedules to try to retain people. We compete with retail and food-service businesses. We are trying to sell a career, not a job. The new generation is looking for a quick buck. We are looking for a very different person.

In the late 1990s and early 2000s, Baltimore was clearly Southwest's biggest challenge with regard to staffing turnover. As Southwest had experienced with its Los Angeles operation in the early 1990s, Baltimore's growth was outpacing management's ability to attract and train employees. Southwest's growth in Baltimore came up against staffing shortages given the tight labor markets of the late 1990s, and became a source of concern for top management. According to Jim Wimberly, Southwest's executive vice president of operations:

Baltimore plays an important role in our system, competitively, given its location in the center of the East Coast. We've had a lot of serious discussions internally about how much more Baltimore can take given the facility constraints that we have, and the shortage of employees that we have there. In fact, we deferred some of our growth there last summer because it was just too much hassle to do. It's a customer service issue because we don't want to put our customers through that type of experience in an airport where we can't deliver the type of product that our reputation stands on.[5]

Matt Hafner, regional director, explained the challenge he faced when he became the station manager of Baltimore in 1998:

Our first challenge was stabilizing an understaffed operation—we were 179 short for a staff normally running 500, and we were short 80 on the ramp alone. Baltimore had a really tight labor market, and we were having a lot of problems getting and keeping people. We ended up assigning a lot of mandatory overtime, including some 16-hour days. It took a toll on morale here. Our people were really tired. We got into some bad habits.[6]

According to an operations agent at the Baltimore station, who had been with Southwest for 20 years:

We're still understaffed. We've never been understaffed like this before. Due to the expansion, we were using overtime too much. . . . It makes it tough to get fully staffed.

Baltimore's station manager, Mike Miller, explained the challenge:

We want people to see a long-term career opportunity with us. [But] people coming in to start generally have the worst shifts and they are the lowest-paid individuals. The lack of a long-term vision is the problem. People don't want to start at the bottom. They don't look at the long-term payoff. We have agents here with 20-plus years at Southwest. They have huge retirement funds and are very well off.

Another long-time Southwest employee gave his perspective on Baltimore's staffing challenge.

These are just growing pains. I tell the other [employees]: "you've got to chip in. If you don't work it, it won't be here. We *made* this thing. I'm not going to let you ruin it." I just try to set an example.

As we would expect, given their relationships of shared goals, shared knowledge, and mutual respect, Southwest's longer-term staff appeared to be cushioning the blow of the company's growing pains. Time would soon tell, as the Baltimore station was poised to continue its growth and possibly become Southwest's largest station by 2003, outpacing Phoenix and Las Vegas. Beyond the Baltimore station, growth is a challenge for Southwest more generally. Southwest's growing scale has increased both the importance of strong relationships, and the difficulty of maintaining them.

Response to the Crisis of September 11, 2001[7]

On top of these growing pains, Southwest along with the rest of the airline industry faced the devastating losses brought by the September 11, 2001, terrorist attacks. See Exhibit 17–1 for industrywide declines in passenger traffic following the attacks. According to Kevin Murphy, airline industry analyst for Morgan Stanley, "If there was ever a stress test for a good business, this is it."[8] The day after the attacks, the major airlines were in front of Congress seeking relief in the form of federal assistance. Fifteen billion dollars were immediately allocated to the industry, some in the form of outright grants to cover the loss of operating revenue in the days after the attacks when the industry was shut down by federal order. The rest of the $15 billion allocation was made available in the form of loan guarantees to be allocated according to rules established by the Air Transport Stabilization Board.

Even with this federal assistance, however, the industry was losing millions of dollars on a daily basis because of the slow rate of passenger return. In response to these losses, the major airlines cut their flights by 20 percent and laid off 16 percent of their workforces in the weeks following the attacks. Even though all of the major airlines were devastated about equally in terms of the initial decline in passenger traffic, they did not respond in the same way. In particular, there were differences in the extent of their flight reductions (see Exhibit 17–2) and layoffs (see Exhibit 17–3).

There were also differences in organizational performance, when observed a year later. Stock prices for all major U.S. airlines dropped after September 11, but a year later there were substantial differences in the extent to which individual airline stock prices (Exhibit 17–4) and passenger traffic (Exhibit 17–5) had recovered.

US Airways' Response

US Airways' leaders conducted the highest level of layoffs in the industry, at 24 percent compared to the industry average of 16 percent. Worse, US Airways leaders appeared to take advantage of the September 11 tragedy to accomplish some goals they had not previously been able to accomplish:[9]

> Despite US Airway's huge losses, President Rakesh Gangwal said he is optimistic about the airline's future. Specifically, he said the September 11

Exhibit 17–1 Decline in Revenue Passenger Miles (RPMs) after September 11, 2001

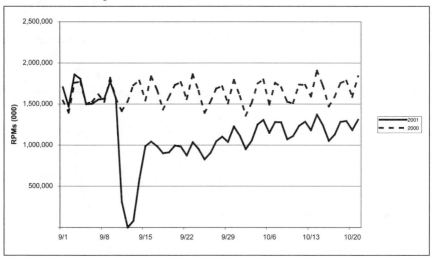

(*Source:* Air Transport Association)

Exhibit 17–2 Flight Reductions after September 11, 2001

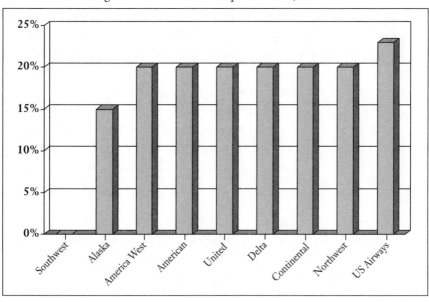

(*Source:* Air Transport Association)

Exhibit 17–3 Employee Layoffs after September 11, 2001*

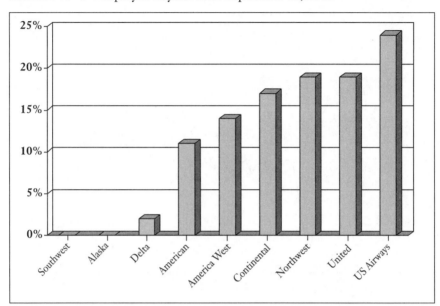

* (Data obtained from layoffs reported in press after September 11, divided by year-end employment for 2000 as reported by Bureau of Transportation Statistics.)

attacks have allowed the airline to restructure and downsize in ways that would have been impossible otherwise. Specifically, the attacks allow the airline to invoke "force majeure" clauses in union contracts and eliminate unprofitable routes. Force majeure is the legal term for an uncontrollable event that releases a party from its contractual obligations.

Gangwal said he expects the changes to be permanent. "I don't want to take advantage of the situation, but we have to do what is right for the company," Gangwal said in a conference call with analysts. "And the events of September 11 have opened certain doors for the company that were pretty much closed before."

Employees responded negatively to this rank opportunism on the part of US Airways' leadership, and their representatives filed a series of grievances against the airline related to its use of the force majeure clause. The head of the pilots' union noted:

> We've been saying all along that management has been using force majeure not as an opportunity to get through a crisis, but to take advantage of a crisis.[10]

Exhibit 17–4 Change in Stock Values from September 10, 2001 to September 10, 2002*

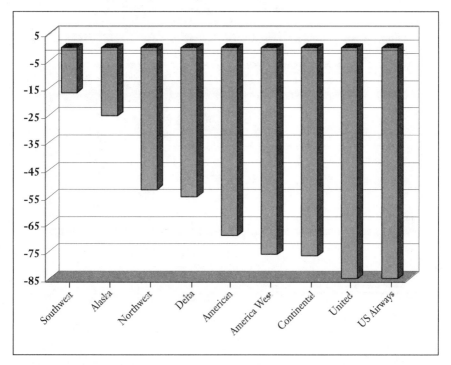

* Percent change in stock price.
(*Source:* Yahoo Financials)

Whether the actions taken by US Airways were legal or not, they are expected to do lasting damage to organizational relationships, as well as to undermine the credibility of its leadership. Indeed, US Airway's leadership was replaced in early 2002 due in part to its loss of credibility with employees throughout the company in its response to the crisis of September 11.

American Airlines' Response

Though less obviously opportunistic, other U.S. airlines attempted to use similar clauses in their labor contracts reqarding national emergencies or extraordinary circumstances to avoid making severance payments, including both American Airlines and Northwest Airlines.[11] According to a spokesperson at American Airlines:[12]

Exhibit 17–5 Change in Revenue Passenger Miles from August 2001 to August 2002

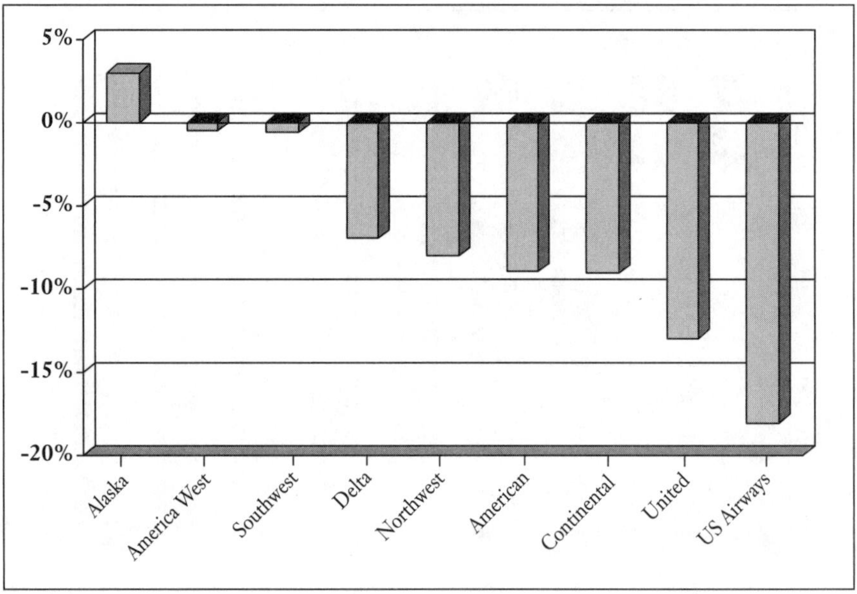

(*Source:* Air Transport World.)

> In the past when we've gone through periods where we're eliminating jobs, we've tried to do it so it'll have as minimal an impact as possible. In this instance, the financial situation is such that we're just not able to do that.

Union leaders were quick to criticize this approach, saying:[13]

> It's outrageous that American would ask the workers to support them on getting this massive federal bailout and then turn around to slap the workers in the face by failing to honor its commitments.

American responded to this criticism by pointing out that:[14]

> The reason for using these provisions is because of the dire financial condition of the industry. We're furloughing 20,000 employees because of the 20 percent reduction in our flight schedule, which of course occurred suddenly. Right now the issue is the survival of the company.

According to American CEO Don Carty:[15]

> The losses we face are truly staggering. They exceed anything we ever imagined at American. Right now, it's survival, not profitability, that is our core challenge.

Carty sought to soften the blow of no severance payments for American's laid-off employees, however, by saying he would personally take no pay for the three remaining months of 2001.

Continental Airlines' Response

Continental Airlines took a different approach in the wake of September 11. Like nearly every other U.S. major airline, Continental announced substantial layoffs—20 percent of its workforce—and in addition it was one of the first airlines to do so. However, Continental conducted these layoffs in a way that demonstrated caring and showed a regard for maintaining critical relationships. Continental's CEO Gordon Bethune announced 2 weeks after the attacks that the organization would stand behind all severance and furlough pay provisions in its labor contracts.[16] In addition, some of the announced layoffs were subsequently translated into voluntary leaves of absence, so that ultimately only 18 percent of Continental's workforce faced layoffs.

Continental had a high debt load due to leveraging decisions made by its previous leaders, so this decision to avoid force majeure arguments and honor all employee contracts was financially speaking a painful one. Some of Continental's payments to holders of aircraft-backed certificates were late in the immediate post-September 11 period, indicating that the airline was indeed experiencing financial hardship. Yet Bethune stuck to his guns, saying it was not proper to break commitments to Continental's employees. "We believe that employees should always be treated with dignity and respect, especially when we are forced to make these tough decisions," said Bethune in September 2001.[17]

Based on subsequent interviews with Continental employees, Bethune's caring approach appears to have lessened the negative impact of the layoffs, allowing Continental to increase its chance of short-term survival without a dramatic negative impact on its longer-term viability.

Southwest Airlines' Response

Southwest had its own unique approach for responding to this crisis. Southwest demonstrated caring by avoiding layoffs altogether, and by couching its decision in terms of "taking care of our people." One would expect that avoiding layoffs in the face of a dramatic decline in demand would jeopardize Southwest's short-term well-being. Maintaining relationships among employees in order to build organizational resilience and long-term prospects for success is one thing, but what of corporate survival? Indeed, the company was reportedly losing "millions of dollars per day"[18] in the weeks following the terrorist attacks. "Clearly we can't continue to do this indefinitely," said Southwest's CEO Jim Parker. Still, he said, "we are willing to suffer some damage, even to our stock price, to protect the jobs of our people."[19] Southwest was apparently willing to suffer these short-term losses in order to achieve longer-term performance.

As a result, while other airlines shed both employees and unprofitable routes, Southwest maintained a steady presence in the wake of the attacks, refusing to lay off its employees. Indeed, Southwest instead saw these difficult times as an opportunity to increase its presence and expand the availability of its product to the flying public. According to one industry observer: "They're doing what they do best, which is to shine in the hours of trouble."[20]

Southwest's no-layoff response to September 11 served to remind its employees of Southwest's tradition of caring for its people. According to the president of the Transport Workers Union local representing Southwest's ramp and operations employees:

> What may have seemed like really big issues a month ago maybe aren't quite the big issues now. . . . When it gets bad everywhere else, it's good here.[21]

Asked about Southwest's efforts to avoid layoffs in the wake of the September 11 attacks, the Director of the Office of Financial Analysis explained:

> It's part of our culture. We've always said we'll do whatever we can to take care of our people. So that's what we've tried to do.

Kelleher explained his philosophy regarding layoffs in early 2001, before the crisis of September 11 hit:[22]

> Nothing kills your company's culture like layoffs. Nobody has ever been furloughed [at Southwest], and that is unprecedented in the airline industry. It's been a huge strength of ours. It's certainly helped us negotiate our union contracts. One of the union leaders—a Teamsters leader—came in to negotiate one time and he said, "We know we don't need to talk with you about job security."
>
> We could have furloughed at various times and been more profitable, but I always thought that was shortsighted. You want to show your people that you value them and you're not going to hurt them just to get a little more money in the short term.
>
> Not furloughing people breeds loyalty. It breeds a sense of security. It breeds a sense of trust. So in bad times you take care of them, and in good times they're thinking, perhaps, "We've never lost our jobs. That's a pretty good reason to stick around."

Layoffs as a Response to Crisis

As a response to a crisis, layoffs are almost always included in the short-term responses of organizations. The trouble is, almost all downsizing is interpreted as unfair, personally harmful, and a violation of an implied work covenant.[23] Consequently, organizational resilience is sapped, and the organization becomes weaker over time, jeopardizing the organization's longer-term success. This scenario represents a dilemma for organizations, in which measures taken for short-term survival appear to undermine the conditions for longer-term success.

However, Southwest's philosophy regarding layoffs is not a popular one in the U.S. business culture of today. As *BusinessWeek* noted:

> Such words would likely make famous job-slashers like Jack Welch and Al Dunlap cringe. But Southwest is a member of a tiny fraternity of contrarian companies that refuse, at least for now, to lay off. . . . In the aftermath of a national tragedy that economists say makes a recession and thousands of additional job cuts inevitable, their stances seem almost noble, an old-fashioned antidote to the make-the-numbers-or-else ethos pervading Corporate America.[24]

The dominant culture, exemplified by GE's former CEO Jack Welch, favors hard-headed job slashing to protect the interests of the shareholder at all costs. The relationship between organizations and their employees is increasingly treated as a contingent one. In the words of human resource scholar Peter Cappelli:

> The old employment system of secure, lifetime jobs with predictable advancement and stable pay is dead. What killed it were changes in the way firms operate that brought markets inside the organization. . . . systematically undermining the complex system of human resource practices that made long-term careers the staple of corporate life.[25]

If Cappelli is right, then no wonder *BusinessWeek* looks at Southwest's no-layoff policy as "almost noble, an old-fashioned antidote to the make-the-numbers-or-else ethos pervading Corporate America." However, Cappelli also observed based on extensive interviews that employers who moved toward a more contingent approach to employment "were shocked by the collapse of employee morale" and often ended up backpedaling to regain the employee commitment without which it was difficult to operate. Similarly, the same *BusinessWeek* article points out some practical benefits of a no-layoff approach, namely, "fierce loyalty, higher productivity, and the innovation needed to enable them to snap back once the economy recovers."[26]

Consistent with these arguments, a simple rank correlation shows that by June 2002, the extent of an airline's September 11 layoffs negatively predicted recovery of its passenger traffic with 99 percent certainty, and negatively predicted recovery of its stock price with 95 percent certainty.[27]

The Role of Financial Reserves

Of course, to make the decision to forgo layoffs, Southwest had to be financially able to sustain short-term losses. This ability was not due to accident or good fortune. Rather it was due to Southwest's long-standing policy of maintaining low debt levels and relatively high levels of cash on hand. As people throughout the company have repeatedly pointed out over the years, "At Southwest, we manage in good times as though we were in bad times." Kelleher explained Southwest's financial policy and how it has enable Southwest to thrive during past downturns:

> Most people think of us as this flamboyant airline, but we're really very conservative from the fiscal standpoint. We have the best balance sheet in the industry. We've always made sure that we never overreached ourselves. We never got dangerously in debt, and never let costs get out of hand. And that gave us a real edge during [the Gulf War crisis of 1990 to 1994].[28]

Southwest's financial reserves are not simply coincidental to this story. At Southwest, the maintenance of financial reserves is seen as integral to the organization's ability to maintain and even strengthen its relationships in the face of crises. Organizations with insufficient financial reserves may be forced to break their commitments with employees and customers when faced with crisis. Exhibits 17–6 and 17–7 show cash on hand and debt–equity ratios at the major U.S. airlines prior to September 11. Organizations with plentiful financial reserves in the form of low debt levels are better positioned to bolster their relationships by maintaining commitments to employees and other stakeholders in times of crisis. Indeed, a simple rank correlation analysis of these data shows that prior cash levels of the airlines did not predict the extent of their layoffs, but their debt–equity ratios predicted the extent of their layoffs with 99 percent certainty.

It appeared that Gordon Bethune of Continental Airlines would have liked very much to suffer the short-term losses after September 11 without resorting to employee layoffs. However, as Bethune had pointed out in 1998, the airline, for all its improvement, was not yet out of the financial woods.[29] In addition to the labor relations legacy of Frank Lorenzo, Bethune has had to overcome the legacy of Continental's multiple bankruptcies, which drained the airline financially and left it with high levels of debt.

Southwest protects its financial reserves by sticking to its policy of gradual steady growth, despite the fact that there is sufficient demand for Southwest's service to permit a far-faster rate of growth. According to John Denison, Southwest's former executive vice president of corporate services:

> We promise the marketplace 10 percent growth, but we are only going to grow as fast as we can manage. Sometimes we have grown faster strategically.

Exhibit 17–6 Days of Cash on Hand Preceding September 11, 2001

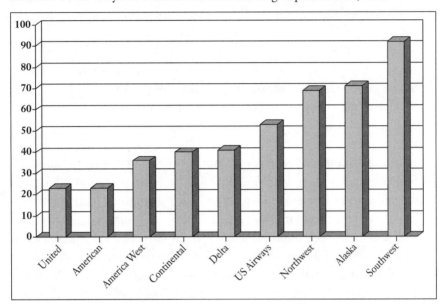

* (*Sources: Aviation Week & Space Technology* and Merrill Lynch.)

We acquired Morris Air in 1994 at the right time to compete. But we try to maintain the balance sheet. It is no accident that we are the only single-A-rated company in the industry.

Indeed, Southwest's leaders have often had to maintain their conservative financial policies in the face of strong pressures from Wall Street to grow faster. According to Matt Hafner, one of Southwest's regional directors:

It is nothing new with Southwest. The "experts" always think we need to expand at a more rapid pace. What these so-called experts express is their desire for Southwest to jump at opportunities at a more rapid clip. Apparently growth excites investors. [But] nobody is pushing us. That could never happen.

The business press reported recently that Southwest's "conservative approach has been criticized by Wall Street analysts, who have argued that the airline should use its extra cash to make acquisitions or buy back stock. Goldman Sachs Airline Analyst Glenn Engel actually calls the bal-

Exhibit 17–7 Debt–Equity Ratios Preceding September 11, 2001

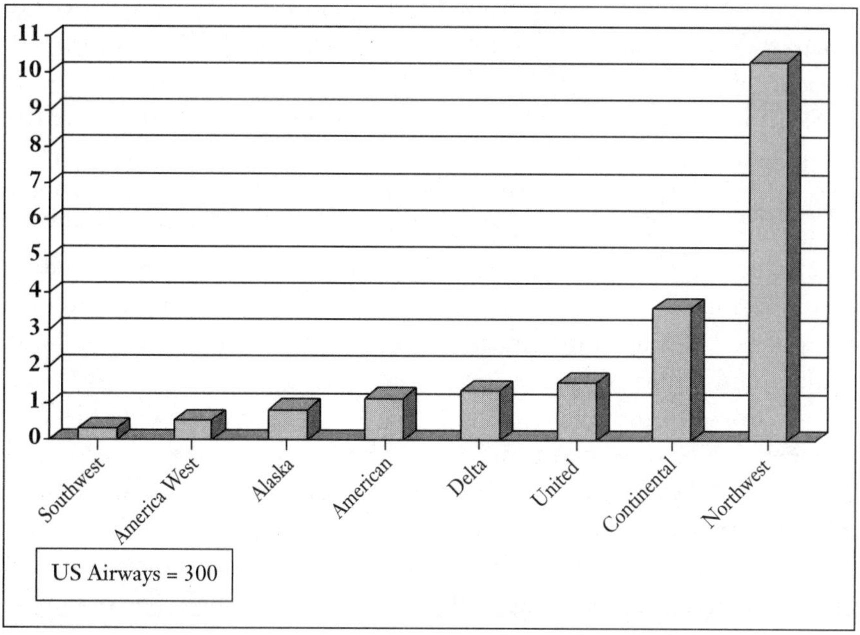

(*Source:* Yahoo Financial and Thomson Financial.)

ance sheet 'too strong' [though] Engel allows, 'this has meant that when times are tough, they have a lot more flexibility.'"[30]

Southwest's policy stands in contrast to accepted wisdom on Wall Street. Southwest's policy also stands in contrast to the policy of People Express, an airline that, like Southwest, also faced tremendous demand for its services and tremendous pressure from Wall Street to grow rapidly and take advantage of every opportunity. While Southwest has experienced 31 years of disciplined, steady, profitable growth, always maintaining plenty of financial reserves to flourish in times of crisis, People Express under the leadership of Donald Burr grew at an exponential rate from 1981 to 1986 and then simply collapsed into its own wreckage.

Summing Up

Resilience, the ability to be strengthened rather than weakened by difficult challenges, is a trait that psychologists have identified in some individuals. Similarly some organizations, such as Southwest Airlines, appear to be more resilient than others. Little is known about the sources of organizational resilience, although resilience is expected to require reserves of some sort. Previous research on the auto industry and on the U.S. Army suggests that organizational resilience depends at least partly on a reserve of a particular form of human capacity. The downsizing research[31] and the threat-rigidity research[32] clearly point out that most organizations deteriorate in performance after experiencing trauma. Twelve negative, dysfunctional attributes tend to arise which produce a deterioration of performance over time—for example, declining innovation, deteriorating communication, escalating conflict, scapegoating leaders, and centralizing decisions.[33]

According to the theory of relational coordination presented in Part 1, relationships of shared goals, shared knowledge, and mutual respect are a powerful source of high performance. Actions that undermine these relationships can therefore be expected to take a significant toll on organizational performance. Exhibit 17–8 depicts the normal sequence of events. A crisis such as the September 11 tragedy occurs. The organization responds with layoffs and cutbacks. The organization's performance suffers because of the resulting deterioration in relationships.

Exhibit 17–8 Financial Reserves, Relationships, and Resilience

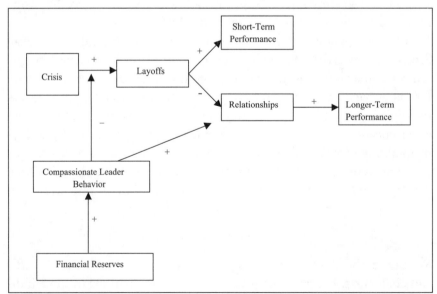

In some exceptional organizations, a reserve exists of a special form of human capacity that tends to produce resilience in the face of crisis. Southwest Airlines is clearly one of these exceptional organizations. Its commitment to long-term relationships helps to explain its resilience in the face of the Gulf War crisis, in the face of growing competition, in the face of staffing challenges, and in the face of the September 11 tragedy.

As every CEO knows, however, *wanting* to maintain commitments in the face of crisis is only half of the story. The other half is being able to do so, which requires having financial reserves in place for that very purpose. The relationship-based performance of Southwest Airlines therefore flies in the face of the leveraged buyout movement of the 1980s and 1990s, in which corporate leaders were encouraged to rid their organizations of financial reserves, with the promise that this would make them "fit" and "lean" and more accountable to shareholders. The fact that there would be few reserves in place to preserve commitments in the face of crises was an untold part of the story that needs to be understood and reconsidered. The Southwest Airlines Way, though apparently old-fashioned in this respect, may well be just plain good sense.

Implementing High Performance Relationships in Your Organization

W E HAVE SEEN HOW relationships based on shared goals, shared knowledge, and mutual respect have contributed to Southwest Airlines' extraordinary performance, and how these relationships can help to create high performance in other industry settings (Part 1). We have examined 10 organizational practices that Southwest uses to build relationships between managers and frontline employees, among frontline employees, with unions, and with suppliers (Part 2). We have gained insight into how these organizational practices work together—and how they have helped Southwest thrive in times of crisis (Part 3).

This final chapter offers guidance for implementing high performance relationships in your organization. It describes key steps for introducing these 10 supporting organizational practices to your organization or department, and some common obstacles you will need to overcome to be successful. One obvious challenge arises from the fact that these practices are complementary—they work together rather than in isolation (Chap. 15). Therefore investments in these practices will not be fully realized until they are all in place. You will need to reevaluate current practices in terms of whether they help to support or undermine relationships based on shared goals, shared knowledge, and mutual respect. If your organization is a typical one, with little systematic consideration of how organizational practices either support or undermine relationships, you may need to change on multiple fronts simultaneously. We will consider each of the 10 practices one by one, then end with the challenge of sustaining them over time.

Lead with Credibility and Caring

One critical step is for leaders in your organization, including yourself, to begin building credibility with employees throughout the organization (Chap. 5). Credibility is a valuable resource that cannot be achieved overnight, but rather must be developed over time. As we saw in the case of Southwest, Herb Kelleher (chairman and founder) and Colleen Barrett (president and chief operating officer) achieved high levels of credibility through repeated, consistent episodes of "telling it straight," whether the news was good or bad. "If it's bad, they'll tell you," said one employee. Credibility cannot be built overnight. It is the classic problem of the boy who cried wolf. A leader who decides to deliver bad news to the organization but who does not have a reputation for credibility runs the risk that his employees will believe he is trying once again to trick them to win an advantage. For example, former American CEO Bob Crandall's so-called Transition Plan—a thinly veiled threat to take American out of the airline business and into information systems and management services if employees did not cooperate—met with employee disbelief. His credibility with his board and with Wall Street was coming into question at the same time, due largely to his inability to establish credibility with frontline employees.

To develop credibility, one must simply "tell it straight" for long enough that people come to trust what you say. However, credibility is not sufficient—it must also be clear to your employees that their top leadership cares deeply about their well-being. This is the element of compassion that is so apparent in Southwest's leadership—not only in what they say, but what they do, epitomized by the no-layoff record they have worked to maintain throughout the 32 years since the organization's founding. American's Bob Crandall, by contrast, not only lacked credibility when he rolled out the Transition Plan, he also suggested by this move that he did not care about the future well-being of his employees. He was not deeply committed to making the company, in which employees still took a great deal of pride and on which they depended for their livelihood, a success. By contrast, Southwest employees repeatedly emphasize to outsiders that "If you have a problem, Herb cares." The same is also said of Colleen Barrett, who is legendary for taking personal action to help employees solve personal problems and is said by employees to be "up there with Jesus Christ."

To develop caring is just as critical as developing credibility, but it is less straightforward. How does one become a compassionate leader? You must care deeply for the well-being of your employees *and* find a way to demonstrate that caring—crossing boundaries of power and hierarchy to do so. It is difficult to show compassion every day, when there are no traumatic events to help crystallize and pull everyone together, but one clear message from Southwest's employees is the "everydayness" of the caring that is demonstrated by their leaders. The first step is to become a caring person—the second step is to find ways to communicate this caring on an everyday basis as well as in times of extreme crisis. Ultimately this may require a new, expanded set of criteria for leader selection in your organization.

Invest in Frontline Leadership

Leadership does not happen only at the top levels of the organization. Rather it is a distributed process that occurs throughout the organization, with a particularly critical leadership role to be played by frontline supervisors who can work side by side with frontline employees, providing them with meaningful coaching and feedback (Chap. 6). As Southwest's leaders have said, "Next to Herb, our frontline supervisors are our most important leaders."

The critical ingredients in building frontline leadership, as we saw at Southwest, are generous staffing levels for frontline supervisors and training that helps them to engage in active coaching and feedback rather than simply monitoring for noncompliance. Both of these ingredients require investment in additional resources, particularly increasing supervisory staffing levels. High staffing levels for supervisors are a direct charge against the bottom line, to be paid off over time through improved operational performance. However, it will make even more sense economically if job descriptions are flexible enough to allow supervisors to step in and help with the work of frontline employees as needed. Working side by side with frontline employees gives supervisors additional credibility for engaging in coaching and feedback, since it gives them an intimate firsthand understanding of the work in which employees are engaged. In addition, daily interactions between supervisors and frontline employees help to support the relationships between top leadership and frontline employees that are so difficult to maintain as an organization grows.

Besides the investment required for increasing supervisory staffing, the other major obstacle you will face is the lingering belief among many of your colleagues that supervision is antithetical to teamwork. Managers who were trained in the 1970s and 1980s have come to believe that reducing supervisory staff is a path to employee empowerment. You will have to make the case, as shown in Chap. 6, that supervision reconceived as coaching and feedback helps to build teamwork rather than undermine it.

Hire and Train for Relational Competence

Hiring is one of the most critical things an organization can do to shape its performance, particularly in service organizations in which people are the primary input to production (Chap. 7). The tendency to hire and train for functional expertise rather than for relational competence is very common, particularly for jobs that require high levels of functional expertise. Yet people in these jobs require equally high levels of relational competence to contribute their full value to the organization—otherwise we observe the all-too-common scenario of experts whose expertise serves as a barrier rather than a resource to the organization.

Southwest's focus on relational skills in the hiring process is legendary. Pilots throughout the industry tell the story of the pilot who was rude to the administrative assistant during the course of his interview process at Southwest. "He didn't get the job," the story concludes. Such a shift in hiring practices should be fairly easy to achieve in your own organization, one would think. It is not a matter of *discounting* the traditional markers of skill, when they are indeed relevant to what you are trying as an organization to achieve. Instead, it is a matter of identifying selection tools that will uncover the relational competencies that enable an employee to integrate his or her expertise into the work process, to achieve the outcomes that the organization and its customers care about.

There are three obstacles to hiring for relational competence, however. First, these new hiring criteria may threaten deeply held beliefs about the overriding importance of individual expertise, particularly in occupations such as medicine, engineering, or the law. The mystique of individual excellence is not easily overridden, even when research demonstrates the importance of relational competence. Taking care not to downgrade the importance of expertise, but rather to portray relational competence as necessary to realize the potential contributions of individual experts, can help to avoid unnecessary conflicts.

Second, it is not easy to identify soft skills like relational competence in the hiring process. Human resource departments may not feel comfortable screening for skills that are not readily amenable to objective measurement. One method used at Southwest and more recently at Jet-Blue for identifying these softer attributes is target selection, also known in some settings as behavioral interviewing. In target selection, a candidate is asked to recall an incident from a previous work experience in which he or she worked with others to solve a problem, for example. After walking through the incident, the candidate is then asked in-depth questions about the incident—what happened next, how did others react, what was the outcome of the incident? Based on the candidate's account of the incident, multiple interviewers rate the candidate on the target attribute. Candidates who are unanimously rated highly by multiple interviewers on that target attribute then move forward in the hiring process.

So although it is challenging to identify soft skills like relational competence, it can be done. The additional benefit of target selection is that candidates become very aware of the qualities that are valued by the organization, and they have had to provide evidence that they too have these special qualities. The hiring process thus creates a bond between the organization and the newly hired employee around the qualities that the organization values most highly.

The final obstacle to hiring for relational competence is that it is not a quick fix and it almost certainly cannot work by itself. It is an investment that can take a long time to pay off, particularly in a time of slow organizational growth, when new hires are few and far between. New people can quickly become jaded by the behaviors and attitudes of more senior employees who were selected under a different set of criteria. It is therefore particularly important that this practice not be attempted in isolation from the others.

Use Conflicts to Build Relationships

Conflicts are typically thought of as negative events to be avoided in the name of organizational harmony. However, we saw a different, more proactive approach to conflict at Southwest Airlines, stemming from the view that conflicts are normal, expected events, particularly given the time pressure and interdependence of the flight departure process (Chap. 8). We saw that conflicts can be lifted up, examined, and used as a learning experience that will ultimately strengthen relationships of shared goals, shared knowledge, and mutual respect between the conflicting parties and beyond, given the "ripple effect" of such learning. The more typical organizational approach to conflicts is to submerge them and hope that they go away. This approach is understandable given the potentially destructive nature of conflict.

How can your organization develop a proactive approach to conflict resolution and begin to treat conflicts as opportunities for learning? One key ingredient is to make conflict resolution an explicit part of the managerial role and to talk about and praise occasions when conflicts were resolved in a way that led to stronger relationships among the conflicting parties. Second, organizations that seek to learn from conflict need to develop and inculcate the view that conflicts are not the basis for disciplinary action, but the inability to learn from a conflict could very well be. As Southwest's managers attested, when the attempt to bring the parties in a conflict together fails to result in learning by either party, it is often taken as a sign that neither belongs at Southwest.

Finally, to make this proactive, learning approach to conflict truly pay off, the organization needs to promulgate the "ripple effect," whereby the story gets told and retold throughout the organization about how the flight attendant and the gate agent were brought together to work out a conflict, and came away with a whole new appreciation of the challenges involved in the other's role. This "ripple effect" ensures that the learning achieved from the individual incident is leveraged throughout the organization, so that the same conflict need not occur repeatedly for all to learn its lessons.

Bridge the Work/Family Divide

One model for strong working relationships comes from the family, where people can ideally be themselves and connect with each other based on their true selves (Chap. 9). Southwest employees often refer to family ties in describing their interactions with each other—"she is like a sister to me"— and refer to their work responsibilities as though they are on the same level as their family responsibilities—"I have a responsibility for a family, a house, and for this company." Giving work ties the intensity of family ties can help to bring an employee's best energies into the service of the organization. How can your organization create the strength of familylike ties at work?

There are several key ingredients. The first is encouraging people to bring their true selves when they come to work at your organization, allowing them to interject their own personalities into the work process, for example, personalizing their work spaces and interacting with customers in a way that reflects their own personalities. Second, related to the first, is to regularly recognize your employees' personal tragedies and triumphs, extending help and compassion to them in times of trouble, and celebrating the everyday occurrences in their lives. When people feel they must only bring part of themselves to the organization and leave the rest at home, their work identities are less holistic and their relationships with each other are weaker as a result. Finally, by engaging employees in acts of giving to the community, as in Southwest's Culture Committee, you can forge an organizational identity that builds upon and leverages employees' identities as members of a larger community.

One obstacle to creating these familylike ties at work, however, is the concern by employees that familylike ties at work may supplant or weaken ties with their own families—leading to conflicting loyalties that are hard to manage. You can reduce this hazard, as Southwest has done, through practices that consistently support your employees' family commitments—providing help in times of emergency, making flexible schedules available to all employees to accommodate their families' needs, and getting family members involved in your organization's extended family, "so they don't feel left out."

Create Boundary Spanners

In your organization, you will likely find boundaries—based on differences in goals, knowledge, and status—between the functions that must work together smoothly to deliver reliable service for your customers. These boundaries can be bridged through informal ties that may simply emerge in the process of working together, or through formal teams that include members from each function. Alternatively, you can create boundary spanners, as we saw at Southwest Airlines, people whose job it is to bring together information from multiple functions in a timely way to meet performance objectives (Chap. 10). At its most effective, the boundary spanner does more than transfer information among parties who are involved in the same work process. He or she also helps to build relationships of shared goals, shared knowledge, and mutual respect among them.

How can you create boundary spanners in your organization, and what are the likely obstacles that would prevent you from doing so? The design of the boundary spanner role is fairly straightforward. The first step is to identify a work process whose performance is critical for the organization's success, and one that requires inputs from multiple functions. The second step is to create a new role, either to be filled by an existing function that already tends to play an integrative role or to create a new job altogether. Finally, you need to staff and support the boundary spanner role based on the understanding that the job involves more than the transfer and integration of information; it involves building connections among all parties involved in the work process. This means staffing the role adequately to create a workload small enough to support the relational work of an effective boundary spanner. This also means selecting employees into the job who have the ability and desire to do more than information processing—they understand and are well suited to carry out the relational work of a boundary spanner as well, bringing people together around a shared understanding of the work process and the important role that each party plays in it.

There are likely to be obstacles to creating this boundary spanning role. If the job does not already exist in some form, there is likely to be resistance on the part of existing personnel to the creation of a new job that appears to overlap with and perhaps encroach upon their own jobs. The job needs to be well respected in the organization to be carried out effectively, creating the additional potential for status conflict with existing employees. If the job already exists in some form and simply needs to be extended to play a more relational role, the obstacles will be somewhat different. People who are accustomed to playing a hands-off, information processing role, often carried out primarily through an information systems interface, may resist the redefinition of their job to include a less well understood relational component. They may also feel ill-equipped to carry out the more intensive interaction, much of it face-to-face, involved in building relationships of shared understanding around the work process. They have likely been hired and trained for their current job in a way that does not include the broader skill requirements of an effective boundary spanner.

Finally, the investment required to staff this role adequately will serve as an additional obstacle. When managers in other airlines heard about Southwest's staffing levels for the operations agent position, they often expressed disbelief, saying, "What a waste!" or "That is so inefficient!" And yet the evidence outlined in Chap. 10 suggests that there are performance payoffs to investing in this key role. Furthermore, there is no reason to believe that this particular investment will take a long time to pay off. Once boundary spanners have been hired, trained, and adequately staffed to perform their expanded role, they should be able to add value fairly quickly.

A core, underlying objection to the boundary spanner role is the belief that "what really matters is transmitting the information itself, and we can solve that problem with IT." But we know from years of research, cited in Chap. 10, that much critical information cannot be transmitted effectively through information technology alone, and that strong ties among participants are required to use and share that information effectively. Boundary spanners help to forge those ties.

Measure Performance Broadly

The traditional approach to performance measurement is to break down performance into its discrete components or behaviors, consistent with functional departmental structures. The problem is that an organization's most critical work processes tend to span multiple functional or departmental boundaries, and the outcomes of those work processes depend not on any one function but on the actions that are taken by people in each of those functions. When performance measures try to separate out the contributions of individual functions, rather than focusing on overall outcomes, the result can be a great deal of unproductive finger pointing, when each function that is "blamed" can point to an action or inaction by another function that contributed to the outcome. As we saw in Chap. 11, Southwest attempts to short-circuit the cycle of blaming by instituting a "team delay," allowing multiple functional groups to take joint responsibility for a delay, rather than assigning it to one and only one department. The idea was to focus on the problem itself, and to create more openness around understanding its sources, by taking away the measurement system that had focused employee attention on blaming and blame avoidance.

How can your organization change its performance measurement system to end the cycle of blaming, and what are the likely obstacles to doing so? It is fairly straightforward to design a performance measurement system that focuses on process outcomes rather than functional outcomes. One simply measures on-time performance for the whole station, rather than measuring on-time performance separately for the flight attendants, for the pilots, for the baggage handlers, for the mechanics, for the gate agents, and so on.

The obstacles, of course, are tremendous. The first obstacle is the concern that much valuable information will be lost in the move toward broader performance measures. "How will we be able to identify and fix the problem if we don't know which department was at fault?" This objection assumes, however, that the functionally based performance measurements currently in place yield accurate information about the cause of a problem. A long-held tenet of quality improvement, first stated by W. Edwards Deming, is that functionally based performance measures lead to information hiding, rather than information sharing. Paradoxically, using functional performance measures to learn about the root cause of problems often leads to less useful information, rather than more. Measures that focus on overall process performance, rather than functional accountability, take the focus off individuals and place it on the process, creating the safety to share information and learn from mistakes.

The second major obstacle is related to the first, but it is found at a deeper level. It is the belief that detailed performance measures are the only way that control can be achieved. The measurement system at American Airlines was hard to relinquish because of this belief, deeply held by former CEO Bob Crandall and promulgated throughout the company. If you do not fundamentally trust your people, nor do they trust you, it is particularly hard to imagine how your organization can be run successfully without the element of fear and oversight of a detailed performance measurement system. In some organizations, it can be risky even to suggest such a change. The ruin of a promising young executive's career at American, recounted in Chap. 11, hinged on her questioning of the system of performance measurement and its suitability for a work process that required teamwork.

There is some truth to each of these objections. Indeed, performance measures that focus on overall process performance rather than individual or departmental failure cannot work by themselves. In isolation from other relationship-building organizational practices, broad, team-based performance measures may indeed create the outcomes their detractors claim—a lack of detailed information for quality improvement, and a refusal of anyone to take responsibility for problems. This practice should not be attempted in isolation.

Keep Jobs Flexible at the Boundaries

There are good reasons why organizations tend to draw boundaries around jobs, delineating clear areas of responsibility for particular functional groups. Such boundaries help to increase role clarity, focus employee attention on their particular contribution to a broader work process, and avoid the employee burnout that can result from trying to accomplish too many ill-defined objectives. And yet the flip side of this practice is the all too common, and often annoying, statement—"It's not my job." This attitude can slow down a work process, preventing employees from switching roles even when doing so would prevent an unnecessary delay. More important, clear job boundaries can produce employees who know their own jobs very well, but who do not have a clue how their jobs relate to those of others, even others who are intimately involved in the same work process. These employees cannot readily visualize how their jobs relate to those of others, cannot readily integrate their work with others, and cannot readily solve problems or adapt to unexpected contingencies.

Southwest's solution, as we saw in Chap. 12, is to have very clearly defined jobs, but to also make clear in each job description that part of the job is to do whatever is necessary to make the operation successful. This simple statement, and its constant reinforcement by the other organizational practices, transforms an ordinary job into a job with broad responsibilities. Flexible job descriptions ask employees to focus on doing their own specific job very well, while at the same time asking them to remain open to the larger picture of what the organization is trying to accomplish. They open employees up to the possibility of jumping in to help others as needed to achieve overall performance objectives. Flexible job descriptions also help to reduce status barriers between jobs, as when baggage handlers (called "ramp rats" at other airlines) come upstairs from the ramp to help check in customers, or when pilots help to load bags or clean the cabin between flights (derided as "pillow fluffing—a woman's job" at other airlines). In short, flexible job descriptions help to foster relationships of shared goals, shared knowledge, and mutual respect between functions that traditionally have had little in common.

For organizations that already have clearly specified job descriptions for all employees, it seems quite straightforward to add Southwest's "whatever else is needed" clause to each job description. In reality, the potential obstacles are tremendous. First, if unions are present, job descriptions are subject to negotiation and must be changed through negotiation. Southwest has been a highly unionized company since its origin, demonstrating that flexible job descriptions are indeed possible under these circumstances. Still, Southwest managers emphasize that job flexibility is not simply a management choice, but rather the repeated outcome of negotiation. In unionized workplaces, achieving flexible job descriptions therefore depends on the quality of the labor/management relationship (see next section for more on achieving this).

Even in nonunion settings, employees can have considerable leverage, either through formal channels or simply due to the ample opportunities that exist for effective informal resistance. Employees must trust that these broader job descriptions will not be used to take advantage of them, creating responsibilities that they simply cannot meet. More fundamentally, employees must come to terms with a potential weakening of their occupational identities, which have often served as a tremendous source of pride. Pilots who are expected to help load bags, or come into the cabin between flights to clean newspapers from the aisle, must place their organizational identity above their occupational identity in order to be comfortable with the expanded job description. "I am a pilot" must be superceded by "This is my company."

Achieving flexible job descriptions is therefore dependent on other organizational practices discussed in this book, including selection of employees for relational competence, using conflict resolution as an

opportunity to build relationships, and especially measuring performance of the overall process rather than that of individual functions.

Make Unions Your Partners, Not Adversaries

In any organization in which employees are represented by unions, there
is an additional party that must be considered in achieving flexible job
descriptions, or in building high performance relationships more generally—the unions themselves. Southwest's history suggests that unions
can serve as partners rather than as adversaries and that managers can
influence whether the relationship will be one of partnership or adversarialism. How can you create effective partnerships with the unions that
represent your employees, and what are the likely obstacles to doing so?

The first key step is to accept unions as the legitimate representatives
of your employees and welcome them as partners in your organization.
This step seems incredibly obvious and straightforward, but in reality the
traditional antiunion bias in U.S. culture presents a major obstacle.
There is no point moving further if you cannot take this first key step,
since the relationship is bound to be adversarial, implicitly if not explicitly, if you do not accept unions as the legitimate representatives of your
employees. When your employees are in the process of choosing a union
to represent them, it is particularly important to stand back and take the
position that, as Southwest COO and President Colleen Barrett put it,
"We really want them to have whoever they want." Taking this position
demonstrates trust in your employees and their judgment, and sets the
stage for a potentially positive relationship with the union they ultimately choose to represent their interests.

The other obstacle to partnering with unions is a fear that, legitimate
or not, a union will vie for your employees' loyalty, making them less
concerned with the company's well-being and less likely to identify
strongly with it. If you take the position that you trust your employees'
judgment and do not see the union as an adversary, you increase the
chances that your employees will keep their union representatives in line
and prevent them from taking positions that are destructive to the company. The union activists at Southwest who were interviewed for this
book expressed intense loyalty and ownership of the company and
explained how they got rid of one union because it "was trying to hurt
the company." Trying to hurt the company was considered by Southwest

employees to be unacceptable union behavior. "We belong to this company," one union activist explained. Another union activist explained, "We made this company, and we are not going to let you ruin it." Of course, this intense loyalty is not only a reward for trusting your employees to make their own decisions regarding union representation. It is also the product of other practices that create strong relationships between employees and their managers, particularly leading with credibility and caring, and fostering frontline leadership.

The final obstacle to creating partnerships with the unions that represent your employees is the deeply held belief that unionization signifies management failure. As one of JetBlue's leaders said, "If we need unions, then boy have we failed." Nobody likes to fail, and if unions signify failure, they will be avoided with intensity and passion, particularly by the high achievers who tend to seek positions of managerial responsibility. This belief is partly a function of our business culture, which places individual striving above the collective good, and which assumes the stockholder to be the only stakeholder to whom managers can legitimately respond. If other stakeholders are seen as a constraint on performing one's legitimate managerial function, they will be resisted at all costs. This obstacle to building high performance relationships can be ascribed in part to the training that managers receive in traditional MBA programs, suggesting the need to reexamine our MBA programs for the biases they promulgate.

Southwest's experience suggests that it is not union representation itself, but the nature of the labor/management relationship, which determines performance. The labor/management relationship in turn is heavily influenced by managers' respect for employee choices regarding union representation, and by their willingness to welcome unions as their partners.

Build Relationships with Your Suppliers

The traditional approach to supplier relations is to keep suppliers in line by avoiding reliance on any one of them, pitting them against each other to achieve the upper hand in bargaining. While this approach gives management a sense of security and power over its suppliers, other advantages are lost. As shown in Chap. 14, Southwest gains multiple advantages from its long-term supplier relationships, including the ability to turn to those suppliers to solve problems jointly, to respond quickly to opportunities, and to come up with ideas that would not have occurred to either party in isolation. How might your company build supportive long-term relationships with your suppliers, and what are the potential obstacles to doing so?

The "how-to" is not difficult. Once you have developed strong relationships of shared goals, shared knowledge, and mutual respect *within* your organization, it is simply a matter of choosing carefully the suppliers who are critical to your success and making them part of that web of relationships, treating them as you would any colleague with whom you are mutually dependent.

However this step suggests the first potential obstacle—if you don't have strong relationships internally, it is much harder to extend them to encompass your key suppliers. For one thing, the skills and experience for doing so are not likely to be widespread throughout your organization. In addition, representatives of your organization will not be able to speak easily *for* the organization without going through a huge bureaucracy, thus inhibiting their ability to partner freely with external suppliers.

Once you do have a strong, well-functioning set of internal relationships, there is a second key obstacle—a suspicion of outsiders and an assumption that their interests are somehow in conflict with those of your own organization. Indeed, these feelings of "us versus them" can be even more intense in organizations that have developed strong internal relationships, and can serve to block your efforts to make suppliers part of the team. One way to overcome this obstacle with your colleagues is to be very selective about which suppliers really should become part of the team. Only those on whom your organization is highly dependent for its success need be cultivated as part of the team. And even when the *intent* is to forge a long-term relationship, it is best to keep in mind what are the circumstances under which your organization would exit from this relationship.

Once these obstacles are overcome, your organization can enjoy the fruits of collaborating with external suppliers, particularly the generation of new solutions and the quick adaptation to external shocks, as exemplified by Southwest and Manchester Airport after the events of September 11, 2001.

Maintain Financial Reserves

The relationship-building practices described above can be put into place in most if not all organizations. But how does one maintain a commitment to something as intangible as relationships in times of crisis, when external stakeholders are demanding attention to the bottom line?

Certainly it is times of crisis when the sustainability of relationship-based performance is most at risk. As we saw in Chap. 17, however, times of crisis are also when the value of relationships becomes most apparent. We saw evidence that relationships themselves can serve as a tremendous source of organizational resilience. Organizations with strong relationships of shared goals, shared knowledge, and mutual respect, like Southwest, have a powerful "relational reserve" that enables them to thrive under pressure.

The problem is that crisis often forces managers to put short-term survival ahead of long-term performance. This often means layoffs and other actions that undermine or destroy relationships, just when they are most needed for the organization to deal successfully with the crisis at hand. One obvious solution is to maintain financial reserves for this very purpose—to allow the organization to survive in the face of crisis without damaging the relationships that are so critical both for responding to the crisis at hand, and for achieving performance over the long term. However, these financial reserves will be hard to maintain.

Why should it be so difficult for organizations to maintain financial reserves for the purpose of sustaining relationships in times of crisis? After all, it is known with certainty that crises will come. The obstacles are twofold. First, it is not widely believed that relationships are such a powerful driver of performance that they need to be nurtured and sustained through good times and bad. This book is an effort to make this case. Others have made the same argument in different ways, and more will follow, resulting eventually in a revitalization and renewal of business culture around the critical importance of relationships.

The other obstacle is the high-leverage financial strategies that have become the norm in Corporate America. There was a concerted effort in the late 1980s to leverage firms highly to make them more vulnerable and more directly accountable to their financial stakeholders, removing the slack that would allow firms to maintain their commitments to other stakeholders in good times and bad. As we saw in the airline industry post-September 11, a strong, highly significant predictor of airline layoffs was the debt–equity ratio of the individual airline prior to September 11. To sustain the practices that support high performance relationships, it is essential to have financial reserves in place for that purpose.

Summing Up

Far from being a pie-in-the-sky, soft approach to management, this book has shown that attention to relationships is simply good management practice. However, as competitors know, replicating the Southwest model is challenging to say the least. The "Southwest Airlines way" involves more than pursuing a particular product market strategy. For Southwest's leaders, taking care of business literally means taking care of relationships. They see these relationships—with their employees, among their employees, and with outside parties—as the foundation of competitive advantage, through good times and bad. They see the quality of these relationships not as a success factor, but as the most *essential* success factor. They believe that to develop the company, they must constantly invest in these relationships.

Is this enough to carry Southwest through the challenging realities that lay ahead? This book suggests that the relationships in which Southwest has so carefully invested will provide a powerful impetus for continued success.

Appendixes

APPENDIX 3–1

A Nine-Site Study of Relational Coordination*

	AMR1† n = 35	AMR2 n = 40	SWA1 n = 33	SWA2 n = 38	CON1 n = 39	CON2 n = 46	UAL1 n = 35	UAL2 n = 31	UAL3 n = 12	Total n = 315	Std. Dev.
Relational coordination	.33	.27	.62	.48	.46	.35	.43	.41	.55	.42	.20
Frequent communication	.30	.28	.47	.36	.29	.28	.31	.29	.29	.32	.23
Timely communication	.40	.24	.56	.39	.48	.37	.39	.38	.38	.40	.26
Problem-solving communication	.35	.33	.66	.45	.52	.39	.56	.44	.75	.46	.31
Shared goals	.31	.28	.85	.67	.49	.44	.54	.50	.75	.50	.38
Shared knowledge	.25	.18	.52	.42	.39	.28	.31	.36	.38	.33	.24
Mutual respect	.35	.33	.68	.57	.59	.35	.48	.51	.72	.48	.30

* This table shows the results of an employee survey that was administered at nine airline sites. Survey questions asked about communication and relationships between 12 functions—pilots, flight attendants, gate agents, ticket agents, baggage handlers, mechanics, and so on—at each site. Each number in the table indicates the percentage of communication and relationship ties that were rated as "strong" or "very strong" among employees at that particular site. All relationship and communication dimensions were highly correlated with each other, and were combined into a single index called relational coordination, coordination carried out through relationships of shared goals, shared knowledge, and mutual respect. See Chap. 3 for details of the study.

† AMR1 = American Airlines in Boston; AMR2 = American Airlines in Los Angeles; SWA1 = Southwest Airlines in Chicago; SWA2 = Southwest Airlines in Los Angeles; CON1 = Continental Airlines in Boston; CON2 = Continental Airlines in Cleveland; UAL1 = United Airlines in Boston; UAL2 = United Airlines in Los Angeles; UAL3 = United Shuttle in Los Angeles; n = number of employees who were surveyed.

APPENDIX 3–2

A Nine-Site Study of Relational Coordination: Differences in Performance and Product Characteristics*

	AMR1† n = 12	AMR2 n = 12	SWA1 n = 12	SWA2 n = 12	CON1 n = 12	CON2 n = 12	UAL1 n = 12	UAL2 n = 12	UAL3 n = 3	Total n = 99	Std. Dev.
Performance											
Turnaround time	65.5	88.5	22.9	22.7	43.1	38.6	62.5	66.1	32.6	50.7	22.1
Staff time per passenger	99.4	131.3	35.9	37.4	76.6	72.0	88.6	83.5	42.1	77.0	32.4
Customer complaints	50.5	47.1	0.5	0.5	23.4	27.7	25.5	23.3	20.7	24.7	18.9
Lost baggage	5.4	6.1	3.9	4.1	5.3	6.4	4.4	6.9	7.3	5.4	1.6
Late arrivals	22.5	17.8	15.3	20.0	27.0	26.1	21.7	19.2	13.5	21.0	8.0
Product characteristics											
Flights per day	36	51	76	84	36	98	22	99	57	63	30
Average flight length	1348	1984	319	387	447	523	1463	1459	330	971	608
Passengers per flight	110	123	73	81	73	61	110	121	80	94	24
Cargo per flight	3.8	6.2	.15	.49	.94	.66	2.9	4.6	.10	2.4	2.2
Passenger connections	1.0	3.9	10.4	3.5	1.0	31.2	1.0	3.9	1.0	6.8	9.6

* This table shows performance and product characteristics of the nine airline sites that were included in the study of relational coordination. Exhibit 3–3 provides exact definitions of these performance and product measures. See Chap. 3 for details of the study.

† AMR1 = American Airlines in Boston; AMR2 = American Airlines in Los Angeles; SWA1 = Southwest Airlines in Chicago; SWA2 = Southwest Airlines in Los Angeles; CON1 = Continental Airlines in Boston; CON2 = Continental Airlines in Cleveland; UAL1 = United Airlines in Boston; UAL2 = United Airlines in Los Angeles; UAL3 = United Shuttle in Los Angeles; n = number of months over which these measures were tracked. UAL3 data were collected for only 3 months because at the time of the study, UAL3 (the United Shuttle) had been in operation for only 3 months.

A Nine-Site Study of Relational Coordination: Impact of Relational Coordination on Flight Departure Performance[‡]

	Flight Departure Performance				
	Turnaround Time	Staff Time per Passenger	Customer Complaints	Lost Bags	Late Arrivals
Relational coordination	-0.21*** (0.000)	-0.42*** (0.000)	-0.64*** (0.000)	-0.31* (0.042)	-0.50** (0.001)
Flights/day	-0.19*** (0.000)	-0.37*** (0.000)	-0.30*** (0.000)	0.13 (0.287)	-0.22+ (0.065)
Flight length, passengers and cargo per flight	0.79*** (0.000)	0.45*** (0.081)	0.13 (0.188)	0.12 (0.471)	-0.54** (0.001)
Passenger connections	0.12** (0.004)	0.19** (0.008)	0.09 (0.329)	0.13 (0.287)	0.00 (0.987)
R^2	.94	.81	.69	.19	.20

[‡] This table shows the impact of relational coordination on flight departure performance. Relational coordination, coordination carried out through relationships of shared goals, shared knowledge, and mutual respect, is measured as the percentage of cross-functional ties that are "strong" or "very strong," based on an employee survey. Flight departure performance includes quality—customer complaints, mishandled bags, and late arrivals—as well as efficiency—turnaround time per departure and staff time per passenger. Exact definitions of performance and product measures are shown in Exhibit 3-3. See Chap. 3 for details of the study.

All models are random effects regressions with site/month as the unit of analysis ($n = 99$) and site ($n = 9$) as the random effect. Statistical significance is denoted: [+]$p < 0.10$, [*]$p < 0.05$, [**]$p < 0.01$, [***]$p < 0.001$, and suggests the certainty that a change in relational coordination will produce a change in performance, where a smaller p value suggests a higher certainty. R^2 denotes the percentage of the variation in performance that is explained by the model.

A Nine-Hospital Study of Relational Coordination*

	Hosp 1 n = 49	Hosp 2 n = 49	Hosp 3 n = 33	Hosp 4 n = 38	Hosp 5 n = 13	Hosp 6 n = 24	Hosp 7 n = 30	Hosp 8 n = 34	Hosp 9 n = 42	Total n = 313	Std. Dev.
Relational coordination	0.72	0.67	0.73	0.83	0.80	0.81	0.75	0.78	0.76	0.76	0.19
Frequent communication	0.66	0.59	0.72	0.81	0.70	0.72	0.72	0.78	0.65	0.70	0.28
Timely communication	0.77	0.72	0.72	0.85	0.95	0.87	0.78	0.81	0.78	0.79	0.26
Accurate communication	0.86	0.77	0.85	0.96	0.90	0.87	0.86	0.94	0.89	0.88	0.22
Problem-solving communication	0.63	0.46	0.52	0.81	0.60	0.77	0.63	0.76	0.75	0.66	0.34
Shared goals	0.78	0.83	0.81	0.88	0.92	0.86	0.78	0.84	0.81	0.83	0.25
Shared knowledge	0.65	0.65	0.72	0.78	0.78	0.80	0.76	0.63	0.71	0.71	0.28
Mutual respect	0.65	0.66	0.78	0.75	0.73	0.77	0.76	0.65	0.70	0.71	0.31

* This table shows the results of an employee survey that was administered in nine hospitals. Survey questions asked about communication and relationships between five functions—physicians, nurses, physical therapists, case managers, and social workers—working with joint replacement patients in each hospital; n is the number of employees working with joint replacement patients who were surveyed in each hospital. Each number in the table indicates the percentage of communication and relationship ties that were rated as "strong" or "very strong" among employees working with joint replacement patients in that particular hospital. All relationship and communication dimensions were highly correlated with each other, and were combined into a single index called relational coordination, coordination carried out through relationships of shared goals, shared knowledge, and mutual respect. See Chap. 4 for details of the study.

APPENDIX 4–2

A Nine-Hospital Study of Relational Coordination: Differences in Performance and Product Characteristics*

	Hosp 1 n = 109	Hosp 2 n = 93	Hosp 3 n = 125	Hosp 4 n = 135	Hosp 5 n = 65	Hosp 6 n = 67	Hosp 7 n = 97	Hosp 8 n = 70	Hosp 9 n = 48	Mean n = 809	Std. Dev.
Performance measures											
Length of stay (days)	5.6	5.8	5.9	4.4	4.2	4.4	5.6	4.3	5.0	5.1	2.1
Patient satisfaction	3.89	3.98	4.01	4.34	4.28	4.21	4.01	4.27	4.01	4.10	0.64
Post-op freedom from pain	72.3	71.1	78.7	77.6	74.8	79.6	73.8	77.3	76.5	75.8	20.8
Post-op mobility	72.2	68.6	74.6	74.2	73.0	76.5	71.2	74.9	76.7	73.3	19.8
Patient characteristics											
Age	66.3	67.2	67.2	67.3	67.6	65.9	66.4	67.2	66.6	66.9	11.1
Co-morbidities index	1.5	1.7	1.4	1.4	1.3	1.7	1.6	1.5	1.7	1.5	1.3
Psychological well-being	3.2	3.1	3.2	3.2	3.2	3.2	3.3	3.3	3.4	3.2	1.0
Pre-op freedom from pain	43.3	38.9	44.8	45.1	43.9	42.4	41.9	46.6	43.5	43.5	19.6
Pre-op mobility	48.6	40.6	46.8	48.6	48.9	48.5	44.5	49.2	48.5	47.0	21.2
Days since surgery	78	85	83	80	75	80	84	78	76	81	17
% female	61	66	58	50	60	49	62	63	58	58	49
% African-American	13	11	5	2	0	6	6	9	0	6	24
% Hips	24	45	59	43	43	48	40	47	40	43	50
% Married	64	52	73	62	77	50	68	65	63	64	48
Hospital characteristics											
Surgical volume	458	362	920	527	400	363	501	353	400	510	186

* This table shows performance and product characteristics of the nine hospitals that were included in the study of relational coordination; *n* is the number of joint replacement patients whose outcomes were tracked in each hospital. See Chap. 4 for definitions of these measures and for details of the study.

APPENDIX 4–3

A Nine-Hospital Study of Relational Coordination: Impact of Relational Coordination on Patient-Care Performance[‡]

	Patient-Care Performance			
	Length of Stay	Patient Satisfaction	Post-op Freedom from Pain	Post-op Mobility
Relational coordination	−0.31***	0.22***	−0.07*	−0.05
	(0.000)	(0.000)	(0.047)	(0.139)
Patient age	−0.02	0.13**	−0.01	−0.05
	(0.554)	(0.003)	(0.803)	(0.178)
Co-morbidities	0.08*	−0.04	−0.013	−0.04
	(0.038)	(0.424)	(0.723)	(0.229)
Pre-op status	0.03	−0.15**	0.20***	0.28***
	(0.392)	(0.002)	(0.000)	(0.000)
Surgical procedure	−0.00	0.07	0.22***	0.11**
	(0.977)	(0.102)	(0.000)	(0.002)
Psychological well-being	−0.08*	0.11*	0.41***	0.41***
	(0.042)	(0.024)	(0.000)	(0.000)
Gender	0.05	−0.06	−0.03	−0.01
	(0.167)	(0.217)	(0.382)	(0.751)
Race	0.02	0.02	−0.03	−0.06+
	(0.586)	(0.628)	(0.382)	(0.071)
Marital status	0.02	0.10*	0.020	0.023
	(0.670)	(0.030)	(0.586)	(0.515)
Surgical volume	0.17***	−0.04	0.05	0.019
	(0.000)	(0.326)	(0.144)	(0.561)
R^2	.17	.11	.37	.39

[‡] This table shows the impact of relational coordination on patient-care performance. Relational coordination, coordination carried out through relationships of shared goals, shared knowledge, and mutual respect, is measured as the percent of cross-functional ties that are "strong" or "very strong," based on an employee survey. Patient-care performance includes quality—patient satisfaction, post-operative freedom from pain and post-operative functioning—as well as efficiency— length of stay in the hospital. Performance and control measures are defined in Chap. 4.

All models are random effects regressions with patient as the unit of analysis (n = 599 for length-of-stay model, n = 491 for patient satisfaction model, n = 539 for post-operative pain model, and n = 531 for post-operative mobility model). Hospital (n = 9) is the random effect. Statistical significance is denoted: $^+p < 0.10$, $^*p < 0.05$, $^{**}p < 0.01$, $^{***}p < 0.001$, and suggests the certainty that a change in relational coordination will produce a change in performance, where a smaller p value suggests a higher certainty. R^2 denotes the percentage of the variation in performance that is explained by the model.

APPENDIX 6-I

Impact of Supervisory Staffing on Relational Coordination[‡]

	Relational Coordination
Supervisory staffing	0.46[***]
	(0.000)
Flights/day	−0.34[**]
	(0.001)
Gate agent	0.32[***]
	(0.000)
Baggage agent	0.12[*]
	(0.020)
Operations agent	0.39[***]
	(0.000)
Ramp agent	0.32[***]
	(0.000)
R^2	.29

[‡] Supervisory staffing is measured as the number of supervisors per hundred front-line employees. Relational coordination, coordination carried out through relationships of shared goals, shared knowledge, and mutual respect, is measured as the percentage of cross-functional ties that are "strong" or "very strong," based on an employee survey. These findings are discussed in Chap. 6.

All models are random effects regressions with employee as the unit of analysis ($n = 317$) and site ($n = 9$) as the random effect. Functional identity of the respondent is included as a control variable to reflect differences in relational coordination as experienced by different functions, treating pilots as the baseline function. Standardized regression coefficients are shown. Statistical significance is denoted: $+p < 0.10$, $^*p < 0.05$, $^{**}p < 0.01$, $^{***}p < 0.001$, and suggests the certainty that a change in supervisory staffing will produce a change in relational coordination, where a smaller p value suggests a higher certainty. R^2 denotes the percentage of the variation in relational coordination that is explained by the model.

APPENDIX 6-2

Impact of Supervisory Staffing on Flight Departure Performance‡

	Flight Departure Performance				
	Turnaround Time	Staff Time per Passenger	Customer Complaints	Lost Bags	Late Arrivals
Supervisory staffing	-0.31^{***}	-0.31^{**}	-0.84^{***}	-0.69^{**}	-0.25
	(0.000)	(0.001)	(0.000)	(0.002)	(0.168)
Flights/day	-0.08^{*}	-0.30^{***}	-0.00	0.43^{**}	-0.20
	(0.049)	(0.000)	(0.976)	(0.002)	(0.199)
Flight length, passengers and cargo per flight	$.76^{***}$	0.59^{***}	0.09	-0.10	-0.30^{+}
	(0.000)	(0.000)	(0.308)	(0.525)	(0.075)
Passenger connections	0.16^{***}	0.35^{***}	0.23^{**}	0.13	0.22^{+}
	(0.000)	(0.000)	(0.002)	(0.284)	(0.096)
R^2	$.95$	$.77$	$.71$	$.43$	$.17$

‡ Supervisory staffing is measured as the number of supervisors per hundred frontline employees. Flight departure performance includes quality—customer complaints, mishandled bags, and late arrivals—as well as efficiency—turnaround time per departure and staff time per passenger. Exact definitions of performance and product measures are shown in Exhibit 3–3. These findings are discussed in Chap. 6.

All models are random effects regressions with site/month as the unit of analysis ($n = 99$) and site ($n = 9$) as the random effect. Statistical significance is denoted: $^{+}p < 0.10$, $^{*}p < 0.05$, $^{**}p < 0.01$, $^{***}p < 0.001$, and suggests the certainty that a change in supervisory staffing will produce a change in performance, where a smaller p value suggests a higher certainty. R^2 denotes the percentage of variation in performance that is explained by the model.

APPENDIX 7–1

Impact of Hiring for Relational Competence on Relational Coordination[‡]

	Relational Coordination
Hiring for relational competence	0.35***
	(0.000)
Flights/day	−0.07
	(0.474)
Gate agent	0.32***
	(0.000)
Baggage agent	0.13*
	(0.018)
Operations agent	0.38***
	(0.000)
Ramp agent	0.32***
	(0.000)
R^2	.28

[‡] Hiring for relational competence is measured as the number of functions for which relational competence is an important hiring criterion. Relational coordination, coordination carried out through relationships of shared goals, shared knowledge, and mutual respect, is measured as the percent of cross-functional ties that are "strong" or "very strong," based on an employee survey. These findings are discussed in Chap. 7.

All models are random effects regressions with employee as the unit of analysis ($n = 317$) and site ($n = 9$) as the random effect. Functional identity of the respondent is included as a control variable to reflect differences in relational coordination as experienced by different functions, treating pilots as the baseline function. Standardized regression coefficients are shown. Statistical significance is denoted: $^+p < 0.10$, $^*p < 0.05$, $^{**}p < 0.01$, $^{***}p < 0.001$, and suggests the certainty that a change in hiring practices will produce a change in relational coordination, where a smaller p value suggests a higher certainty. R^2 denotes the percentage of the variation in relational coordination that is explained by the model.

Impact of Hiring for Relational Competence on Flight Departure Performance[‡]

	Flight Departure Performance					
	Turnaround Time	Staff Time per Passenger	Customer Complaints	Lost Bags	Late Arrivals
Hiring for relational competence	−0.37*** (0.000)	−0.43*** (0.000)	−0.56*** (0.000)	−0.68*** (0.000)	−0.66*** (0.000)
Flights/day	−0.15*** (0.000)	−0.37*** (0.000)	−0.32*** (0.000)	0.21[+] (0.060)	−0.18 (0.131)
Flight length, passengers and cargo per flight	0.65*** (0.000)	0.43*** (0.000)	0.18 (0.159)	−0.22 (0.227)	−0.70*** (0.000)
Passenger connections	−0.02 (0.680)	0.13 (0.153)	0.06 (0.598)	−0.17 (0.319)	−0.18 (0.307)
R^2	.96	.79	.62	.27	.22

[‡] Hiring for relational competence is measured as the number of functions for which relational competence is an important criterion. Flight departure performance includes quality—customer complaints, mishandled bags, and late arrivals—as well as efficiency—turnaround time per departure and staff time per passenger. Exact definitions of performance and product measures are shown in Exhibit 3–3. These findings are discussed in Chap. 7.

All models are random effects regressions with site/month as the unit of analysis ($n = 99$) and site ($n = 9$) as the random effect. Statistical significance is denoted: [+]$p < 0.10$, [*]$p < 0.05$, [**]$p < 0.01$, [***]$p < 0.001$, and suggests the certainty that a change in hiring practices will produce a change in performance, where a smaller p value suggests a higher certainty. R^2 denotes the percentage of the variation in performance that is explained by the model.

APPENDIX 8–1

Impact of Proactive Conflict Resolution on Relational Coordination[‡]

	Relational Coordination
Conflict resolution	0.39***
	(0.000)
Flights/day	–0.20*
	(0.048)
Gate agent	0.32***
	(0.000)
Baggage agent	0.13*
	(0.017)
Operations agent	0.38***
	(0.000)
Ramp agent	0.32***
	(0.000)
R^2	.30

[‡] Proactive conflict resolution is assessed on a 1-to-5 scale. Relational coordination, coordination carried out through relationships of shared goals, shared knowledge, and mutual respect, is measured as the percentage of cross-functional ties that are "strong" or "very strong," based on an employee survey. These findings are discussed in Chap. 8.

All models are random effects regressions with employee as the unit of analysis ($n = 317$) and site ($n = 9$) as the random effect. Functional identity of the respondent is included as a control variable to reflect differences in relational coordination as experienced by different functions, treating pilots as the baseline function. Standardized regression coefficients are shown. Statistical significance is denoted: $^+p < 0.10$, $^*p < 0.05$, $^{**}p < 0.01$, $^{***}p < 0.001$, and suggests the certainty that a change in conflict resolution will produce a change in relational coordination, where a smaller p value suggests a higher certainty. R^2 denotes the percent of the variation in relational coordination that is explained by the model.

APPENDIX 8-2

Impact of Proactive Conflict Resolution on Flight Departure Performance‡

	Flight Departure Performance				
	Turnaround Time	Staff Time per Passenger	Customer Complaints	Lost Bags	Late Arrivals
Conflict resolution	-0.37*** (0.000)	-0.52*** (0.000)	-1.03*** (0.000)	-0.30 (0.162)	-0.68** (0.001)
Flights/day	-0.04 (0.335)	-0.19* (0.024)	0.11 (0.228)	0.22 (0.185)	0.04 (0.809)
Flight length, passengers and cargo per flight	0.68*** (0.000)	0.40*** (0.000)	-0.14 (0.204)	0.14 (0.473)	-0.66** (0.001)
Passenger connections	-0.01 (0.910)	0.08 (0.379)	-0.24* (0.023)	0.11 (0.552)	-0.17 (0.359)
R^2	.95	.79	.74	.17	.20

‡ Proactive conflict resolution is assessed on a 1-to-5 scale. Flight departure performance includes quality—customer complaints, mishandled bags, and late arrivals—as well as efficiency—turnaround time per departure and staff time per passenger. Exact definitions of performance and product measures are shown in Exhibit 3–3. These findings are discussed in Chap. 8.

All models are random effects regressions with site/month as the unit of analysis ($n = 99$) and site ($n = 9$) as the random effect. Statistical significance is denoted: $^{+}p < 0.10$, $^{*}p < 0.05$, $^{**}p < 0.01$, $^{***}p < 0.001$, and suggests the certainty that a change in conflict resolution will produce a change in performance, where a smaller p value suggests a higher certainty. R^2 denotes the percentage of the variation in performance that is explained by the model.

APPENDIX 10-1

Impact of Boundary Spanner Staffing on Relational Coordination[‡]

	Relational Coordination
Boundary spanner staffing	0.34[**]
	(0.001)
Flights/day	−0.15
	(0.127)
Gate agent	0.32[***]
	(0.000)
Baggage agent	0.13[*]
	(0.019)
Operations agent	0.38[***]
	(0.000)
Ramp agent	0.32[***]
	(0.000)
R^2	.26

[‡] Boundary spanner staffing is measured as the number of boundary spanners on staff per daily flight departure. Relational coordination, coordination carried out through relationships of shared goals, shared knowledge, and mutual respect, is measured as the percentage of cross-functional ties that are "strong" or "very strong," based on an employee survey. These findings are discussed in Chap. 10.

All models are random effects regressions with employee as the unit of analysis ($n = 317$) and site ($n = 9$) as the random effect. Functional identity of the respondent is included as a control variable to reflect differences in relational coordination as experienced by different functions, treating pilots as the baseline function. Standardized regression coefficients are shown. Statistical significance is denoted: $^+p < 0.10$, $^*p < 0.05$, $^{**}p < 0.01$, $^{***}p < 0.001$, and suggests the certainty that a change in boundary spanner staffing will produce a change in relational coordination, where a smaller p value suggests a higher certainty. R^2 denotes the percentage of the variation in relational coordination that is explained by the model.

APPENDIX 10-2

Impact of Boundary Spanner Staffing on Flight Departure Performance‡

	Flight Departure Performance				
	Turnaround Time	Staff Time per Passenger	Customer Complaints	Lost Bags	Late Arrivals
Boundary spanner staffing	-0.21^{***} (0.000)	-0.18^{*} (0.004)	-0.48^{***} (0.000)	-0.30^{*} (0.002)	-0.21^{+} (0.084)
Flights/day	-0.20^{***} (0.000)	-0.43^{***} (0.000)	-0.36^{***} (0.000)	0.11 (0.340)	-0.29^{*} (0.013)
Flight length, passengers and cargo per flight	0.81^{***} (0.000)	0.67^{***} (0.000)	0.33^{***} (0.000)	-0.17 (0.206)	-0.27^{*} (0.049)
Passenger connections	0.18^{***} (0.000)	0.38^{***} (0.000)	0.32^{**} (0.000)	0.23^{+} (0.063)	0.23^{+} (0.076)
R^2	.95	.76	.68	.20	.14

‡ Boundary spanner staffing is measured as the number of boundary spanners on staff per daily flight departure. Flight departure performance includes quality—customer complaints, mishandled bags, and late arrivals—as well as efficiency—turnaround time per departure and staff time per passenger. Exact definitions of performance and product measures are shown in Exhibit 3–3. These findings are discussed in Chap. 10.

All models are random effects regressions with site/month as the unit of analysis ($n = 99$) and site ($n = 9$) as the random effect. Statistical significance is denoted: $^{+}p < 0.10$, $^{*}p < 0.05$, $^{**}p < 0.01$, $^{***}p < 0.001$, and suggests the certainty that a change in boundary spanner staffing will produce a change in performance, where a smaller p value suggests a higher certainty. R^2 denotes the percentage of the variation in performance that is explained by the model.

APPENDIX I I – I

Impact of Performance Measurement on Relational Coordination[‡]

	Relational Coordination
Cross-functional performance measurement	0.42***
	(0.000)
Flights/day	–0.21*
	(0.011)
Gate agent	0.33***
	(0.000)
Baggage agent	0.13*
	(0.019)
Operations agent	0.38***
	(0.000)
Ramp agent	0.32***
	(0.000)
R^2	.30

[‡] Cross-functional performance measurement is measured as the number of functions that could be held jointly accountable for a flight delay. Relational coordination, coordination carried out through relationships of shared goals, shared knowledge, and mutual respect, is measured as the percentage of cross-functional ties that are "strong" or "very strong," based on an employee survey. These findings are discussed in Chap. 11.

All models are random effects regressions with employee as the unit of analysis ($n = 317$) and site ($n = 9$) as the random effect. Functional identity of the respondent is included as a control variable to reflect differences in relational coordination as experienced by different functions, treating pilots as the baseline function. Standardized regression coefficients are shown. Statistical significance is denoted: [+]$p < 0.10$, [*]$p < 0.05$, [**]$p < 0.01$, [***]$p < 0.001$, and suggests the certainty that a change in performance measurement will produce a change in relational coordination, where a smaller p value suggests a higher certainty. R^2 denotes the percentage of the variation in relational coordination that is explained by the model.

APPENDIX 11–2

Impact of Performance Measurement on Flight Departure Performance[‡]

	Flight Departure Performance				
	Turnaround Time	Staff Time per Passenger	Customer Complaints	Lost Bags	Late Arrivals
Cross-functional performance measurement	-0.30^{***} (0.000)	-0.38^{***} (0.001)	-0.66^{***} (0.000)	-0.54^{***} (0.002)	-0.42^{**} (0.002)
Flights/day	-0.07^{*} (0.012)	-0.26^{***} (0.000)	-0.10 (0.215)	0.35^{**} (0.006)	-0.11 (0.434)
Flight length, passengers and cargo per flight	0.76^{***} (0.000)	0.54^{***} (0.000)	0.21^{**} (0.007)	0.01 (0.954)	-0.41^{**} (0.004)
Passenger connections	$0.05+$ (0.089)	0.20^{**} (0.006)	0.05 (0.524)	0.01 (0.916)	0.03 (0.819)
R^2	.96	.81	.74	.28	.19

[‡] Cross-functional performance measurement is measured as the number of functions that could be held jointly accountable for a flight delay. Flight departure performance includes quality—customer complaints, mishandled bags, and late arrivals—as well as efficiency—turnaround time per departure and staff time per passenger. Exact definitions of performance and product measures are shown in Exhibit 3–3. These findings are discussed in Chap. 11.

All models are random effects regressions with site/month as the unit of analysis ($n = 99$) and site ($n = 9$) as the random effect. Statistical significance is denoted: $^{+}p < 0.10$ $^{*}p < 0.05$ $^{**}p < 0.01$ $^{***}p < 0.001$, and suggests the certainty that a change in performance measurement will produce a change in performance, where a smaller p value suggests a higher certainty. R^2 denotes the percentage of the variation in performance that is explained by the model.

APPENDIX 12-1

Impact of Job Flexibility on Relational Coordination[‡]

	Relational Coordination
Job flexibility	0.36[***]
	(0.000)
Flights/day	−0.22[***]
	(0.000)
Gate agent	0.31[***]
	(0.000)
Baggage agent	0.13[*]
	(0.016)
Operations agent	0.43[***]
	(0.000)
Ramp agent	0.34[***]
	(0.000)
R^2	.27

[‡] Job flexibility is assessed on a 1-to-5 scale. Relational coordination, coordination carried out through relationships of shared goals, shared knowledge, and mutual respect, is measured as the percentage of cross-functional ties that are "strong" or "very strong," based on an employee survey. These findings are discussed in Chap. 12.

All models are random effects regressions with employee as the unit of analysis ($n = 317$) and site ($n = 9$) as the random effect. Functional identity of the respondent is included as a control variable to reflect differences in relational coordination as experienced by different functions, treating pilots as the baseline function. Standardized regression coefficients are shown. Statistical significance is denoted: [+]$p < 0.10$, [*]$p < 0.05$, [**]$p < 0.01$, [***]$p < 0.001$, and suggests the certainty that a change in job flexibility will produce a change in relational coordination, where a smaller p value suggests a higher certainty. R^2 denotes the percentage of the variation in relational coordination that is explained by the model.

Impact of Job Flexibility on Flight Departure Performance[‡]

	Flight Departure Performance				
	Turnaround Time	Staff Time per Passenger	Customer Complaints	Lost Bags	Late Arrivals
Job flexibility	−0.55*** (0.000)	−1.36*** (0.000)	−1.41*** (0.000)	−0.10 (0.648)	−0.67 (0.122)
Flights/day	−0.14** (0.004)	−0.62*** (0.000)	−0.14 (0.220)	0.07 (0.552)	0.21+ (0.060)
Flight length, passengers and cargo per flight	0.32** (0.006)	−0.81*** (0.000)	−0.71** (0.006)	0.29 (0.224)	−0.83* (0.045)
Passenger connections	0.06 (0.574)	0.34+ (0.056)	0.32+ (0.077)	0.31* (0.012)	0.46+ (0.078)
R^2	.85	.44	.64	.15	.09

[‡] Job flexibility is assessed on a 1-to-5 scale. Flight departure performance includes quality—customer complaints, mishandled bags, and late arrivals—as well as efficiency—turnaround time per departure and staff time per passenger. Exact definitions of performance and product measures are shown in Exhibit 3–3. These findings are discussed in Chap. 12.

All models are random effects regressions with site/month as the unit of analysis ($n = 99$) and site ($n = 9$) as the random effect. Statistical significance is denoted: $^+p < 0.10$, $^*p < 0.05$, $^{**}p < 0.01$, $^{***}p < 0.001$, and suggests the certainty that a change in job flexibility will produce a change in performance, where a smaller p value suggests a higher certainty. R^2 denotes the percentage of the variation in performance that is explained by the model.

Endnotes

Chapter I

1. Katrina Brooker (2001). "The Chairman of the Board Looks Back," *Fortune*, May 28.
2. Roger Hallowell (1997). Harvard Business School Doctoral Dissertation.
3. Steven Spear and Kent Bowen (1999). "Decoding the DNA of the Toyota Production System," *Harvard Business Review*, September–October; James P. Womack, Daniel T. Jones, and Daniel Roos (1990). *The Machine That Changed the World: The Story of Lean Production*. New York: Rawson-Macmillan.
4. Rigas Doganis (2001). *The Airline Business in the 21st Century*. London: Routledge.
5. U.S. Department of Transportation. Air Carrier Traffic Statistics Monthly. Domestic Scheduled Services Traffic.
6. Melanie Trottman (2001). "Up in the Air: Amid Crippled Rivals, Southwest Again Tries to Spread its Wings—Low-Fare Airline Maintains Service, Mulls Expansion in Risky Bid for Traffic—Tapping $475 Million in Credit," *Wall Street Journal*, October 11.
7. This analysis of Southwest's position in 1994 and the competitive threats it posed, and faced, can be found in Jody Hoffer Gittell (1995). "Cross-Functional Coordination and Control: Influencing Employee Behavior and Process Outcomes through Organizational Design in the Airline Industry." Massachusetts Institute of Technology Doctoral Dissertation.
8. Randall D. Bennett and James M. Craun (1993). *The Airline Deregulation Evolution Continues: The Southwest Effect*. U.S. Department of Transportation, Office of Aviation Analysis.
9. Anthony L. Velocci, Jr. (1995). "More City Pairs Await Southwest," *Aviation Week and Space Technology*, August 7.
10. Edwin McDowell (1993). "No Business Trip Bedrolls, Yet: Economizing on Business Travel," *New York Times*, November 5.
11. Martha Brannigan, Susan Carey, and Scott McCartney (2001). "First-Class Mutiny: Fed up with Airlines, Business Travelers Start to Fight Back," *Wall Street Journal*, August 28.
12. Ibid.
13. Melanie Trottman and Scott McCartney (2002). "The Age of 'Wal-Mart' Airlines Crunches the Biggest Carriers," *Wall Street Journal*, June 18.

14. Ibid.
15. Jim Wimberly, quoted in: Jody Hoffer Gittell (2001). "Investing in Relationships," *Harvard Business Review*, June.
16. Deborah Ancona, Thomas A. Kochan, Maureen Scully, John Van Maanen, and Eleanor Westney (forthcoming). *Managing for the Future: Organizational Behavior and Procedures*, 3d ed., Southwestern.
17. Jeffrey Pfeffer (1996). *Competitive Advantage through People: Unleashing the Power of the Work Force*. Boston: Harvard Business School Press; James Heskett, Earl Sasser, and Leonard Schlesinger (1997). *The Service Profit Chain: How Leading Companies Link Profit and Growth to Loyalty, Satisfaction and Value*. New York: The Free Press.
18. Howard Banks (1994). "A Sixties Industry in a Nineties Economy," *Forbes*, May 5.
19. James P. Womack, Daniel T. Jones, and Daniel Roos (1990). *The Machine That Changed the World: The Story of Lean Production*. New York: Rawson-Macmillan.
20. Frederick Abernathy, John Dunlop, Janice Hammond, and David Weil (1999). *A Stitch in Time: Lean Retailing and the Transformation of Manufacturing*. New York: Oxford University Press.
21. Jody Hoffer Gittell (1998). "Coordinating Services across Functional Boundaries: The Departure Process at Southwest Airlines," in *Best Practices in Customer Service: Case Studies and Strategies*, Ron Zemke and John Wood (Eds.). Amherst, MA: HRD Press.
22. Janice Hammond (1992). "Coordination as the Basis for Quick Response: A Case for 'Virtual' Integration in Supply Networks," Harvard Business School Working Paper No. 92-007.
23. John Paul MacDuffie (1995). "Human Resource Bundles and Manufacturing Performance: Organizational Logic and Flexible Production Systems in the World Auto Industry," *Industrial and Labor Relations Review*, 58: 197–221.
24. Steven Spear and Kent Bowen (1999). "Decoding the DNA of the Toyota Production System," *Harvard Business Review*, September–October; James Womack, Daniel Jones, and Daniel Roos (1990). *The Machine That Changed the World: The Story of Lean Production*. New York: Rawson-Macmillan.
25. Rose Batt (1999). "Work Design, Technology, and Performance in Customer Services and Sales," *Industrial and Labor Relations Review*, 52(4): 539–564.
26. Marco Iansiti and Kim Clark (1994). "Integration and Dynamic Capability: Evidence from Product Development in Automobiles and Mainframe Computers," *Industrial and Corporate Change*, 3(3): 557–605.
27. Frederick Abernathy, John Dunlop, Janice Hammond, and David Weil (1999). *A Stitch in Time: Lean Retailing and the Transformation of Manufacturing—Lessons from the Apparel and Textile Industries*. New York: Oxford University Press; John Dunlop and David Weil (1996). "Diffusion and Performance of Modular Production in the US Apparel Industry," *Industrial Relations*, June, pp. 334–355.

Chapter 2

1. This point is not widely understood. As Herb Kelleher pointed out in 1995, "Delta is doing a terrific job of cutting its costs so that by 1997 they will be at 7.5 cents per available seat mile. Some people are saying, 'Holy mackerel, Herb! Delta is closing the gap with Southwest.' People forget that Delta's average stage length is 901 miles. If our average stage length were 901 miles, or nearly double what it is now, our actual costs would be 4.6 cents per available seat mile." Quoted in Anthony L. Velocci, Jr. (1995). "More City Pairs Await Southwest," *Aviation Week and Space Technology*, August 7.
2. Terran Melconian and John-Paul Barrington Clarke (2001). *Effects of Increased Non-Stop Routing on Airline Cost and Profit.* MIT International Center for Air Transportation, Report No. ICAT-2001-4.
3. Howard Banks (1994). "A Sixties Industry in a Nineties Economy," *Forbes*, May 5.
4. Ibid.
5. Peter Coy (2002). "The Airlines: Caught Between a Hub and a Hard Place," *BusinessWeek*, August 5.
6. Randall D. Bennett and James M. Craun (1993). *The Airline Deregulation Evolution Continues: The Southwest Effect.* U.S. Department of Transportation, Office of Aviation Analysis.

Chapter 3

1. I conducted field research in the mid-1990s to discover how organizational factors influence flight departure performance. In order to understand the flight departure process, I attended meetings, shadowed employees in each function, and asked them to explain what they were doing and why. I became interested in exploring interactions among employees, as well as the formal organizational practices that had been established by management. At each site, I observed employees in each of the 12 functions involved in flight departures.

I shadowed employees as they carried out their tasks related to flight departures and observed their interactions with each other. I also interviewed them in their break rooms, asking them to explain things I had observed while shadowing them. Interviews were unstructured and typically lasted from 15 to 30 minutes. I took notes recording my observations and their comments and typed them up within a week of each visit. In typing up my notes, related observations were brought to mind and were recorded along with those captured in the original notes. My goal was to understand the nature of interactions among participants in the flight departure process. I conducted 28 interviews and 8 days of observations at AMR1, and 20 interviews and 5 days of observations at SWA1.

To analyze the data collected at each site, I followed traditional guidelines for qualitative methods (B. Glaser and A. Strauss, 1967, *The Discovery of Grounded Theory: Strategies of Qualitative Research*. London: Wiedenfield and Nicholson), developing empirically grounded sets of categories related to coordination of the flight departure process. I followed an iterative process, first developing hunches, then comparing those ideas to new data from the site, and further using the new data to decide whether to retain, revise, or discard the inferences. My goal was not to impose a category scheme from the existing literature but rather to identify empirically the relevant dimensions of coordination. My criteria for identifying dimensions of coordination in this research setting were the following. First, that they described interactions among participants directly relevant to integrating tasks in the flight departure process. This criterion resulted in a focus on interactions that occurred across functional boundaries, rather than within functional areas, because that is where the critical task interdependencies were expected to be. Second, that they had a plausible link to outcomes of the flight departure process. For example, when my notes recorded a participant mentioning the need for timely communication with other functions, or when I recorded observing timely communication or a lack of timely communication, I noted "timeliness" in the margin. I went back through previous notes to find other occasions where timely communication had been an issue but I had not made note of it. I then focused on timeliness in subsequent interviews and observations to discover whether or not it emerged consistently as a theme. I focused on timeliness in the sense that when the issue arose, I asked follow-up questions and requested examples in order to develop a comparison with the site where timeliness had already emerged as a theme.

After the initial site visits, I compared my field notes across the two sites, looking at each site for evidence regarding types of interactions that I had flagged in the other site. For some, I noted I had plentiful data from one site and little from the other. I had become sensitized to some issues at the second site that I had not noticed in the first. I then perused my notes from the first site, looking further for data that addressed that particular dimension. As I returned to each of the two sites for additional observations and interviews, I focused on the dimensions that had been overlooked. Again, I focused on these dimensions in the sense that when they arose in my observations or interviews, I asked follow-up questions and requested examples in order to develop a comparison with the other site.

Because these interviews were conducted in the mid-1990s and changes have occurred at both airlines in the meantime, particularly at American Airlines, the interviews in this chapter do not necessarily reflect the current state of affairs at either airline.

2. K. D. Benne and P. Sheats (1948). "Functional Roles of Group Members," *Journal of Social Issues*, 4: 41–19.

3. Thomas Allen (1984). *Managing the Flow of Technology*. Cambridge, MA: MIT Press; Deborah G. Ancona and David F. Caldwell (1992). "Bridging the Boundary: External Activity and Performance in Organizational Teams," *Administrative Science Quarterly*, 37: 634–665; Linda Argote (1982). "Input Uncertainty and Organizational Coordination in Hospital Emergency Units," *Administrative Science Quarterly*, 27(3): 420–434; R. Katz and Michael Tushman (1979). "Communication Patterns, Project Performance and Task Characteristics: An Empirical Evaluation and Integration in an R&D Setting," *Organizational Behavior and Human Performance*, 23: 139–162; James D. Thompson (1967). *Organizations in Action: Social Science Bases of Administrative Theory*. New York: McGraw-Hill; Andrew Van de Ven, A. Delbecq, and R.

Koenig, Jr. (1976). "Determinants of Coordination Modes within Organizations," *American Sociological Review*, 41: 322–338.

4. Wanda J. Orlikowski and Joanne Yates (1991). "Genre Repertoire: The Structuring of Communicative Practices in Organizations," *Administrative Science Quarterly*, 394: 541–574; Mary J. Waller (1999). "The Timing of Adaptive Group Responses to Non-routine Events," *Academy of Management Journal*, 42(2): 127–137.

5. Saul Rubinstein (2000). "The Impact of Co-management on Quality Performance: The Case of the Saturn Corporation," *Industrial and Labor Relations Review*, 53(1): 197–220.

6. W. Edwards Deming (1986). *Out of the Crisis*. Cambridge, MA: MIT Press.

7. James G. March and Herbert A. Simon (1958). *Organizations*. New York: Wiley.

8. Richard Saavedra, P. Christopher Earley, and Linn Van Dyne (1993). "Complex Interdependence in Task-Performing Groups," *Journal of Applied Psychology*, 78(1): 61–72; Ruth Wageman (1995). "Interdependence and Group Effectiveness," *Administrative Science Quarterly*, 40: 145–180.

9. Deborah Dougherty (1994). "Interpretive Barriers to Successful Product Innovation in Large Firms," *Organization Science*, 3(2): 179-202.

10. John Van Maanen and Steve R. Barley (1984). "Occupational Communities: Culture and Control in Organizations." In B. M. Staw and L. L. Cummings (eds.), *Research in Organizational Behavior*, 6: 287–365. Greenwich, CT: JAI Press.

11. Albert H. Rubenstein, Richard T. Barth, and Charles F. Douds (1971). "Ways to Improve Communications between R&D Groups," *Research Management*, 14: 49; Eric Eisenberg (1990). "Jamming: Transcendence through Organizing," *Communication Research*, 17: 139–164.

12. At each site, I administered the survey in person on a single day to employees working the morning shift. All surveys were conducted on weekdays between Tuesday and Thursday, to avoid disrupting the operations and to increase the number of surveys completed, because passenger loads were typically lighter on these three days. Respondents typically required 20 minutes to complete the survey. Four hundred surveys were administered with a response rate of 89 percent, yielding 354 surveys.

   The survey questions reflected the six dimensions of relational coordination: the frequency, timeliness, and problem-solving nature of communication between participants, and the degree to which their relationships were characterized by shared goals, shared knowledge, and mutual respect. Respondents were asked to answer the questions with respect to each of the 12 functions involved in flight departures, including the functions that were not surveyed—pilots, flight attendants, freight agents, mechanics, cabin cleaners, caterers, and fuelers. Responses were captured on a 5-point Likert-type scale.

13. Turnaround time is costly because it represents time that an aircraft is occupying valuable gate space and not earning revenue. Long turnaround times reduce the return on both the aircraft and the gate. Based on lost revenues from the aircraft alone, I have shown that a 5-minute reduction in turnaround time resulted in an average annual savings of $1.6 billion, or $4700 per employee, for the 10 major U.S. airlines over a 1-year period. See Jody Hoffer Gittell

(1995). "Cost/Quality Tradeoffs in the Departure Process? Evidence from the Major U.S. Airlines," *Transportation Research Record*, 1480: 25–36.

14. These variables were chosen based on advice from industry experts at MIT's Flight Transportation Lab and were included in a model of flight departure performance developed and tested in an earlier study of the flight departure process. See Jody Hoffer Gittell (1995). "Cost/Quality Tradeoffs in the Departure Process? Evidence from the Major U.S. Airlines," *Transportation Research Record*, 1480: 25–36.

15. Correlations among the six dimensions of relational coordination were all greater than 0.23 and significant at the 99 percent level or higher. Cronbach's alpha for the relational coordination construct was 0.803, suggesting a reasonably high level of construct validity.

16. Statistical analyses confirmed that there were significant differences between airlines in the strength of relational coordination, and that in addition there were significant differences between the sites within airlines. Using one-way analysis of variance, I found cross-airline differences in relational coordination that were significant at the 99.9 percent level. Jointly testing the significance of cross-airline and cross-site differences, I also found cross-site differences in relational coordination that were significant at the 99.9 percent level. See Appendix 3-1 for site-level means for relational coordination.

17. Statistical analyses confirmed that cross-site differences in product and performance variables were significant at the 99.9 percent level. See Appendix 3-2 for site-level means for product and performance variables.

18. Random-effects models, also known as mixed, hierarchical linear, or multi-level models, were used to accommodate the multilevel structure of the data. Site/month served as the unit of analysis, with site as the random effect. Regression coefficients, standard errors, and the overall R^2 for random-effects models reflect statistical associations both within and across sites.

19. See Appendix 3-3 for specific results.

20. The impact of relational coordination on turnaround time, staffing productivity, and customer complaints is significant at the 99.9 percent level. The impact of relational coordination on flight delays is significant at the 99 percent level, while the impact of relational coordination on baggage losses is significant at the 95 percent level. The higher the level of significance, the more certain it is that changes in relational coordination will result in changes to the performance measures in question.

21. Janice Hammond (1992). "Coordination as the Basis for Quick Response: A Case for 'Virtual' Integration in Supply Networks," Harvard Business School Working Paper.

22. Jurgen Habermas (1971). *Knowledge and Human Interest.* Boston: Beacon Press; Michel Foucault (1972). *The Archaeology of Knowledge.* New York: Harper Colophon; Kenneth J. Gergen (1994). *Realities and Relationships: Soundings in Social Construction.* Cambridge, MA: Harvard University Press.

23. Jean Baker Miller (1978). *Toward a New Psychology of Women.* Boston: Beacon Press; Judith V. Jordan, Alexandra G. Kaplan, Jean Baker Miller, Irene P. Stiver, and Janet L. Surry (1991). Women's Growth in Connection: Writings from the Stone Center. New York: Guilford Press.

24. Joyce Fletcher (1999). *Disappearing Acts: Gender, Power and Relational Practice at Work*. Cambridge, MA: MIT Press.
25. Carrie Leana and Harry Van Buren, III (1999). "Organizational Social Capital and Employment Practices," *Academy of Management Review*, 24: 538–555; Janine Nahapiet and Sumantra Ghoshal (1998). "Social Capital, Intellectual Capital and the Organizational Advantage," *Academy of Management Review*, 23: 242–266.
26. Adam Smith (1776). *The Wealth of Nations*. New York: Modern Library (2000).
27. Karl Marx (1845). "The German Ideology." In L. Feuer (Ed.), *Marx and Engels: Basic Writings on Politics and Philosophy*. New York: Anchor (1959); Sigmund Freud (1927). *Civilization and Its Discontents*. New York: Norton (1989).

Chapter 4

1. John Kenagy, Don Berwick, and Miles Shore (1999). "Service Quality in Health Care," *Journal of the American Medical Association*, 281:661–665; Regina Herzlinger (1997). *Market Driven Health Care: Who Wins and Who Loses in the Transformation of America's Largest Service Industry*. Reading, MA: Addison-Wesley.
2. Anselm Strauss, Shizuko Fagerhaugh, Barbara Suczek, and Carolyn Wiener (1985). *Social Organization of Medical Work*. Chicago: University of Chicago Press.
3. Linda Argote (1982). "Input Uncertainty and Organizational Coordination in Hospital Emergency Units," *Administrative Science Quarterly*, 27: 420–434; William A. Knaus, Elizabeth A. Draper, Douglas Wagner, and Jack E. Zimmerman (1986). "An Evaluation of Outcomes from Intensive Care in Major Medical Centers," *Annals of Internal Medicine*, 104: 410–418; Judith Gedney Baggs, Sheila A. Ryan, Charles E. Phelps, J. Franklin Richeson, and Jean E. Johnson (1992). "The Association between Interdisciplinary Collaboration and Patient Outcomes in a Medical Intensive Care Unit," *Heart and Lung*, 21: 18–24; Stephen M. Shortell, Jack E. Zimmerman, Denise E. Rousseau, Robin R. Gillies, Douglas P. Wagner, Elizabeth A. Draper, William A. Knaus, and Joanne Duffy (1994). "The Performance of Intensive Care Units: Does Good Management Make a Difference?" *Medical Care*, 32: 508–25; Gary Young, Marty Charns, Kamal Desai, Shukri F. Khuri, Maureen G. Forbes, William Henderson, and Jennifer Daley (2000). "Patterns of Coordination and Clinical Outcomes: A Study of Surgical Services," *Health Services Research*, 33: 1211–1236.
4. Jody Hoffer Gittell, Kathleen Fairfield, Benjamin Bierbaum, William Head, Robert Jackson, Michael Kelly, Richard Laskin, Stephen Lipson, John Siliski, Thomas Thornhill, and Joseph Zuckerman (2000). "Impact of Relational Coordination on Quality of Care, Post-operative Pain and Functioning, and the Length of Stay: A Nine-Hospital Study of Surgical Patients," *Medical Care*, 38(8): 807–819.

5. Amy Edmondson (1996). "Learning from Mistakes is Easier Said than Done: Group and Organizational Influences on the Detection and Correction of Human Error," *Journal of Applied Behavioral Science*, 32(1): 5-28.

6. Peggy Barry Martin (1996). "Review of Coordination of Care Issues in CRICO Claims," *Forum*. Risk Management Foundation of the Harvard Medical Institutions, Inc., 17(4): 2–14.

7. Margaret Gerteis, Susan Edgman-Levitan, Jennifer Daley, and Thomas Delbanco (1993). *Through the Patient's Eyes: Understanding and Promoting Patient-Centered Care*. San Francisco: Jossey-Bass.

8. Surveys were sent to all eligible care providers in the five core disciplines who had clinical or administrative responsibilities for joint-replacement patients during the study period: physicians, nurses, physical therapists, social workers, and case managers (known in some departments as care coordinators). Providers were asked to comment on ongoing, day-to-day coordination occurring in their units. A total of 338 surveys were returned out of 666, for an overall provider response rate of 51 percent.

9. Jon Chilingerian (2000). "Evaluating Quality Outcomes against Best Practice: A New Frontier." In J. R. Kimberly and E. Minvielle (Eds.), *The Quality Imperative: Measurement and Management of Quality in Health Care*. London: Imperial College Press, 141–167.

10. Margaret Gerteis, Susan Edgman-Levitan, Jennifer Daley, and Thomas Delbanco (1993). *Through the Patient's Eyes: Understanding and Promoting Patient-Centered Care*. San Francisco: Jossey-Bass.

11. Marsha Gold and Judith Wooldridge (1995). "Surveying Customer Satisfaction to Assess Managed Care Quality: Current Practices," *Health Care Financing Review*, 16(4): 155–173; Don Berwick (1996). "The Year of 'How': New Systems for Delivering Health Care," *Quality Connections*, 5(1): 1–4; John Kenagy, Don Berwick, and Miles Shore (1999). "Service Quality in Health Care," *Journal of the American Medical Association*, 281:661–665.

12. Patients were selected at random from among those admitted to one of the nine hospitals for primary, elective unilateral total joint replacement during the study period with a diagnosis of osteoarthritis. All patients were mailed surveys between 6 and 10 weeks postdischarge. A total of 878 surveys were returned out of 1367, for an overall patient response rate of 64 percent. To measure performance outcomes, a service quality index was constructed from 15 survey items regarding service quality in the in-patient hospital setting. Postoperative pain and functional status were assessed from the patient survey, using the 5 items relating to pain and 17 items relating to physical functioning from the WOMAC, a validated osteoarthritis instrument.

13. Correlations among the seven dimensions of relational coordination were all greater than .24 and significant at the 99.9 percent level or higher. Cronbach's alpha for the relational coordination construct was 0.849, suggesting a reasonably high level of construct validity.

14. Statistical analyses confirmed that there were significant differences between hospitals in the strength of relational coordination. Using one-way analysis of variance, cross-hospital differences in relational coordination were found to be significant at the 99.9 percent level. See Appendix 4-1 for hospital-level means for relational coordination.

15. Statistical analyses confirmed that cross-hospital differences in performance variables were significant at the 99.9 percent level. See Appendix 4-2 for hospital-level means for performance variables.
16. Random-effects models, also known as mixed, hierarchical linear, or multilevel models, were used to accommodate the multilevel structure of the data. Patient served as the unit of analysis, with hospital as the random effect. Regression coefficients, standard errors, and the overall R squares for random-effects models reflect statistical associations both within and across hospitals.
17. See Appendix 4-3 for specific results.
18. The impact of relational coordination on length of stay and service quality is significant at the 99.9 percent level. The impact of relational coordination on postoperative freedom from pain is significant at the 95 percent level, while the impact of relational coordination on postoperative mobility is significant at the 85 percent level. The higher the level of significance, the more certain it is that changes in relational coordination will result in changes to the performance measures in question.
19. James D. Thompson (1967). *Organizations in Action: Social Science Bases of Administrative Theory.* New York: McGraw Hill.
20. Andrew Van de Ven, Andre Delbecq, and R. Koenig, Jr. (1976). "Determinants of Coordination Modes within Organizations," *American Sociological Review*, 41: 322–338; Linda Argote (1982). "Input Uncertainty and Organizational Coordination in Hospital Emergency Units," *Administrative Science Quarterly*, 27(3): 420–434.
21. Paul Adler (1995). "Interdepartmental Interdependence and Coordination: The Case of the Design/Manufacturing Interface," *Organization Science*, 6:147–167.

Part 2

1. John Paul MacDuffie (1995). "Human Resource Bundles and Manufacturing Performance: Organizational Logic and Flexible Production Systems in the World Auto Industry," *Industrial and Labor Relations Review*, 48: 197–221.
2. John T. Dunlop and David Weil (1996). "Diffusion and Performance of Modular Production in the U.S. Apparel Industry," *Industrial Relations*, July, 334–355.
3. Casey Ichniowski, Kathryn Shaw, and Giovanna Prennushi (1996). "The Effects of Human Resource Practices on Manufacturing Performance: A Study of Steel Finishing Lines," *American Economic Review*, 87(3): 291–313.
4. Rose Batt (1999). "Work Design, Technology, and Performance in Customer Services and Sales," *Industrial and Labor Relations Review*, 52(4): 539–564.
5. These studies, like the one reported in this book, were fostered by the Sloan Industry Centers under the auspices of the Alfred P. Sloan Foundation. The Sloan Industry Centers are intended to develop a deep understanding of performance in particular industry settings, and to transfer learning from one industry setting to the others. See "The Sloan Industry Centers: Understanding the Critical Issues That Affect Business and Commerce Today," www.sloan.org.

Chapter 5

1. Matthew Brelis (2000). "Herb's Way," *Boston Globe*, November 5, p. F4.
2. Ralph M. Stogdill (1974). *Handbook of Leadership: A Survey of the Literature.* New York: Free Press, p. 259.
3. J. K Hemphill and A. E. Coons (1957). "Development of the Leader Behavior Description Questionnaire." In Ralph M. Stogdill and A. E. Coons (Eds.), *Leader Behavior: Its Description and Measurement.* Columbus, OH: Bureau of Business Research, Ohio State University.
4. T. O. Jacobs and E. Jacques (1990). "Military Executive Leadership." In K. E. Clark and M. B. Clark (Eds.), *Measures of Leadership.* West Orange, NJ: Leadership Library of American, p. 281.
5. Katrina Brooker (2001). "The Chairman of the Board Looks Back," *Fortune*, May 28.
6. "Continental Airlines' Turnaround," *The News Hour with Jim Lehrer*, transcript, March 19, 1998.
7. Ibid.
8. Ibid.
9. Julie Schmit (1994). "UAL's New Leader Is Accustomed to Risk—Greenwald Must Keep Morale High While Cutting Pay," *USA Today*, July 15.
10. Perry Flint (1994). "United in Battle," *Air Transport World*, October.
11. Ibid.
12. Ibid.
13. Michael J. McCarthy (1994). "United Names as President Edwardson, Ameritech CFO with Airline Experience," *Wall Street Journal*, July 15.
14. Katrina Brooker (2001). "The Chairman of the Board Looks Back," *Fortune*, May 28.
15. Margaret Allen (2001). "Southwest Airlines' Head Takes Flight with Ground Control," *Houston Business Journal*, August 27.
16. See interview with Southwest's top management team regarding new challenges, conducted with R. John Hansman and Anne Dunning and reported in Jody Hoffer Gittell (2001). "Investing in Relationships," *Harvard Business Review*, June, pp. 28–30.
17. L. J. Bourgeouis and Kathleen Eisenhardt (1998). "Strategic Decision Processes in High Velocity Environments: Four Cases in the Microcomputer Industry," *Management Science*, 34(7): 816–835; Jon Katzenbach (1998). *Teams at the Top: Unleashing the Power of Both Teams and Individual Leaders.* Boston: Harvard Business School Press; Michael Tushman, Donald Hambrick, and David Nadler (1998). *Navigating Change: How CEOs, Top Teams and Boards Steer Transformations.* Boston: Harvard Business School Press.
18. Robert J. House. "A 1976 Theory of Charismatic Leadership." In J. G. Hunt and L. L. Larson (Eds.), *Leadership: The Cutting Edge.* Carbondale, IL: Southern Illinois University Press.

Chapter 6

1. Phillip Selznick (1949). *TVA and the Grass Roots.* Berkeley, CA: Berkeley University Press; Abner Gouldner (1954). *Patterns of Industrial Bureaucracy.*

Glencoe, IL: Free Press; Robert Merton (1957). *Social Theory and Social Structure*. Glencoe, IL: Free Press; Stephen Marglin (1974). "What Do Bosses Do? The Origins and Functions of Hierarchy in Capitalist Production," *Review of Radical Political Economy*, 6(2): 60–112; Katherine Stone (1976). "The Origins of Job Structure in the Steel Industry," *Review of Radical Political Economy*, 6(2): 113–173; Richard Edwards (1979). *Contested Terrain: The Transformation of the Workplace in the Twentieth Century*. New York: Basic Books; Samuel Bowles (1985). "The Production Process in a Competitive Economy: Neoclassical, Neohobbesian and Marxian," *American Economic Review*, 75(1): 16–36.

2. Michael Piore and Charles Sabel (1984). *The Second Industrial Divide*. New York: Basic Books; Richard Walton (1985). "From Control to Commitment in the Workplace," *Harvard Business Review*, March/April, 76–84; Shoshona Zuboff (1988). *In the Age of the Smart Machine: The Future of Work and Power*. New York: Basic Books; Eileen Appelbaum and Rose Batt (1994). *The New American Workplace*. Ithaca, NY: ILR Press; Charles Heckscher and Anne Donnellon (Eds.) (1994). *The Post-Bureaucratic Organization*. Thousand Oaks, CA: Sage.

3. David Gordon (1996). *Fat and Mean: The Corporate Squeeze of Working Americans and the Myth of Managerial "Downsizing."* New York: Free Press; Michael Handel (2000). "Models of Economic Organization and the New Inequality in the United States." Doctoral Dissertation, Harvard Sociology Department.

4. Deborah Ancona, Thomas A. Kochan, Maureen Scully, John Van Maanen, and Eleanor Westney (forthcoming). *Managing for the Future: Organizational Behavior and Procedures*, 3d ed. Mason, OH: South-Western Publishing.

5. These ideas were previously published in: Jody Hoffer Gittell (2001). "Supervisory Span, Relational Coordination and Flight Departure Performance: A Reassessment of Post-Bureaucracy Theory," *Organization Science*, 12(4): 467–482.

6. Matthew Brelis (2000). "Herb's Way," *Boston Globe*, November 5, F1.

7. Supervisory staffing is measured as the number of supervisors per hundred frontline employees. It ranged from 2.4 at an American Airlines site to 13.0 at a Southwest Airlines site.

8. See Appendixes 6-1 and 6-2 for detailed results.

9. Richard Hackman and Gregory Oldham (1980). *Work Redesign*. New York: Addison-Wesley; Richard Mowday, L. Porter, and R. Steers (1982). *Employee Organization Linkages*. New York: Academic Press; Richard Walton (1985). "From Control to Commitment in the Workplace," *Harvard Business Review*, March/April, 76–84; Richard Walton and Richard Hackman (1986). "Groups under Contrasting Management Strategies." In Paul Goodman and Associates (Eds.), *Designing Effective Work Groups*, San Francisco: Jossey-Bass.

10. Richard Hackman and Gregory Oldham (1980). *Work Redesign*. New York: Addison-Wesley, 209.

11. Richard Walton and Leonard Schlesinger (1979), "Do Supervisors Thrive in Participative Work Systems?" *Organizational Dynamics*, 7(3): 25–38.

12. T. D. Wall, N. J. Kemp, P. R. Jackson, and C. W. Clegg (1986). "Outcomes of Autonomous Workgroups: A Long-Term Field Experiment," *Academy of Management Journal*, 29(2): 280–305.

13. R. I. Beekun (1989). "Assessing the Effectiveness of Sociotechnical Interventions: Antidote or Fad?" *Human Relations*, 47: 877–897.
14. Douglas McGregor (1960). *The Human Side of Enterprise*. New York: McGraw-Hill, 206.
15. Rensis Likert (1961). *New Patterns of Management*. New York: McGraw-Hill; Arnold Tannenbaum (1968). *Control in Organizations*. New York: McGraw-Hill.
16. Frederick Winslow Taylor (1911). *The Principles of Scientific Management*. Toronto: Dover (1998), 75.
17. Lyman W. Porter and Edward E. Lawler (1964). "The Effects of 'Tall' versus 'Flat' Organization Structures on Managerial Job Satisfaction," *Personnel Psychology*, 135–148.
18. Jeffrey D. Ford (1981). "Department Context and Formal Structure as Constraints on Leader Behavior," *Academy of Management Journal*, 24: 274–288.
19. Barry E. Goodstadt and David Kipnis (1970). "Situational Influences on the Use of Power," *Journal of Applied Psychology*, 54: 201–207.
20. Frank A. Heller and Gary Yukl (1969). "Participation, Managerial Decision-Making and Situational Variables," *Organizational Behavior and Human Performance*, 4: 227–241.
21. David Kipnis and Joseph Cosentino (1969). "Use of Leadership Powers in Industry," *Journal of Applied Psychology*, 53: 460–466; David Kipnis and William P. Lane (1962). "Self Confidence and Leadership," *Journal of Applied Psychology*, 46: 291–295.
22. Deborah G. Ancona (1990). "Outward Bound: Strategies for Team Survival in an Organization," *Academy of Management Journal*, 33(2): 334–365; John C. Henderson and Soonchul Lee (1992). "Managing I/S Design Teams: A Control Theories Perspective," *Management Science*, 38(6): 757–777; Kathleen Eisenhardt and Behnam N. Tabrizi (1995). "Accelerating Adaptive Processes: Product Innovation in the Global Computer Industry," *Administrative Science Quarterly*, 4: 84–110; Y. Kim and B. Lee (1995). "R&D Project Team Climate and Team Performance in Korea: A Multidimensional Approach," *R&D Management*, 25(2): 179–196.
23. Joan Woodward (1965). *Industrial Organization: Theory and Practice*. New York: Oxford University Press.

Chapter 7

1. David Day and Stanley Silverman (1989) "Personality and Job Performance: Evidence of Incremental Validity," *Personnel Psychology*, 42(1): 25–36; Robert Hogan (1991). "Personality and Personality Measurement," in Marvin Dunnette and Leanna Hough (Eds.), *The Handbook of Industrial and Organizational Psychology*, 2d ed., Volume 2. Palo Alto: Consulting Psychologists Press.
2. Leonard Schlesinger and James Heskett (1991). "The Service-Driven Service Company," *Harvard Business Review*, September/October, 71–84.
3. Peter Cappelli and N. Rogovsky (1994). "New Work Systems and Skill Requirements," *International Labour Review*, 133(2): 205–220.
4. Gianni Lorenzoni and Andrea Lipparini (1999). "The Leveraging of Interfirm Relationships as a Distinctive Organizational Capability: A Longitudi-

nal Study," *Strategic Management Journal*, 20: 317–338.

5. Joyce Fletcher (1999). *Disappearing Acts: Gender, Power and Relational Practice at Work*. Cambridge, MA: MIT Press.

6. James Heskett (1993). "Southwest Airlines: 1993 (A)," *Harvard Business School Case 694-023*. Boston: Harvard Business School Publishing.

7. Matthew Brelis (2000). "Herb's Way," *Boston Globe*, November 5, F1.

8. Southwest's actions in this case were consistent with the principles outlined in Leonard Schlesinger and James Heskett (1991). "Breaking the Cycle of Failure in Services," *Sloan Management Review*, 32(3): 17–28.

9. At American Airlines, two groups at the smaller station (Boston) and no groups at the larger station (Los Angeles) were hired for relational competence. At United Airlines, two groups at the smaller station (Boston) and no groups at the larger station (Los Angeles) were hired for relational competence. However, at the United Shuttle, also in Los Angeles, eight groups were hired for relational competence, in the sense that they had self-selected from the regular operations into the Shuttle, knowing teamwork was a condition of entry. This was not the case with the fuelers and ticketing agents, however, who worked across the mainline and Shuttle operations and did not have the option of self-selecting to the Shuttle. At Continental Airlines, four groups at the smaller station (Boston) and no groups at the larger station (Cleveland) were explicitly hired for relational competence. At Southwest, ten groups at the Los Angeles station and nine groups at the Chicago station (fueling was outsourced) were explicitly hired for relational competence.

10. See Appendixes 7-1 and 7-2 for detailed results.

11. Exhibit 3–4 illustrates that the United Shuttle (denoted by UAL3) also out-performed United's non-Shuttle sites in the study (denoted by UAL1 and UAL2), due in part to the higher levels of relational coordination that were achieved in the Shuttle operations.

12. Some of the training potential was lost due to a lack of employee involvement in the design of the new product. Unlike the United Shuttle, frontline employees were not involved in the design of the Continental Lite—instead, the design of Continental Lite had been carried out in a highly secretive way. The Cleveland station manager explained the process: "It was very confidential and very high level. They rented an office and were sworn to secrecy. It was unveiled in the fall. Each station sent people to headquarters to be trained in the concept, then bring it back."

Chapter 8

1. Paul Lawrence and Jay Lorsch (1967). *Organization and Environment: Managing Differentiation and Integration*. Boston: Harvard Business School Press; Louis Pondy (1967). "Organizational Conflict: Concepts and Models," *Administrative Science Quarterly*, 297–320; Richard Walton and John Dutton (1967). "The Management of Interdepartmental Conflict: A Model and Review," *Administrative Science Quarterly*, 73–83; Andrew Van de Ven (1976). "A Framework for Organization Assessment," *Academy of Management Review*, 1: 64–78.

2. Deborah Dougherty (1992). "Interpretive Barriers to Successful Product Innovation in Large Firms," *Organization Science*, 3(2): 179–202.
3. Deborah Gladstein (1984). "A Model of Task Group Effectiveness," *Administrative Science Quarterly*, 29: 499–517; Stuart Schmidt and Thomas Kochan (1972). "Conflict: Toward Conceptual Clarity," *Administrative Science Quarterly*, 17: 359–370.
4. Karen Jehn (1995). "A Multimethod Examination of the Benefits and Detriments of IntraGroup Conflict," *Administrative Science Quarterly*, 40(2): 256–282.
5. The proactiveness of conflict resolution at each of the nine sites was assessed on a 1-to-5 scale. At American Airlines, both sites were rated at 1. At Southwest, both sites were rated at 5. At Continental Airlines the Boston station was rated at 3, while the Cleveland station was rated at 2. At United Airlines, the Shuttle was rated at 5, while the Los Angeles station was rated at 3 (because of its proximity to the Shuttle, some of the conflict-resolution practices had begun to spread), and the Boston station was rated at 2.
6. See Appendixes 8–1 and 8–2 for detailed results.
7. "Continental Airlines' Turnaround," *The News Hour with Jim Lehrer*, transcript, March 18, 1998.
8. Deirdre Wicks (1998). *Nurses and Doctors at Work: Rethinking Professional Boundaries*. Philadelphia: Taylor and Francis, Inc.
9. Dana Weinberg (2003). *Code Green: Money-Driven Hospitals and the Dismantling of Nursing*. Ithaca, NY: ILR/Cornell University Press.
10. Louis Pondy (1967). "Organizational Conflict: Concepts and Models," *Administrative Science Quarterly*, 319.
11. Andrew Van de Ven (1976). "A Framework for Organization Assessment," *Academy of Management Review*, 1: 64–78.
12. Andrew Van de Ven and Diane Ferry (1980). *Measuring and Assessing Organizations*. New York: Wiley.
13. Karen Jehn (1995). "A Multimethod Examination of the Benefits and Detriments of IntraGroup Conflict," *Administrative Science Quarterly*, 40(2): 256–282.

Chapter 9

1. James Heskett (1993). "Southwest Airlines: 1993 (A)," *Harvard Business School Case 694-023*. Boston: Harvard Business School Publishing, 3.
2. Michael Pratt (1998). "To Be or Not to Be: Central Questions in Organizational Identification." In David Whetten and P. Godfrey (Eds.), *Identity in Organizations: Developing Theory through Conversations*. Beverly Hills, CA: Sage, 171–207; Michael Pratt, K. W. Rock, and J. Kaufmann (2001). "Making Sense of Socialization: How Multiple Social Identities Shape Members' Experiences of Work," *Academy of Management Proceedings*, MOC: A1–A6.
3. Peter J. Frost (2002). *Toxic Emotions at Work*. Boston: Harvard Business School Press; Jacoba Lilius (2001). Personal communication.
4. Laura Morgan (2001). "We Wear the Mask: The Strategic Enactment of Racioethnic Identity in Professional Contexts," University of Michigan Business School Working Paper.

5. Erving Goffman (1959). *The Presentation of Self in Everyday Life*. New York: Anchor Books Doubleday.
6. Arlie Russell Hochschild (1983). *The Managed Heart: Commercialization of Human Feeling*. Berkeley, CA: University of California Press. See also: R. L. Kahn, D. M. Wolfe, Robert P. Quinn, J. Snoek, and R. A. Rosenthal (1964). *Organizational Stress: Studies in Role Conflict and Ambiguity*. New York: Wiley.
7. T. R. Tyler (1998). "Why People Cooperate with Organizations: An Identity-Based Approach." In Barry M. Staw and Robert Sutton (Eds.), *Research in Organizational Behavior*. Greenwich, CT: JAI Press.
8. Blake Ashforth and Michael G. Pratt (2001). "Institutionalized Spirituality: A Paradox?" In R. A. Giacalone and C. L. Jurkiewicz (Eds.), *The Handbook of Workplace Spirituality and Organizational Performance*. New York: M. E. Sharpe.
9. This argument is foreshadowed in: Leslie Perlow (1998). *Finding Time: How Corporations, Individuals and Families Can Benefit from New Work Practices*. Ithaca, NY: Cornell University Press; Leslie Perlow (1998). "Boundary Control: The Social Ordering of Work and Family Time in a High-Tech Corporation," *Administrative Science Quarterly*, 43: 328–357.
10. Arlie Russell Hochschild (1997). *The Time Bind: When Work Becomes Home and Home Becomes Work*. New York: Metropolitan Books.
11. Matthew Brelis (2000). "Herb's Way," *Boston Globe*, November 5, F1.
12. Kevin Freiberg and Jackie Freiberg (1996). *Nuts: Southwest Airlines' Crazy Recipe for Business and Personal Success*. Austin, TX: Bard Press.
13. Peter J. Frost (2002). *Toxic Emotions at Work*. Boston: Harvard Business School Press; Jacoba Lilius (2001). Personal communication.
14. Joyce Fletcher (1998). "Relational Practice: A Feminist Reconstruction of Work," *Journal of Management Inquiry*, 7(2): 163–186.

Chapter 10

1. Jay Galbraith (1973). *Designing Complex Organizations*. Reading, MA: Addison-Wesley.
2. Harold Aldrich and D. Herker (1977). "Boundary Spanning Roles and Organization Structure," *Academy of Management Review*, 2(2): 217–230; R. Katz and Michael Tushman (1983). "A Longitudinal Study of The Effects of Boundary Spanning Supervision on Turnover and Promotion in Research and Development," *Academy of Management Journal*, 26(3): 437–456.
3. Jay Galbraith (1994). *Competing with Flexible Lateral Organizations*. Reading, MA: Addison-Wesley.
4. Boundary spanner staffing was measured for each of the nine sites as the number of operations agents on staff divided by the number of daily flight departures. Staffing levels for operations agents varied from 0.11 operations agents per daily flight departure at American's Boston site to 0.48 operations agents per daily flight departure at Southwest's Chicago site.
5. See Appendixes 10–1 and 10–2 for detailed results.
6. Harold Aldrich and D. Herker (1977). "Boundary Spanning Roles and Organization Structure," *Academy of Management Review*, 2(2): 217–230; R. Katz

and Michael Tushman (1983). "A Longitudinal Study of the Effects of Boundary Spanning Supervision on Turnover and Promotion in Research and Development," *Academy of Management Journal*, 26(3): 437–456.

7. Deborah G. Ancona and David F. Caldwell (1992). "Bridging the Boundary: External Activity and Performance in Organizational Teams," *Administrative Science Quarterly*, 37: 634–665; M. J. Dollinger (1984). "Environmental Boundary Spanning and Information Processing Effects on Organizational Performance," *Academy of Management Journal*, 27(2): 351–371; Michael L. Tushman (1977). "Special Boundary Roles in the Innovation Process," *Administrative Science Quarterly*, 22(4): 587–605; Michael L. Tushman and R. Katz (1980). "External Communication and Project Performance: An Investigation into the Role of Gatekeepers," *Management Science*, 26(11): 1071–1085; Michael L. Tushman and Elaine Romanelli (1983). "Uncertainty, Social Location and Influence in Decision Making: A Sociometric Analysis," *Management Science*, 29(1): 12–23; Michael L. Tushman and T. J. Scanlan (1981). "Characteristics and External Orientations of Boundary Spanning Individuals," *Academy of Management Journal*, 24(1): 83–98; Michael L. Tushman and T. J. Scanlan (1981). "Boundary Spanning Individuals: Their Role in Information Transfer and Their Antecedents," *Academy of Management Journal*, 24(2): 289–305.

8. Michael L. Tushman and R. Katz (1980). "External Communication and Project Performance: An Investigation into the Role of Gatekeepers," *Management Science*, 26(11): 1071–1085.

9. Deborah G. Ancona and David F. Caldwell (1992). "Bridging the Boundary: External Activity and Performance in Organizational Teams," *Administrative Science Quarterly*, 37: 634–665.

10. R. N. Ashkenas and S. C. Francis (2000). "Integration Managers: Special Leaders for Special Times," *Harvard Business Review*, 78(6): 108–116; C. M. Leighton and R. G. Tod (1969). "After the Acquisition: Continuing Challenge," *Harvard Business Review*, 47(2): 90–102.

11. Jody Hoffer Gittell (2002). "Coordinating Mechanisms in Care Provider Groups: Relational Coordination as a Mediator and Input Uncertainty as a Moderator of Performance Effects," *Management Science*, 48(11); Jody Hoffer Gittell and Leigh Weiss (forthcoming, 2004). "Coordination Networks Within and Across Organizations: A Multi-Level Framework," *Journal of Management Studies*, 41(5).

12. R. N. Ashkenas, L. J. DeMonaco, and S. C. Francis (1998). "Making the Deal Real: How GE Capital Integrates Acquisitions," *Harvard Business Review*, 76(1): 165–178.

13. R. N. Ashkenas and S. C. Francis (2000). "Integration Managers: Special Leaders for Special Times," *Harvard Business Review*, 78(6): 108–116.

14. Thomas H. Davenport and Nitin Nohria (1994). "Case Management and the Integration of Labor," *Sloan Management Review*, 35(2): 11–23.

Chapter 11

1. These ideas were previously published in: Jody Hoffer Gittell (2000). "Paradox of Coordination and Control," *California Management Review*, 42(3):

1–17; Rob Austin and Jody Hoffer Gittell (2002). "When It Should Not Work but Does: Anomalies of Performance Measurement," in Andy Neely (Ed.), *Business Performance Measurement*, New York: Cambridge University Press.

2. These differences in performance measurement are reflected by the number of functions that could be held jointly accountable for a delay. At American, only one function could be held accountable for each flight delay. At Continental, up to two functions could be held accountable for each delay. At United, up to three functions could be held accountable for each delay, whereas at the United Shuttle up to four functions could share responsibility. Southwest took the concept of cross-functional accountability furthest with the so-called "team delay," allowing all seven station functions to share responsibility for a flight delay.

3. See Appendixes 11-1 and 11-2 for detailed results.

4. Max Weber (1978). *Economy and Society*. Berkeley, CA: University of California Press; Frederick W. Taylor (1911). *Principles of Scientific Management*. New York: Harper & Row; Chester Barnard (1938). *Functions of the Executive*. Cambridge, MA: Harvard University Press; James March and Herbert Simon (1958). *Organizations*. New York: Wiley; Albert Chandler (1989). *Strategy and Structure*. Cambridge, MA: Massachusetts Institute of Technology Press.

5. James March and Herbert Simon (1958). *Organizations*. New York: Wiley.

6. W. Edwards Deming (1986). *Out of the Crisis*. Cambridge, MA: Massachusetts Institute of Technology Press; Robert Cole (1991). "Different Quality Paradigms and Their Implications for Organizational Learning," presented at the conference: Japan in a Global Economy: A European Perspective, Stockholm School of Economics; Robert Grant, Rami Shani, and R. Krishnan (1994). "TQM's Challenge to Management Theory and Practice," *Sloan Management Review*, 35(2): 25–35; Amy Edmondson (1996). "Learning from Mistakes Is Easier Said Than Done: Group and Organizational Influences on the Detection and Correction of Human Error," *Journal of Applied Behavioral Science*, 32(1): 5–28.

7. Christopher Meyer (1994). "How the Right Measures Help Teams to Excel," *Harvard Business Review*, 72(3): 95–102.

8. Richard Hackman (1987). "The Design of Work Teams," in Jay Lorsch (Ed.), *Handbook of Organizational Behavior*, Englewood Cliffs, NJ: Prentice-Hall, 315–342; Susan Albers Mohrman, Susan Cohen, and Allan Mohrman (1995). *Designing Team-Based Organizations: New Forms for Knowledge Work*. San Francisco: Jossey-Bass; Jay Galbraith (1995). *Competing with Flexible Lateral Organizations*. Reading, MA: Addison-Wesley; Ruth Wageman and George Baker (1997). "Incentives and Cooperation: The Joint Effects of Task and Reward Interdependence on Group Performance," *Journal of Organizational Behavior*, 18(2): 139–158.

Chapter 12

1. Cynthia D. Fisher, Lyle F. Schoenfeldt, and James B. Shaw (1999). *Human Resource Management*, 4th ed., p. 153. New York: Houghton Mifflin.

2. Benjamin Schneider and Andrea Konz (1989). "Strategic Job Analysis," *Human Resource Management*, 28(1): 51–63; James Clifford (1994). "Job Analysis: Why Do It, and How Should It Be Done?" *Public Personnel Management*, 23(2): 321–340; William George (1990). "Internal Marketing and Organizational Behavior: A Partnership in Developing Customer-Conscious Employees at Every Level," *Journal of Business Research*, 20: 63–70.
3. Bob Cardy and Greg Robbins (1992). "Job Analysis in a Dynamic Environment," *Human Resource Division News*, 16(1): 4.
4. Peter Cappelli (1995). *Airline Labor Relations in the Global Era: The New Frontier*. Ithaca, NY: Cornell University Press.
5. David Walsh (1994). *On Different Planes: An Organizational Analysis of Cooperation and Conflict among Airline Unions*. Ithaca, NY: ILR Press.
6. Job flexibility was rated at each site on a scale of 1 to 5. For American Airlines, both sites were rated 1. The United Shuttle was rated 4, while United's mainline stations in Boston and Los Angeles were both rated 3. Both Continental Airlines sites were rated 5. Both Southwest sites were also rated 5.
7. See Appendixes 12–1 and 12–2 for detailed results.
8. Cynthia D. Fisher, Lyle F. Schoenfeldt, and James B. Shaw (1999). *Human Resource Management*, 4th ed., p. 153. New York: Houghton Mifflin.
9. Thomas A. Kochan, Harry Katz, and Robert McKersie (1986). *The Transformation of American Industrial Relations*, p. 29. New York: Basic Books.
10. James March and Herbert Simon (1958). *Organizations*. New York: Wiley.
11. Janice Klein (1991). "Craft Pride: The Key to World Class Maintenance," *Harvard Business School Working Paper No. 91-033*.
12. Gil Preuss (1996). "The Structuring of Organizational Information Capacity: An Examination of Hospital Care," Dissertation Document, Massachusetts Institute of Technology, Cambridge, MA, September.

Chapter 13

1. Jody Hoffer Gittell, Andrew von Nordenflycht, and Thomas A. Kochan (2002). "Mutual Gains or Zero Sum? Labor Relations and Firm Performance in the Airline Industry." Submitted.
2. Masahiko Aoki (1990). "Toward an Economic Model of the Japanese Firm," *Journal of Economic Literature*, 27: 16.
3. Thomas A. Kochan, Harry Katz, and Robert McKersie (1986). *The Transformation of American Industrial Relations*. New York: Basic Books.
4. Richard Walton and Robert McKersie (1965). *A Behavioral Theory of Labor Negotiations*. New York: McGraw-Hill.
5. This point is demonstrated more broadly in: Jody Hoffer Gittell, Andrew von Nordenflycht, and Thomas A. Kochan (2002). "Mutual Gains or Zero Sum? Labor Relations and Firm Performance in the Airline Industry." Submitted.
6. "Continental Airlines' Turnaround," *The News Hour with Jim Lehrer*, transcript, March 19, 1998.
7. Richard M. Weintraub (1994). "Employees Win Control of United; Labor Secretary Calls Airline Deal a 'True Landmark,'" *The Washington Post*, July 13.

8. Adeem S. Husman, Jonathan Histon, and Laura Bogusch (2001). "United Airlines: Analysis of Human Resource Practices," Department of Aeronautics and Astronautics, Massachusetts Institute of Technology, Cambridge, MA.
9. Ibid.
10. CNN, October 28, 2001.
11. Thomas A. Kochan, Harry Katz, and Robert McKersie (1986). *The Transformation of American Industrial Relations*. New York: Basic Books.
12. Jody Hoffer Gittell, Andrew von Nordenflycht, and Thomas A. Kochan (2002). "Mutual Gains or Zero Sum? Labor Relations and Firm Performance in the Airline Industry." Submitted.
13. Richard Freeman and Harry Medoff (1984). *What Do Unions Do?* New York: Basic Books.
14. Masahiko Aoki (1990). "Toward an Economic Model of the Japanese Firm," *Journal of Economic Literature*, 28(16).
15. Thomas A. Kochan and Saul Rubinstein (2000). "Toward a Stakeholder Theory of the Firm: The Saturn Partnership," *Organization Science*, 11(4): 367–386.

Chapter 14

1. Pablo E. Fernandez de la Torre (1999). "Airline Alliances: The Airline Perspective," S.M. thesis. Massachusetts Institute of Technology, Cambridge, MA; Torsten Busacker and John Paul Clarke (2001). "Managing Airline Alliances," in *Handbook of Airline Strategy: Challenges and Solutions, Regulatory Issues and Public Policy*. New York: McGraw-Hill Aviation Week Group.
2. Oliver Williamson (1975). *Markets and Hierarchies*. New York: Free Press.
3. Russell Johnston and Paul R. Lawrence (1988). "Beyond Vertical Integration—The Rise of the Value-Adding Partnership," *Harvard Business Review*, July–August, 94–101.
4. Susan Helper, John Paul MacDuffie, and Charles Sabel (2000). "Pragmatic Collaborations: Advancing Knowledge while Controlling Opportunism," *Industrial and Corporate Change*, 9(3): 443–487.
5. Frederick Abernathy, John Dunlop, Janice Hammond, and David Weil (1999). *A Stitch in Time: Lean Retailing and the Transformation of Manufacturing—Lessons from the Apparel and Textile Industries*. New York: Oxford University Press.
6. Russell Johnston and Paul R. Lawrence (1988). "Beyond Vertical Integration—The Rise of the Value-Adding Partnership," *Harvard Business Review*, July–August, 94–101.
7. Jody Hoffer Gittell and Leigh Weiss (forthcoming, 2004). "Coordination Networks Within and Across Organizations: A Multi-Level Framework," *Journal of Management Studies*, 41(5).
8. Rosabeth Moss Kanter (1989). *When Giants Learn to Dance*. New York: Simon & Schuster; Rosabeth Moss Kanter (1988). "The New Alliances: How Strategic Partnerships Are Reshaping American Business," in H. L. Sawyer (ed.), *Business in the Contemporary World*. Lamson, MD: University Press of America.

9. Susan Helper, John Paul MacDuffie, and Charles Sabel (2000). "Pragmatic Collaborations: Advancing Knowledge while Controlling Opportunism," *Industrial and Corporate Change*, 9(3): 443–487.
10. Gianni Lorenzoni and Andrea Lipparini (1999). "The Leveraging of Inter-firm Relationships as a Distinctive Organizational Capability: A Longitudinal Study," *Strategic Management Journal*, 20: 317–338.

Chapter 15

1. John Paul MacDuffie (1995). "Human Resource Bundles and Manufacturing Performance: Organizational Logic and Flexible Production Systems in the World Auto Industry," *Industrial and Labor Relations Review*, 48(2): 197–221.
2. John T. Dunlop and David Weil (1996). "Diffusion and Performance of Modular Production in the US Apparel Industry," *Industrial Relations*, 35(3) 334–355.
3. Casey Ichniowski, Kathryn Shaw, and Giovanna Prennushi (1996). "The Effects of Human Resource Practices on Manufacturing Performance," *American Economic Review*, 87(3): 291–313.
4. Rose Batt (1999). "Work Design, Technology, and Performance in Customer Services and Sales," *Industrial and Labor Relations Review*, 52(4): 539–564.
5. These studies, like the one reported in this book, were fostered by the Sloan Industry Centers under the auspices of the Alfred P. Sloan Foundation. The Sloan Industry Centers are intended to develop a deep understanding of performance in particular industry settings, and to transfer learning from one industry setting to the others. See "The Sloan Industry Centers: Understanding the Critical Issues That Affect Business and Commerce Today," www.sloan.org.
6. Paul Lawrence and Jay Lorsch (1967). *Organizational Environment: Managing Differentiation and Integration.* Boston: Harvard Business School Press.
7. Jay Galbraith (1973). *Designing Complex Organizations.* Reading, MA: Addison-Wesley; David A. Nadler and Michael L. Tushman (1997). *Competing by Design: The Power of Organizational Architecture.* New York: Oxford University Press.
8. Paul Milgrom and John Roberts (1990). "The Economics of Modern Manufacturing: Technology, Strategy, and Organizations," *American Economic Review*, 80(6): 511–528; Paul Milgrom and John Roberts (1993). "Complementarities and Fit: Strategy, Structure and Organizational Change," Working Paper, Stanford University, Stanford, CA; Bengt Holmstrom and Paul Milgrom (1994). "The Firm as an Incentive System," *American Economic Review*, 84(4): 972–991.
9. Paul Osterman (1994). "How Common Is Workplace Transformation and How Can We Explain Who Adopts It? Results from a National Survey," *Industrial and Labor Relations Review*, 47(2): 173–188; Paul Osterman (2000). "Work Reorganization in an Era of Restructuring: Trends in Diffusion and Effects on Employee Welfare," *Industrial and Labor Relations Review*, 53(2): 179–196; Casey Ichniowski, Thomas Kochan, David Levine, Craig Olson,

and George Strauss (1996). "What Works at Work: Overview and Assessment," *Industrial Relations*, 35(3): 299–333.

10. Casey Ichniowski, Kathryn Shaw, and Giovanna Prennushi (1996). "The Effects of Human Resource Practices on Manufacturing Performance," *American Economic Review*, 87(3): 291-313; John Paul MacDuffie (1995). "Human Resource Bundles and Manufacturing Performance: Organizational Logic and Flexible Production Systems in the World Auto Industry," *Industrial and Labor Relations Review*, 48(2): 197–221; Jan Rivkin (2000). "Imitation of Complex Strategies," *Management Science*, 46(6): 824–844.

11. Neil Siggelkow (2001). "Change in the Presence of Fit: The Rise, the Fall and the Renaissance of Liz Claiborne," *Academy of Management Journal*, 44(4): 838–857.

Chapter 16

1. Frederick Abernathy, John Dunlop, Janice Hammond, and David Weil (1999). *A Stitch in Time: Lean Retailing and the Transformation of Manufacturing—Lessons from the Apparel and Textile Industries*. New York: Oxford University Press.

2. Technically, airlines are not supposed to limit another airline's access to any airport. However, their dominant presence at an airport makes competing airlines think twice before entering a market, because of their loyal customer base, high frequencies, and strong relationships with airport operator and local communities. In some instances the dominant airline may also use certain tricks to prevent other airlines from entering certain markets.

3. Howard Banks (1994). "A Sixties Industry in a Nineties Economy," *Forbes*, May 5.

4. Michael Levine (1995). Remarks at the Center for Transportation Studies, Massachusetts Institute of Technology, Cambridge, MA, Spring Seminar Series.

5. *New York Times* (1993). "American Airlines to Lease San Jose Gates to Reno Air," May 13.

6. Bridget O'Brian (1994). "AMR's Profit in 3rd Quarter Jumped 74%—But Carrier Says Reductions in Costs Are Still Needed; Givebacks Are Sought," *Wall Street Journal*, October 20.

7. Howard Banks (1994). "A Sixties Industry in a Nineties Economy," *Forbes*, May 5.

8. *USA Today* (1993). "Continental May Unveil Discount Airline Today," September 10.

9. Wendy Zellner (1993). "Continental: In for the Short Haul," *BusinessWeek*, December 6.

10. Perry Flint (1994). "Continental Divide," *Air Transport World*, September.

11. Bridget O'Brian (1995). "Continental's Continental Lite Hits Some Turbulence in Battling Southwest," *Wall Street Journal*, January 10.

12. Perry Flint (1994). "Continental Divide," *Air Transport World*, September.

13. Bridget O'Brian (1994). "Flying Continental through Turbulent Times," *Wall Street Journal*, October 27.

14. *USA Today* (1994). "More Cheap Seats," October 26.
15. *CO Times* (1995). January 16.
16. Julie Schmidt (1994). "No-Frills Airline: Will It Fly?" *USA Today*, July 26.
17. Perry Flint (1994). "United in Battle," *Air Transport World*, October.
18. Bruce A. Smith (1994). "United Shuttle Takes on Southwest," *Air Transport World*, October 17.
19. Agis Salpukus (1993). "United Air Gets Tough on Unions," *New York Times*, May 10.
20. Adam Bryant (1993). "United Air's Design for New Carrier," *New York Times*, October 27.
21. *Labor Relations Advisor* (1994). "Changing of Corporate Culture at United Benefits All," April.
22. Perry Flint (1994). "United in Battle," *Air Transport World*, October.
23. Chris Woodyard (2001). "United Drops Shuttle Flights, Abandons Low-Fare Model," *USA Today*, October.
24. This section draws upon: Jody Hoffer Gittell and Charles O'Reilly (2001). "JetBlue Airways: Starting from Scratch," *Harvard Business School Case 801354*. Boston, MA: Harvard Business School Publishing.

Chapter 17

1. Melanie Trottman (2002). "Vaunted Southwest Slips in On-Time Performance," *Wall Street Journal*, September 25.
2. Dorothy Leonard-Barton (1995). *Wellsprings of Knowledge: Building and Sustaining the Sources of Innovation*: Boston, MA: Harvard Business School Press; Dorothy Leonard-Barton (1994). "Core Capabilities and Core Rigidities," pp. 26–56, in *The Perpetual Enterprise Machine*, H. Kent Bowen, Kim B. Clark, Charles A. Holloway and Steven C. Wheelwright (Eds.). Oxford, UK: Oxford University Press; Joseph Bower and Clay Christensen (1995). "Disruptive Technologies: Catching the Wave," *Harvard Business Review*, 73(1): 43–53.
3. This account is taken from: James Heskett, "Southwest Airlines: 1993 (A)," *Harvard Business School Case No. 694-023*. Boston: Harvard Business School Publishing.
4. *BusinessWeek* (2001). "The Top Entrepreneurs," January 8.
5. Rogelio Oliva and Jody Hoffer Gittell (2002). "Southwest Airlines in Baltimore," *Harvard Business School Case No. 9-602-156*. Boston: Harvard Business School Publishing.
6. Ibid.
7. This section is based largely on: Jody Hoffer Gittell and Kim Cameron (2002). "Compassion, Relationships and Resilience: The Role of Relational and Financial Reserves in Responding to Crisis," presented at the Academy of Management Meetings, Denver, CO.
8. Presentation at MIT's Sloan School of Management, October 2001.
9. Matthew Barakat (2001). "US Airways Loses $766 Million in Third Quarter, Worse Than Analysts Expected," *Arlington Journal*, October 31.
10. Ibid.

11. Steven Greenhouse (2001). "Unions at Airlines Assail Management for Denying Benefits," *New York Times*, September 26.
12. "Airlines Weigh Severance," *CNNfn*, September 26, 2001.
13. Steven Greenhouse (2001). "Unions at Airlines Assail Management for Denying Benefits," *New York Times*, September 26, 2001.
14. "Airlines Weigh Severance," *CNNfn*, September 26, 2001.
15. Melanie Trottman (2001). "Up in the Air: Amid Crippled Rivals, Southwest Again Tries to Spread Its Wings—Low-Fare Airline Maintains Service, Mulls Expansion in Risky Bid for Traffic—Tapping $475 Million in Credit," *Wall Street Journal*, October 11.
16. "Airlines Weigh Severance," *CNNfn*, September 26, 2001.
17. Ibid.
18. *Wall Street Journal* (2001). "Southwest Mulls Cuts, Halts Boeing Deliveries," September 21.
19. Michelle Conlin (2001). "Where Layoffs Are a Last Resort," *BusinessWeek*, October 8.
20. Melanie Trottman (2001). "Up in the Air: Amid Crippled Rivals, Southwest Again Tries to Spread Its Wings—Low-Fare Airline Maintains Service, Mulls Expansion in Risky Bid for Traffic—Tapping $475 Million in Credit," *Wall Street Journal*, October 11.
21. Ibid.
22. Katrina Brooker (2001). "The Chairman of the Board Looks Back," *Fortune*, May 28.
23. Kim S. Cameron (1997) "Downsizing and the New Work Covenant." *Exchange*, Spring: 6–10.
24. Michelle Conlin (2001). "Where Layoffs Are a Last Resort," *BusinessWeek*, October 8.
25. Peter Cappelli (1999). *The New Deal at Work: Managing the Market-Driven Workforce*. Boston: Harvard Business School Press.
26. Michelle Conlin (2001). "Where Layoffs Are a Last Resort," *BusinessWeek*, October 8.
27. This analysis was conducted using Spearman rank correlation, with each of the nine major U.S. airlines as an observation. The results were as follows: correlation between the extent of layoffs in September 2001 and passenger traffic recovery by August 2002 ($r = -0.798$, $p < 0.01$) and correlation between the extent of layoffs in September 2001 and airline stock price recovery by September 2002 ($r = -0.790$, $p < 0.05$).
28. Katrina Brooker (2001). "The Chairman of the Board Looks Back," *Fortune*, May 28.
29. "Continental Airlines' Turnaround," *The News Hour with Jim Lehrer*, transcript, March 19, 1998.
30. Ian Mount (2002). "Southwest's Gary Kelly: A Tip of the Hat to the CFO at the One Airline Still Making Money," *Business 2.0*, March.
31. Kim S. Cameron (1998). "Strategic Organizational Downsizing: An Extreme Case," *Research in Organizational Behavior*, 20: 185–229; James R. Morris, Wayne F. Cascio, and Clifford E. Young (1999). "Downsizing after All These Years: Questions and Answers about Who Did It, How Many Did It, and Who Benefited from It." *Organizational Dynamics*, Winter: 78–87.

32. Barry Staw, Lance Sandelands, and Jane Dutton (1981). "Threat-Rigidity Effects in Organizational Behavior: A Multi-Level Analysis," *Administrative Science Quarterly*, 26: 501–524.

33. Kim S. Cameron, Myung U. Kim, and David A. Whetten (1987). "Organizational Effects of Decline and Turbulence." *Administrative Science Quarterly*, 32: 222–240.

Index

About the Author

Jody Hoffer Gittell is an assistant professor of management at Brandeis University's Heller School for Social Policy and Management and a faculty member of MIT's Global Airline Industry Program. She received her Ph.D. from the MIT Sloan School of Management, and she served for 5 years on the faculty of the Harvard Business School. Professor Gittell's research and teaching focus on human resource and service operations management and, in particular, on coordination within and across organizations. She has developed a theory of relational coordination—coordinating work through relationships of shared goals, shared knowledge, and mutual respect. She has identified quality and efficiency outcomes of relational coordination and a set of organizational practices that foster it.

Professor Gittell has published over 20 articles, chapters, and cases, and she frequently presents her results to managers, researchers, and policymakers. She serves as co-chair of the Human Resource Network of the Industrial Relations Research Association, vice chair of the board of directors for Families First Health and Support Center, and is an active member of the Academy of Management. She lives in Portsmouth, New Hampshire, with her husband, Ross, and their daughters, Rose and Grace.